D0898040

TWENTIETH CENTURY POLISH THEATRE

TWENTIETH CENTURY POLISH THEATRE

Edited by Bohdan Drozdowski
English translations edited by Catherine Itzen

JOHN CALDER · LONDON
RIVERRUN PRESS · DALLAS

Published in collaboration with
Gambit International Theatre Review, 1979.

This edition first published in the UK, 1979, by
John Calder (Publishers) Ltd.,
18 Brewer Street, London W1R 4AS
and in the USA, 1980, by
riverrun press Inc.,
Suite 247, 2800 Routh Street,
Dallas, Texas 75201

This translation *Cuttlefish* © Daniel C. and Eleanor S. Gerould,
1969, 1979

This translation *Hamlet 70* © Catherine Mulvaney and Mariusz Tchorek, 1979

© John Calder (Publishers) Ltd 1979

ALL RIGHTS RESERVED

BRITISH LIBRARY CATALOGUING DATA

Twentieth century Polish theatre.
 1. Theater - Poland - History - 20th century
 I. Drozdowski, Bohdan
 792'.09438   PN2859.P6   79-41172

ISBN 0 7145 3738 1 cased

No part of this publication may be reproduced, stored in a
retrieval system, or transmitted in any form by any means,
electronic, mechanical, photo-copying, recording or otherwise,
except brief extracts for the purpose of review, without the
prior written permission of the copyright owner and the
publisher.

Any paperback edition of this book whether published
simultaneously with, or subsequent to, the casebound
edition, is sold subject to the condition that it shall not,
by way of trade, be lent, resold, hired out, or otherwise
disposed of, without the publishers' consent, in any form
of binding or cover other than that in which it is published.

Typeset by Gilbert Composing Services Ltd., Leighton Buzzard
Printed in Great Britain by Hillman Printers (Frome) Ltd., Somerset

CONTENTS

LIST OF ILLUSTRATIONS

INTRODUCTION
Catherine Itzin

Mention Polish theatre and most people will think of Grotowski. Others will know of Kantor, especially after his visit to the Edinburgh Festival in 1976 with his extraordinary *The Dead Class.* Cognoscenti will have heard of the playwright Mrozek, perhaps Rozewicz, thanks in part to John Calder's diligence in publishing Eastern European playwrights. Academics, at least, know of Stanislaw Witkiewicz, the great gothic avant-garde writer of the twenties and thirties. Beyond these, however, there is a wealth of untapped classic and contemporary Polish drama still little known in the West.

One purpose, therefore, of this collection of essays and plays (compiled by Bohdan Drozdowski, the Polish critic, editor and play-wright whose *Hamlet 70* is included in this volume) is to provide a survey of classic and contemporary Polish theatre, spotlighting its most notable and best-known practitioners (Szajna and Tomaszewski as well as Wajda, Grotowski and Kantor) and introducing those not yet so well-known, though no less notable (Wyspkianski, Gombrowicz, Slowacki, Mickiewicz, Przybyszewska, Swinarski, Hanuszkiewicz and Krasowski).

To understand Polish theatre it is necessary to appreciate that it is all 'subsidised', organised from training to product within the centrally-planned state structure. There is no alternative or fringe theatre as we know it in England. Experiment—and it is important to remember that Poland is now known world-wide for its theatrical experiment—occurs within the 'established' system, where there is arguably more latitude for individual innovation, particularly directorial, than there is in comparable theatres in England. Poland is also famous for its theatre festivals—regional, national and international—which often operate as its 'fringe'.

It is also necessary to set Polish drama against the struggles for power in which Poland has been a pawn from the nineteenth century to the Nazi occupation and destruction of Warsaw, to its present position as a Soviet 'satellite'. For the historical struggles have been particularly harsh and are invariably reflected in the theatre. As a consequence, Polish playwrights and directors seem more acutely conscious of the 'politics of everything'—from the cost of the Nazi terror to the current price of meat in a centrally-planned economy, to the shadow of Big Brother. While the Polish repertoire may thus naturally, almost instinctively, reflect the political realities (both historical and contemporary), it does not use the direct, 'literal' agit-prop methods that are being popularised in England, but relies instead on subject matter, symbolism and the development of the dramatic art form itself—in contemporary plays and in contemporary interpretations of the classics.

When censorship is explicit, criticism and social comment must be subtly implicit. Perhaps for this reason Polish theatre has been the domain of the director: the visual can speak as loudly and clearly as words, while being much less compromising. The magnificent romantic/grotesque tradition in Polish drama particularly lends itself to such directorial virtuosity and social commentary as, ironically, does Shakespeare whose 'disorder in the kingdom', canon has been so suitable for an exploration of Polish politics, that Shakespeare is popularly referred to as one of the Polish 'national' playwrights.

In the first essay in this volume, Elzbieta Wysinska deals specifically with directors' theatre, describing the ways in which the nineteenth century national classics are produced today to comment on crucial contemporary issues and showing how different directors have plundered the romantic repertoire and used it to illuminate the hard facts of history. She synopsises the subject matter of the major plays and chronicles their various interpretations by different directors. Thus she focuses on Mickiewicz's famous *Forefathers* comparing Dejmak's production in the fifties with Swinarski's later version: Swinarski's production of Wyspianski's *Liberation* with others, by Hanuszkiewicz, for example. She looks at Wajda's production of *November Night* (based on the anti-Russian uprising of 1830) and at length at Przybyszewska's *The Danton Case* (set in the French Revolution and dealing with the contradictions inherent in the revolutionary process and the circumstances which determine dictatorship) directed by Wajda, and briefly at the various revivals of Witkacy, at Gombrowicz's *The Marriage* and at Mrozek's *The Slaughterhouse.* It is an essay which fulfills the dual function of providing an annotated 'what's on in Warsaw' with the historical and political background necessary to understand why the plays are produced in the way described.

In a brilliant essay, Konstanty Puzyna then analyses the work of Stanislaw Ignacy Witkiewicz, relating it to its philosophical and literary antecedents and to subsequent developments in European drama. In his own distinctive style, Puzyna describes Witkacy's distinctive and unique style and the recurrent themes. In the process he accomplishes the difficult task of revealing something of Witkacy's now undisputed genius. The value of Jan Blonski's essay on Grotowski is that it undertakes a much-needed and long-overdue critical revaluation of the 'guru'—neither unsympathetic or overly idolatrous. In bravely following this line, Blonski probably does better justice to the man Bohdan Drozdowski refers to in his Foreword as 'the master' than other less critical commentators. This is perhaps the first balanced assessment of Grotowski's contribution to the theatre.

Andrzej Wajda is well-known in the West, for his films if not for his theatre. In the interview in this volume (with Teresa Krzemien) Wajda evaluates the comparative virtues of film and theatre and provocatively concludes that the more ephemeral form of theatre probably has a greater and longer-lasting impact than its more obviously durable celluloid sister-art. He also explains why he is always drawn back 'home' to Poland and to Polish theatre despite his international reputation and the abundant opportunity to work abroad. Wajda's views are authoritative and controversial, certainly by comparison to the rather pretentious seeming pontifications of Jozef Szajna who is perhaps less widely known in the West, though in the theatre world his 'visual artistry' often arouses a zealotry not unlike that associated with Grotowski. Interviewed by his obviously (and overly) sympathetic official biographer Maria Czanerle, Szajna gives some idea of his concept of 'theatre as image' and explains the world view which determines his own idiosyncratic plastic art approach to theatre.

Tadeusz Kantor's *The Dead Class* was a definitive, visionary production (subsequently filmed by Wajda) combining allegory, symbolism, plastic art and politics, about a 'class' of old people who carry the burden of the children they once were, now dead, literally strapped to their backs. It is documented here by Jan Klossowicz in scene by scene detail which comes as near as words perhaps can do to recreating a sense of the original production. It is prefaced by a manifesto by Kantor himself elaborating Craig's concept of the uber-marrionette—and postscripted by Kantor's own account of his 'class' of archetypal characters.

To illustrate the scope of Polish drama—and to remedy somewhat the deplorable lack of Polish plays published in English three plays have been included in this volume. There is Witkiewicz's *The Cuttlefish or The Hyrcanian Worldview,* a typically whimsical Witkacy fantasy reminiscent of Shaw's 'Don Juan in Hell' section of *Man and Superman.* It is Shavian, too, in its dialectics and deliberations, and in its preoccupation with Nietsche's concept of the superman: the Hyrcanian worldview peddled by its super-leader Hyrcan IV aims to put the absolute into effect in everyday life. The fact that Hyrcania is a mysoginist's paradise is another and not altogether irrelevant aspect of the play. The nature of Witkacy's wonderful imagination is perhaps best illustrated by the stage direction which describes 'two old gentlemen dressed in the style of the thirties': the play was written in 1922!

And there is *Ninety-Three* by Stanislawa Przybuszewska whose *The Danton Case* is currently the long-running success of Warsaw. This short play, like all of her work, is set in the French Revolution during the days of the Commune and concerns the incestuous relationship of a revolutionary daughter with her royalist father. It attempts to come to terms with the contradictions between personal destiny (and its psychological determinants) and public duty to a revolutionary cause.

Finally, there is Bohdan Drozdowski's *Hamlet 70*, an unusual play for English and American audiences, written in dramatic verse, and deliberately going back to Elizabethan language. With its many contemporary colloquialisms and even more contemporary situations, it falls on the ear strangely; more so than the verse plays of Christopher Fry and Ronald Duncan. The two characters, a kidnapped ambassador and his guerilla captor, locked in a room together, explore ideology, their relationship to each other and the workings of fate.

Last, but not least, there is a brief survey of Polish opera and an invaluable source of reference in the Bibliography of Polish Plays in English Translation.

Altogether this collection of essays and plays aims to put contemporary Polish theatre in classic perspective and the classic theatre in contemporary perspective. It is intended to provide a sound, basic introduction to Polish theatre: and it should give some indication of the intellectual, aesthetic and political climate in which the work has been written and is produced. If it manages to whet the appetite for more, and to encourage British productions of some of the Polish classics (contemporary as well as historical), it will have more than justified its intentions. England may be infamously insular, and America even more so, but they ignore Polish theatre at their peril.

FOREWORD
Bohdan Drozdowski

The general opinion of theatre in Poland is that is is lively and full of variety. And obviously what foreigners think matters, because despite a tendency to be polite and politic, they are often acute in observing what is noteworthy and innovative. We natives, however, tend to be rather more sceptical. We know what goes on behind the scenes. We know why our theatre is as it is. We also know that it could be different.

The question is—is what ways different? Here opinion begins to divide. Some people say that Polish theatre is too 'experimental'—with too much emphasis on gratuitous interpretive effect. Others say we haven't got enough political theatre. Some believe our theatre to be beyond criticism. To others, this is true only of a few exceptional actors: they feel the rest fail to fulfil expectations.

As far as directors are concerned, Poland can certainly boast some of the most world-eminent. But we also have a host of *would-be* eminent directors, more concerned with aping our few great artists than with coming to their own creative grips with the plays they produce.

All too often these otherwise promising directors want to stage the same plays as Wajda, for example, or Swinarski, saying that they want to do them in 'their own way' because they 'see it differently'. The result is predictably cliché-ridden, devoid of sense, the interpretation forced and fantastic.

Critical response—haphazard and misconceived though it often is—rejects these productions which turn a classical script arbitrarily on its head. Such protests may be rare, but they are significant, warning perhaps of the point of experimentation beyond which it is unwise to venture.

Nevertheless, the number of bizarre, wildly-interpreted productions is always on the increase. And that is because director-worship is so widespread in Poland. Here one hears so often of Hanuszkiewicz's *Hamlet* (rather than Shakespeare's), of Wajda's *The Wedding* (rather than Wyspianski's) that it is almost refreshing to hear of a *Hamlet* by a Kowalski or *The Wedding* by yet another '—icz'. This exclusively and excessively directorial approach to the theatre is not entirely healthy, and is, indeed, the cause of many a failure. Yet it is characteristically Polish that the director should be allowed a free hand. It is only later that one has slightly more critical after-thoughts about this approach.

These cavils aside, one welcomes the opportunity to draw attention

13

to the truly novel and valuable achievements of Polish theatre—those
which are singularly Polish and not to be found anywhere else in
Europe. And there are many directors, designers, actors, innovators
(not to mention actual theatres) who are now deservedly world-famous.
Grotowski, of course, comes top of the list, though the people who
have heard of him far out-number those who have actually seen his
Laboratory Theatre. Another break-through was made by Josef Szajna
with his visionary 'painter's theatre'. It is indicative that an institute in
New York has been named after him, while another has been named
after Grotowski, also similarly commemorated in France. Tomaszewski's
pantomime is now known throughout the world. Axer, Skuszamka,
Wajda and Szajna are regularly invited to perform their work abroad,
as was Swinarski (who died unfortunately and untimely in an air
accident in 1975). Kazimierz Dejmek and Jerzy Krasowski now also
direct throughout the world, as do Adam Hanuszkiewicz and Jerzy
Jarocki. Indeed, the boom in the export of Polish theatre which began
a decade ago continues still today.

In the sixties, the Polish National Theatre under the direction of
Kazimierz Dejmek performed at Peter Daubeny's World Theatre Season,
bringing the unforgettable *History of the Glorious Resurrection of Our
Lord*. This old Polish miracle play won London audiences with its
unhackneyed setting, its formalised acting, scenic dynamics and unconventional pre-Shakespearean script. Some saw in it parallels with the
Japanese Noh plays or the ancient Greek theatre. And a few, uncertain
of what it was all about, predictably voiced misgivings that hidden in
the guise of a respectable religious play was the usual communist
propaganda.

The following year the Teatr Powszechny (The Common Theatre)
under the direction of Adam Hanuszkiewicz brought to London
The Wedding, Columbuses and *Crime and Punishment*. The plays
received a mixed response. What is wrong with Polish theatre, asked
the critics, that it should produce a mediocre play of purely
parochial interest, an adaptation of a contemporary Polish novel and
another adaptation of a classic Russian novel. The objections were not
entirely unfounded except in one respect: *The Wedding* might prove
to be impenetrable to some foreign taste, but it is a national
masterpiece—its stature and universality ultimately revealed in
Wajda's brilliant film based on Wyspianski's play.

It should also be remembered that in Poland at that time, it was a
period of so-called 'directors' literature'. Prominent and ambitious
directors, imitated by minor and derivative directors, had already tried
to 're-animate' the classics and the contemporary avant-garde. So they
turned to adaptations of prose works for something new. And such
novels as Camus's *The Plague*, Kaden-Bandrowski's *General Barcz*,
Brathy's *Columbuses Born in 1920* and Dostoyevsky's *Crime and
Punishment* were adapted for the stage. The theatre was, in fact,
taking its cue from films in popularising the classics and present-day
best sellers.

When an adventurous producer who is a theatre director and a good actor as well, feels like playing Raskolnikov—who would stop him? So when Andrzej Wajda felt like tackling *The Idiot* and spent a few weeks practising with an audience Dostoyevsky's fragment entitled *Nastazya Filipovna*, the results were significant in two respects: as a successful experiment in its own right based on a good text, and as a borrowed theme—a narrative (neither drama nor novel) enacted by two actors in the light of a paraffin lamp. When a famous actress who specialises in monodrama decides to tell a provocative tale, she chooses Rabelais's *Gargantua and Pantagruel* and produces a fine performance, full of piquancy uncommon in today's plays.

Basically, Polish theatre is in a process of search. Sometimes this takes the pecuniary form of making money from other people's texts, sometimes it involves a daring attempt to revitalise old texts with contemporary relevance. The *History of the Glorious Resurrection* was one case in point and later *The Life of Joseph*. Sometimes new life has come from abandoning a script altogether—as is the case with Szajna. A script—all things to Krasowski, Skuszanka, Axer and Dejmek means little to Szajna.

Contemporary classics, too, have been popular in Poland—Sartre Ionesco, Camus, Miller, Osborne, Wesker, Anouilh, Beckett, Brecht, Frisch, Pinter, Shaffer, Adamov, Duerrenmatt and Albee. But the greatest 'recent' discovery has been the neglected, misunderstood, much-maligned Stanislaw Ignacy Witkiewicz, forerunner of them all, to whom a special essay is devoted in this volume. Once 'Witkacy' caught on, he became positively contagious. And every notable director felt duty-bound to do something by him, adapting his work into vaudeville, musical, operetta, farce—and more and worse. Hounded by the philistines before the war, Witkacy has now emerged as the veritable father of modern drama. Before him, it was the 'theatre of the absurd' of Mrozek and Rozewicz that was most fashionable, the absurd being the most politically palatable of styles and therefore most suitable to the Polish theatre. And plays by Broszkiewicz, Grochowiak, Krasinski, Iredynski, Abramov, Sito, and indeed myself, are seen occasionally, but being less abstract, appeal to a narrower public.

One might summarise the idiosyncracy of Polish theatre as its love of the bizarre. So much so that even the revival of a classic romantic drama can be used as an occasion for technical virtuosity. Grotowski, for example, revived 'dead' scripts by using technical tricks—a duel of light beams, ping-pong, see-saw. Now Hanuszkiewicz sits Slowacki's fairly-land characters on Japanese-made Honda motor-bikes and people flock to see them. Critics may sneer, but disciples cheer—apparently oblivious to the oblique meanings of what they obviously regard as outdated and irrelevant content.

Grotowski eventually reached the point where his theatre experiments ended. Since then he has done things which appall many who see them, but which please his long-suffering advocates. And nobody argues his case better than Professor Jan Blonski here in this volume. Ironically when Grotowski was appearing in London and Edinburgh, he was generally distrusted in Poland and his company was threatened with closure. He had little recognition in Poland then, little support in the press and even less audience. Grotowski only had the active support of one fortnightly periodical *Wspolczesnosc (Contemporariety)*, which promoted angry young Polish writers who, like Osborne, made their debut about 1956. The late Jerzy Falkowski, a critic with a keen eye for anything new, used to report at enthusiastic length on Grotowski's latest activities, each report postponing the demise of the Laboratory Theatre. Then Growtowski was invited to London by Peter Brook who translated the directives uttered in French by the master to his actors during his 'black masses'. There followed productions at the Half Moon Theatre (the converted East End synagogue), at the Edinburgh Festival, and at the Polish Arts Festival arranged in cooperation with the North West Arts Association under Alexander Shouvaloff. And Grotowski''s fame spread throughout the world. When Grotowski returned to Poland from his first visit with Brook, he referred to Brook publicly as 'Brook my colleague' and the Polish theatre world laughed derisively and dismissively at the impudence of him speaking of Brook in such intimate terms. Now, of course, Brook can refer to Grotowski as 'his associate' and the Polish theatre laughs up its other sleeve, or, at least, laughs at its peril.

There are now many affectionate anecdotes to be told. When the wheelbarrows, for example, needed for *Akropolis* got lost en route to Edinburgh, there was no alternative but to cancel the performance and look for builders' barrows locally. None were to be found in Scotland, so they were ordered by air from Warsaw. The wheelbarrows were greeted at the airport by Edinburgh Festival VIP's, an indulgence reported with tongue-in-cheek by the Scottish press: 'Grotowski's Wheelbarrows Met at the Airport by VIP'. It was fun as well as funny. And when the powers-that-be turned off the electricity in the theatre hall, over a hundred candles were hurriedly supplied and lit—and then taken by the audience as a special effect dreamt up by the master to create atmosphere!

Tomaszewski's theatre shares a similar chequered history. To begin with there was the problem of the name: 'pantomime' has a different meaning in English than in Polish, and there were fears that English audiences would therefore be put off. In the event, audiences crowded to see Tomaszewski's work. And he has now been seen all over Europe and elsewhere. Tomaszewski invented and then developed his own original form of theatre—'speaking' without words, using only the actors' bodies. It is unique (even Grotowski relies on Dostoyevsky and the Bible) and its impact is enormous.

But repetition dulls interest. When people had had enough of the absurd, when Grotowski 'gave up' and when student theatre grew 'old', the 'new' demand was for political theatre. Jerzy Krasowski, a prominent director of political theatre, unearthed the forgotten writer

16

of the twenties. Stanislawa Przybyszewska, whose father Stanislaw Przybyszewski was the great modernist and leader of young artists at the end of the nineteenth century in Germany, Poland and Scandinavia. Though she wrote exclusively and specifically of the French Revolution, her plays have considerable contemporary relevance. The quality of *The Danton Case, Thermidor* and *93* can not be questioned. Rediscovered—her plays were unsuccessfully produced before the war and she died penniless and neglected—her political ideas, her psychological insights, perfect construction and precision dialogue have earned her a deservedly secure place in the front rank of Polish political drama. After Krasowski, *The Danton Case* was directed by Andrzej Wajda whose production has proved to be the greatest theatrical success of the past ten years. Seats are still booked months in advance.

This introduction to Polish theatre, and particularly to this volume on Polish theatre, cannot end without mentioning Witold Gombrowicz, no longer entirely unknown in the West where his preposterously serious vision has now begun to penetrate. Gombrowicz died in exile in France in the summer of 1969: since then he has begun to be recognised and translated into many languages. Productions of his plays on the Polish stage vary considerably—from the sublime to the ridiculous. For Gombrowicz was a man of wisdom who rendered reality as caricature —madness maybe, but not without method. What doesn't work is the caricature of his caricatures—yet another example of the damage that can be done by directors.

There is only one man in Poland who can do justice to Gombrowicz and that is Tadeusz Kantor, artist, actor and founder and 'animator' of Cricot 2. (Before the war there was the artists' theatre Cricot). Indeed, Kantor is the only director who knows how to do Witkacy. Kantor plays out Witkacy's dizzy-height conceits in dead earnest, but the effect is such as to touch off storms of healthy laughter. Kantor has the perception sadly lacking in the artisans of the conventional theatre, whose only object is to get rid of convention.

These are the 'dramatis personae' of Polish theatre. Now read on . . .

DIRECTORS' THEATRE: MAKING THE CLASSICS CONTEMPORARY
Elzbieta Wysinska
Translated by Mariusz Tchorek

Present-day theatre has developed along two lines, suggested Jean Darcante, Secretary General of the International Theatre Institute (ITI), when he was speaking at the 1975 season of Warsaw's Theatre of Nations. One is the 'royal' road followed by such directors as Bergman, Strehler and Stein; the other—the one which Brook and Grotowski have taken—is the uneasy and untrodden path, exploring relationships between the performer and the audience.

Although the reputation of Polish contemporary theatre is based on the latter, experimental tendency, it also has its representatives of the royal way as well. In this tradition, professionalism goes hand in hand with respect for the literary text; both the validity of the classics and the possibilities offered by modern drama are recognised. This way is, in fact, far from being secure and easy. It does not exclude experimentation any more than it gives precedence to convention before innovation.

In Poland, the theatre achieves its aims to the extent that it is able to respond to current political, ethical, and social issues. And a special characteristic of Polish theatre today is its use of national classics to comment on crucial contemporary issues. So it is not surprising that classic texts play an important part in the Polish repertoire, often, and with good reason, actually functioning as contemporary plays. Works by the romantics and Wyspianski are still useful in evoking experiences in contemporary history. Their poetic, open structure also enables a production to be interpreted in tune with today's meanings and moods.

In the last 15 years the classics which have functioned particularly successfully in this way have included *Forefathers* by Adam Mickiewicz (1798—1855), *Kordian* by Juliusz Sowacki (1809—1849), *The Non-Divine Comedy* by Zygmunt Krasinski (1812—1859), and *Liberation* (with other plays) by Stanislaw Wyspianski (1869—1907). The origins of this 'production tradition' can be traced back to Leon Schiller's success in the mid-war period. Schiller (1887—1954), a remarkable director, an expert on theatrical technique and a friend of Craig's was the Polish Piscator and Meyerhold rolled into one, but

19

still retaining the tradition of 'merry old Poland.' He was fascinated by Mickiewicz's theatrical concepts and Wyspianski's visions of the 'immense theatre'. Before the war he created the modern political, potetical, 'monumental' theatre, in notable productions of *The Non-Divine Comedy, Forefathers,* and *Kordian.* For Schiller's kind of artistic temperament these plays offered immense potential. They had been written by poets in exile after the suppression of the November Uprising of 1830. They were written with prospect of production and were outside any established stage tradition. For this reason they still have a strong appeal combining as they do, poetry with epic construction. And they provide directors with plenty of creative scope.

Polish drama of the twenties and thirties has a similar foothold in the repertoire. The avant-garde of that period beginning with Stanislaw Ignacy Witkiewicz, was concerned with both formal and social matters. And though the avant-garde of that period has now acquired a classic stature it still offers considerable artistic challenge and freedom to the director

What kind of theatre is it then, that so embraces the literature of another century? Perhaps most important, it deals with Poland's liberation from the three partitioning powers, and the struggle of the nonpareil with heaven and earth. It is a theatre relevant to today in following in the tradition of struggle, whether along poetic or grotesque and ironic lines. No wonder that such drama, lofty and poetic, logically absurd and metaphorical, rarely conventionally social or psychological, provides directors with a special challenge. For the director must demonstrate the capacity of the classics to reveal national consciousness and social awareness more precisely and profoundly even than later, more topical drama. Through the director the metaphors used by playwright-poets today can acquire concrete reference. It is the director who is responsible for the 'theatre of interpretation,' in Poland as elsewhere. But what is special about this kind of theatre in Poland is the way in which it has been evolved from historical and political events.

Thus for most of the major directors, the romantic repertoire has offered an outlet for personal views both on theatre and on reality. Productions of the classics have therefore reflected a wide range of different, if not divergent, approaches veering from one extreme to another as for example between the *Forefathers* produced by Kazimierz Dejmek at the Teatr Narodowy (National Theatre) in 1967 and the *Forefathers* of Konrad Swinarski staged in 1973 at Teatr Stary (the Old Theatre) in Krakow. Both of these were major theatrical events in the last decade, eliciting enormous response from both public and critics.

Kazimierz Dejmek was at the turn of the fifties and sixties, responsible for the theatrical renaissance which revived old Polish literature. He saw in native folklore and mystery plays the shape of national style in theatre. He then set about applying that vision in his production of *Forefathers.*

The setting, designed by Andrzej Stopka, was inspired by the staging of miracles, a convention that has survived from the Middle Ages in Nativity puppet shows using two levels and three divisions of the stage. In the visions of the romantics such a stage was regarded as a reflection of the world separated into the perspectives of good and evil. The forefathers' rites took place between the two-storey mansions. Centrally positioned at the back there was a three-winged altar, seen during a single scene only, otherwise hidden behind part of the set.

The pagan mortuary rites came to be combined with those of the Christian 'All Soul's Day'. The peasants, taking at first the role of high moral authority, as guardians of universal values subsequently became silent witnesses to the oppressive actions against the Vilnus youth accused of plotting against the Tsarist régime. Allied with the peasants is Konrad, the romantic hero and protagonist of Mickiewicz's dramatic poem.

The production suggested that the world was subject to moral principles which could be realized of social action. The combination of 'miracle with folklore' and the function of the stage design as an integral part of the dramatic interpretation was the essence of Dejmek's aesthetics as director of the National Theatre (apart, of course, from his artistic policy).

When Konrad Swinarski brought *Forefathers* back to the stage, it was as his fourth production of a great national classic. The first in the series had been *Non-Divine Comedy* by Zygmunt Krasinski (1965), a production in the special style of the then already notable director. Swinarski used the classics to give a perspective to the present. He tried to shock the audience into re-evaluating the classics, commonly venerated as the national bible.

With *Forefathers* this involved the use of devices to produce an effect of alienation. Swinarski juxtaposed the heightened emotional tenor of the grand poetry of *Forefathers,* its love and hatred, with the tough material reality of events (the gaol scene and the Senator Novosilcov scene) enacted on the special elevations across the stage and allowed them to jar. The result had the impact of a running press commentary.

Likewise he let Konrad's mystical, poetic rhetoric clash with the pagan, class-motivated rites of the peasants, making the alliance of the people with the romantic rebel seem most unlikely. This was emphasised by setting a part of the play in the foyer where the peasants conducted their sorcery. Swinarski also saw the play's symbolism in concrete theatrical form. In the text Konrad's inner struggle took the form of a battle between angels and devils for the human soul: on stage this became a brilliant visual pageant with winged spirits acting with operatic magnificence in contrast to the feverish servants of Lucifer spoiling for a fight.

21

Swinarski was attracted by the hard facts of history, but he was also fascinated by the romantic personality, and especially the limitations of freedom imposed by the individual's social conditioning. This was, in fact, a recurrent theme for Swinarski: found in the character of Count Henryk in *The Non-Divine Comedy*, the Count being a poet and the apogee of the doomed aristocracy; found in the poet Fantazy (the title character of Juliusz Sowacki's drama) who having frequented Western drawing rooms returns to a poor Polish province to get married, his intellectuality alienating him from his circumstances. Found last but not least in the protagonist of *Liberation*, whom Stanislaw Wyspianski gave Mickiewicz's name of Konrad, intending to defy not only romantic tradition, but also the political and social conditions of 1902. And to do all this from the stage in a Cracow theatre, where incidently the plot of the play itself takes place.

Liberation, produced by Swinarski in 1974, the year before his tragic death in an air accident, was a truly great production which also turned out to be something of a personal confession. With Wyspianski, Konrad becomes a creative artist. He takes part in the rehearsal of a play entitled 'Contemporary Poland' being rehearsed by a Cracow troupe. For him the play acquires cathartic dimensions—enabling the nation to experience its own errors. During a break in rehearsals, Konrad is assailed and accused by Masques. He feels it is essential to rebut their charges, thus grasping the truth about society and himself. As well as Romantic motifs there are other familiar themes—Prometheus, Orestes and last, but not least, Oedipus and the price of self-knowledge.

Swinarski's achievement was to cut through poetic symbolism to show the struggle of man with himself, his conditions, his life and his ideology. And to show it truthfully and as close as possible to present-day realities. This was the first production in which the romantic hero appeared free from oblique presentation, his quest for truth fully and directly endorsed.

The hero persues his aim individually through art (in a brilliant spectacle including elements of lampoon), and again amidst society, represented as Masques who diagnose him ill (in scenes around a hospital bed). His isolated individual struggle has so little success that it is taken for insanity. Self awareness is anathema. Self-blinded and trapped in a circle drawn around him by Erinyes at the end of the play, Konrad faces defeat brandishing his sword in an empty space. Yet the defeat did not detract from the significance of the contest itself any more than it denied the need for self knowledge. On the contrary, the defeat revealed the grandeur of the human condition.

For today's producer Wyspianski has proved to be an amazing source of inspiration. This was at one time attributed solely to the impact of the artist's theatrical vision alone; for it was clear that he had written some plays of unequalled poetic value. In 1969 however, the centenary of Wyspianski's birth, there were revivals of more than ten of his plays, including some rarely performed on the Polish stage.

This provided the occasion for reappraisal. It was obvious that it was not only his theatrical and artistic vision which had earned him respect and special attention, but also his treatment of national, social, and human issues. Produced regularly throughout the sixties, *Liberation* became something of a running commentary on current affairs (in productions by Adam Hanuszkiewicz and Jan Maciejowski). It also came to be interpreted in the wake of Grotowski's theatre (in Maciej Prus's production). Even if Wyspianski's work has failed to escape the modernist idiosyncracies of its verbal style, it has succeeded in serving as a vehicle for matters of social significance.

The same can be said of *The November Night*, which Andrzej Wajda staged only a few months before the first night of Swinarski's *Liberation*. The play is set at the outbreak of the anti-Russian uprising on a November night in 1830, and is inspired by the scenery of Lazienki Park in Warsaw. With such films by Wajda as *Kanal* and *Ashes* it has now become a tragedy of abortive heroism. Wajda managed—in staging the November events with Greek gods intervening in the human struggle—to give his production a dimension of grandiose symbolism. The gods sang, while the humans spoke; and yet they co-existed naturally. Once the music had established the special status of the gods, and this was recognised by the audience, it was possible for Pallas Athena to be accepted as the leader of the young soldiers, for Kora and Demeter to be in Lazienki Park, and for Charon to take away his cargo of fallen insurrectors. Both the mythological scenes and those charged with national significance, were intrinsically and compatibly theatrical: cadets for example walking into the streets, the scenes of combat, the preparation for departure into the land of shadows. Wajda discovered things in *The November Night* to which he was especially sympathetic: specifically the blending of apotheosis with re-evaluation. He was able, at the Old Theatre, to depict the power and beauty of youthful initiative simultaneously with the mechanisms of defeat and the bitterness of guilt. Following in Wyspianski's footsteps he combined political drama with classical tragedy. Wajda did justice to the tragic mode and therefore prevented over-hasty judgements.

What pre-occupied both Swinarski (in *Liberation*) and Wajda when they were exploring history was the origin of myth, whether the myth of a tragic individual as with Swinarski, or the myth of a collective, as with Wajda. Because of the depth of their reflection and their profound sense of the tragic, neither would ever be tempted to turn their modern interpretations into narrow commentary on current affairs.

A similar approach was used by the outstanding young director Jerzy Grzegorzewski in his production of Wyspianski's *The Wedding* at the Old Theatre in 1977. This play, written in

The Liberation by Stanislaw Wyspianski, directed by Konrad Swinarski, Stary Teatr, Cracow 1974

The Marriage by Witold Gombrowicz at the Teatr Polski, 1977, Wroclaw. *Photo:* Wojciech Plewinski

1901, was based on historical events notably the wedding of a Cracow poet with a girl from a nearby village. With its confrontation of two social classes, the play had often been interpreted as a satire on the 'Young Poland' literati, with their peasant-loving ideology and much talk but no action for independent Poland. *The Wedding* was staged twice in this vein by Hanuszkiewicz, emphasising the folklore with spectacular ostentation. In the screen version, Wajda showed the uniqueness of this play, with its effective social analysis, combined with symbolic insight into history, tradition, and literature. Grzegorzewski was seen to be concerned with class and class-impotence due to intellectual inhibition and social circumstances. Helplessness acquired a tragic dimension.

Grzegorzewski represents a new style in staging the classics, involving a search for a new scenic idiom. As visual artist and designer in his own productions, he uses concrete props only when they harmonise with his allusive overall conceptions.

In the actor-centred production in 1977 of *Kordian*—a biography of the 'innocent' generation from before the November uprising— Erwin Axer returned to the unadorned original text. This production of Slowacki's play marked the 30th anniversary of his direction of the Teatr Wspólczesny (Contemporary Theatre) in Warsaw where his experiments with Bond's *Lear*, Pinter's *Old Times* and Bernhard's *Borys' Holiday* were indicative of his radical approach.

Adam Hanusziewicz, the present director of the National Theatre, also exploits the romantic repertoire, not restricting himself to plays, but plundering as well the non-dramatic poetry of Slowacki, Norwid, and Mickiewicz, mounting productions based on his own scenarios and reaching young audiences with his spirited 'adaptations'.

Although the mid-war years, from the restoration of Poland's independence to the outbreak of war in 1939, were not very productive as far as psychological and social drama were concerned, during this time the specific pre-occupation with the struggle for independence was replaced by general social topics, such as the destiny of civilisation (Witkacy), or the mechanisms of social change (Witkacy, Przybyszewska).

The Case of Danton by Stanislawa Przybyszewska (1901-1935), daughter of the notorious modernist Stanslaw Przybyszewski, has proven more than once to be a valuable retrieval for present-day theatre: first, in 1967, thirty years after its premiere, Jerzy Krasowski mounted *The Case of Danton* at Teatr Polski (The Polish Theatre). Apart from marking a significant repertoire discovery, the production combined clarity with strength, with the juxtaposition of elaborate intellectual discourses and emotionally laden group scenes, such as the opening one in which the people of Paris were shown queuing for their bread rations—an emaciated crowd amidst the blackened scaffolding timber terrorised by hidden informers and commissars. So the people made the revolution, and now those whom the people had brought to power began to take over. Krassowski showed how and why the Danton-Robespierre case developed beyond the control of the people, despite the fact that their ideas still held sway with citizens.

As a result of her painstaking study of the history of the French Revolution, Przybyszewska challenged the established image of the leading figures in Buchner's tragedy *The Death of Danton* and Rolland's drama *Danton*. Her motive was to present the Danton-Robespierre case as a conflict questioning the meaning of revolutionary action. The Danton of Przybyszewska's play is a traitor and a demagogue winning prestige with flattery whilst holding the people in contempt. His case is not so much a matter of revolution devouring its own children, but rather the result of the fear of a new wave of terrorism which sentencing him to death would surely generate. Such is the view taken by Robespierre, the politician and moralist.

Andrzej Wajda's production of the play, staged for the opening of Warsaw's Teatr Powszechny (Common Theatre) after its reconstruction in 1975 laid emphasis on Robespierre's dilemma. In the final act Robespierre is seen talking with Saint-Just after the execution of Danton and his comrades. The moment is one of doubt, of despondency, of questioning, not policy—but the unjust order of the whole world. In a gesture of despair Wajda's Robespierre (played by Wojciech Pszoniak) pulls the blankets of his sick-bed over his face. A sense of commitment makes him rise, however, and attend yet another conference. The unsensational, unobtrusive ending highlighted the central conflict underlying all the scenes of private life and public duty: the price of social progress. The theatre and set (by Andrzej Wajda and Krystyna Zachwatowicz) elaborated this theme, converted to an enormous courtroom with huge painted canvasses on the walls, the public sitting around the central acting space. The play thus became a battle with words for weapons, its target, the power structure which replaced the established order. Unpretentious and unsophisticated, *The Case of Danton* was the first indication of Wajda's break from his spectacular style in favour of actor-centred expression. He continued along the same lines in *When Reason Sleeps* by Buearo Vallero at Warsaw's Teatr na Woli (Theatre in Wola) and especially in *Nastazja Filipovna* based on Dostoyevski's *Idiot*, a moving improvisation for two actors, and contrasting sharply with his earlier *Devils*.

A few avant-garde plays from the twenties have been taken from the academic shelves and successfully put to the test of the stage. One of these, *The Ball of Mannekins* by Bruno Jasienski, a leading intellectual figure of the left and member of The Futurist movement,

The Danton Case by Stanislawa Przybyszewska at the Teatr
Polski, Wroclaw 1967. *Photo:* Grazyna Wysowirska

The Danton Case by Stanislawa Przybyszewska at the Panstwowy
Theatre, 1975, directed by Jerzy Krasowski, with (from left
to right) Jerzy Nowak (Danton), Marian Cebulski (Bourdon),
Romuald Michalewski (Desmoulins), Wojciech Zietarski
(Delacroix), Andrzej Balcerzak (Philippeaux) and Janiz
Ostrowski (Westermann). *Photo:* Wojciech Plewinski

was a splendid production, using rhythm and dance and actors playing
mannekins and humans. Staged by Janusz Warminski, long-time director
of Warsaw's Teatr Ateneum *(Atheneum Theatre),* the production
captured the special literary qualities and social satire of the play.
Warminski was also responsible for the production of *Miss Tutli-Putli*
by Witkacy (1975), staged as a jazz musical, a justifiable approach as
the newly-discovered *Miss Tutli-Putli* (written in 1920) was intended as
an operetta libretto, although with characters reminiscent of other
plays by Witkacy.

Indeed, so similar are his characters that they inspired the collection
of several of Witkacy's plays into one. There was *Witkacy* by Jozef
Szajna and *The Crazy Locomotive* based on Witkacy's *Beelzebub*

The Danton Case by Stanislawa Przybyszewska at the
Panstwowy Theatre, 1975, with Jerzy Nowak as Danton.
Photo: Wojciech Plewinski

Sonata, staged by Krzysztof Jasiński at Cracow's Teatr Stu (Hundred Theatre), one of the leading experimental companies. The production became a musical set in a circus tent and included in its cast some of the popular pop-singers of the day.

This 'Witkacy for the masses' came as something of a surprise following his *Shoemakers* and *The Mother* produced by Jerzy Jarocki at The Old Theatre which had just caused a public stir. Jarocki used multi-media as well: *The Shoemakers,* for example, contained satire, grotesque, cabaret, circus and revue. *The Mother,* on the other hand, was a less exceptional more conventional production. Of the greatest importance was the subject matter: in *Shoemakers,* the process of standardisation of society due to a series of political coups d'état; in *The Mother* the crisis of individualism. Jarocki, a director of great potential and noted for his remarkable productions of Shakespeare *(Cymbeline* 1967 and *King Lear* 1977) and Chekhov *(The Cherry Orchard* 1975) developed his style by producing the avant-garde of the mid-war period and its present-day exemplaries:- Gombrowicz, Rózewicz and Mrozek.

The production of *The Marriage* by Witold Gombrowicz (1904—1969)— a play bridging the mid— and post— war periods—was Jarocki's earliest achievement in this vein. He had staged the play as early as 1960 at a student theatre and came back to it several times before he mounted the official first-night production on the professional stage at Warsaw's Teatr Dramatyczny (Dramatic Theatre) in 1974. His production of *The Marriage* has proven him capable of creating a 'new' theatrical reality blending realistic detail with surrealistic distortion. In the last Warsaw version, Gombrowicz's play was set in a specific moment of history. And though the protagonist Henryk was played as a Polish soldier from the Second World War who dreams in France of his family re-union, Jarocki managed to illuminate hidden areas of the subconscious. The protagonist's attempt to find confirmation of his 'divinity' by forcing others to worship him became a leitmotif of the surrealistic vision.

Even the radically personal and autonomous of Jarocki's productions have a multilayered structure and a complex reference to reality— as in his notorious productions of Rózewicz's *My Daughter* 1968, *The Old Woman Hatches* 1969, *On All Fours* 1972 and recently *Slaughterhouse* by Mrozek. As with Rózewicz so with Mrozek his work began with the preparation of a score. Out of a long-running radio play Jarocki shaped a play for the stage which had its world premiere at Warsaw's Dramatic Theatre. *Slaughterhouse* analyses the social function of art using a musician, his manager, his public and the relationship of all of them to music. Jarocki found a theatrical form for the music: while engaged in virtuosity the Violinist betrayed his dedication with flirtation. The Violinist's fantasies of fame — concerts in the philharmonic hall — were actually shown on stage in full-scale splendour and illustrated the helplessness of culture in the face of the brutality

The Slaughterhouse by Mrozek at the Dramatyczry Theatre,
Warsaw 1977. *Photo:* Marek Holzman

of life. The audience itself became the fictitious audience of the concert
hall, and in the second act assembled at the slaughterhouse to witness
a happening in the making. Woven through this was a 'narrative' of
metaphor, pageant, audience participation and superimposed comment.
Slaughterhouse had a theme in common with *Operetta* by Gombrowicz
staged for the first time in Poland by Kazimierz Dejmek at the Teatr Nowy
(New Theatre) in Lódź in 1975. The theme was that of the artist,
with his commitment to reality, and his ambition to judge history
and art fully aware of the destructive tendencies intrinsic to human
nature.

The artist, represented in *Operetta* by Master Fior, dictator of
fashion, appears helpless in the face of cataclism, though not freed
from the responsibility of essential human values. With such didactic
observation Dejmek shaped this production in keeping with his

outstanding political temperament and moral instinct. It was performed as the author had proposed as a genuine operetta, absurd at first and then swept with the 'wind of history.' The operetta form, elaborated with painstaking detail in set and costumes in the first act, was deliberately distorted in the second, and disintegrated altogether in the third—as a result of war and revolution. But since Dejmek seemed not to believe fully in the decline and fall of the world due to fashion and dressing up, or that it could be saved by the naked youthfulness of Albertynka, he failed to take her sufficiently seriously and over-relied on form in the revue-like finale.

This brief survey of the most important productions in recent Polish theatre has been, confined to the 'mainstage' repertory, most representative of directors' intellectual and ideological interests. It is not an exhaustive survey, nor does it include first rate work from other kinds of repertory. It has not been possible to discuss productions of contemporary foreign drama with which directors such as Zygmunt Hubner, representing intellectual and psychological currents at the Teatr Powszechny (Popular Theatre), achieve great success. One thing is certain however, that the 'traditional' theatre still has much to convey. It is important to realise how and why this theatre maintains its 'royal' rank.

THE GENIUS OF WITKACY (Stanislaw Ignacy Witkiewicz)
Konstanty Puzyna
Translated by Boleslaw Taborski

I

There is a drawing by Linke: a sombre, empty landscape, three black skeletons of withered trees. Against this background—the face of Stanislaw Ignacy Witkiewicz. Looking over his shoulder is another face, another Witkacy. Witkacy would doubtless like that portrait: it elicits the proverbial metaphysical shock. But as for the faces, there are a dozen too few of them.

If the truth be known, all his creative activity, his ideas and fate, his style of life and work make for a peculiar story—a very Polish, a little European and an incredibly confused story. Confused in more ways than one. The very number of disciplines Witkacy cultivated is astonishing: painting, novel, playwriting, theory of art, the orgy of culture, ontology—all these very individual and original, defying summary definition, exciting as intellectual propositions, inter-related, inseparable. The multiplicity of Witkiewicz's creative activities reflects the diversity of his interests.

His work seethes with the dynamics of contradictory tensions. Nearly all of the artistic preoccupations of the twentieth-century avant-garde coincide with pressing political, philosophical and sociological issues. Provocative diagnoses and hypotheses are mixed with a naïve obsession, serious matters with parody or conscious fantasizing Superimposed on this already intense mixture is the Polish national situation, forty stormy years which were not very kind to Witkacy but which gave to his work an additional distinctive significance. Before one's eyes, the emphasis shifts; mocking fantasy becomes observation, observation, an art nouveau myth. And cumulatively all of this takes on a tone of bitterness: the bitterness of being before his times, and, paradoxically, of being too late. There had been no such equally hellish concretion in Polish literature since the Romantics. There are so many threads—and tangled threads at that—in Witkacy, that one can only unravel some of them, in the hope that the whole will, perhaps, become clearer.

At first glance, there is no sign of trouble. Witkacy's position

A photograph of Stanislaw Ignacy Witkiewicz.

seems to have been unassailably established. For some years now he has been in vogue again, after being neglected for a quarter of a century. Theatres produce his plays: exhibitions of his paintings are organised; a new edition of his novel, *Insatiability*,[1] has sold out; young artists, and not only Polish artists, are increasingly interested in Witkacy.

What do they see in him? Something of his appeal has been expressed in the programme note to *The Shoemakers* at Sopot. It is, in fact, somewhat misleadingly extracted from an essay by Andrzej Stawar, selecting what that critic has—albeit reluctantly—positive to say about Witkacy, leaving out all the negative assertions. Witkiewicz's struggle against all the sentimentalising, the devalued emotionality and his interesting theory of acting were ahead of Brecht; Witkacy's catastrophic *weltanschauung* reminds one vividly of Beckett and the so-called black literature of the West; his surrealist, seemingly nonsensical humour rivals that of Ionesco. In our country Witkiewicz strongly influenced the prose of Gombrowicz and Schulz; in him are the roots of Galczynski's *The Green Goose* and Bialoszewski's *Theatre Apart*. And here is another view, that of Roman Ingarden: 'In his basic attitudes, he was an existentialist, many years before that trend emerged in France, and probably at the same time as Heidegger promulgated his views. But, as far as I know he never read Heidegger . . . He had in him—in spite of his profound pessimism—more spontaneous dynamism and original spontaneous generation than the French existentialists, while philosophically he had a more far-reaching ambition to create a complete metaphysical system that they had.'

These views are unambiguous: Witkacy was a dazzling precursor on a European scale, a natural genius long and far ahead—intellectually and artistically—of the directions and tendencies now most vital in Western literature. In spite of the note of exaltation in these quotations it is easy to see that they contain quite true observations and comparisons, with the possible exception of the doubtful parallel with Brecht. No wonder that in artistic circles Witkacy's name is increasingly popular: reappearing in articles and discussions, reverberating in cafés. The enthusiasm for Witkacy, the avant-gardist, is growing. Yet in this sort of situation, no one seems inclined to ask how such a phenomenon has grown from Polish roots.

The problems begin when the enthusiasm confronts its subject. When reading Witkacy's writings, some enthusiasts are puzzled. A precursor he may have been, but how can one compare Witkacy to Ionesco or Sartre! Even though the corpse growing in a room in Ionesco's *Amédée ou comment s'en débarrasser* is an idea lifted straight from Witkacy. And Sartre reminds one of Witkiewicz, not only in his philosophical attitude but sometimes even in his style: the naturalistic-expressionist brutality of *Les Chemins de la liberté*, combined with the constant self-analysis expressed in the conceptual language belongs to the same genre of prose as *Insatiability*. But there are so many longueurs in Witkacy, so much wordiness, diffuseness; how slight often the action in his plays, how great the many interminable debates. Though it is true that Sartre does not do any better on that score, it is also true that Witkacy considered conversation—stage argument—to be a more dramatic element than the events which, at the time of Shaw's success and in opposition to the convention of the well-made play, had their vogue. All this is true—mutters the disenchanted enthusiast—but . . . there is still so much of that annoying turn-of-the century manner in Witkacy.

So consternation grows. Was Witkacy good or bad? Was he a visionary or a charlatan? The disenchanted enthusiast turns to authorities. He finds quite a few of them, because Witkiewicz has been discussed by the most outstanding intellects. But problems increase. Professor Kotarbinski writes that Witkacy was a philosopher of genius, but uneducated, moreover that he 'gave birth not to mature works but rather to embryos of works'. Stawar says: 'an epigone, though a rebellious one.' Tadeusz Boy-Zelenski says: 'I do not hesitate to call that improviser of genius, one of the most powerful and original talents in playwriting, not only in Poland'. Karol Irzykowski says: 'Creative persistence and, maybe, graphomania combined with genius'. What is one to do with such a writer?

And yet these quotations are worth attention, particularly the one from Irzykowski. It could apply equally easily to the work of Stanislaw Wyspianski, Tadeusz Micinski, Stanislaw Przybyszewski, even Stefan Zeromski. What is even more interesting, at least in the case of Wyspianski and Przybyszewski, is that a similar—though perhaps less extreme—diversity of views between Irzykowski and Boy-Zelenski is repeated. This suggests that the argument goes deeper: it concerns not only Witkacy, but the evaluation of a particular intellectual milieu, a particular stylistic circle of the 'Young Poland' movement towards which Irzykowski was antagonistic from the start, and with which Boy-Zelenski was connected artistically and socially. Witkacy undoubtedly emerged from that movement; but he was younger by a generation.

Was he then an epigone, as Stawar would have it? Certainly not. But the notions 'epigone' and 'precursor' are relative: they refer to only a proportion of old and new elements. Precursors do not appear out of nowhere. To analyse Witkacy's position without over-simplification, one would have—with a touch of sheer wantonness—to look to his literary points of departure.

But here new traps await us.

II

The modernist movement, out of which Witkacy grew, had members who might seem odd bed-fellows, if mentioned in one breath, though their total effect is very clear. There are five: I have already mentioned three.

The first is obvious: Miciński. He and Witkacy were personal friends; together they experienced the dazzling impact of Picasso at the Shchukin Gallery in Moscow during the First World War. And the tragic circumstances of Miciński's death made a greater impression on Witkiewicz that it might, at first, seem. He was full of admiration for Miciński's work. He quotes him endlessly, writes articles about him, says that he is 'apart from Wyspiański, the only Polish dramatic genius of our era, since the times of Słowacki, he dedicates *Insatiability* to his memory, announces he will write a bigger work about him. Miciński's influence can be seen in many of Witkacy's works, and his three early plays—*Matthew Korbova, The Pragmatists*[2] and *Tumour Brainard*—abound with obtrusive allusions to Miciński's *Basilissa Teophano*. The shadow of Basilissa herself is to be cast later on many a Witkacy heroine, above all the Duchess Irina Vsevolodovna from *Insatiability* and *The Shoemakers*. In his admiration for Miciński, however, Witkacy follows him passively, uncritically and, as a result, uncreatively. Though in Witkiewicz's later works there develops a deeper inspiration, imaginatively and metaphysically, and the mechanical borrowings disappear.

The second influence is that of Wyspiański. Witkacy rates him next to Miciński, and that means highly; but he treats him in a strange fashion considering what was happening in the twenties. Those were the years when Wyspiański was put on a pedestal as the 'Fourth Seer' (after the three great Romantic poets), who had forecast not only Poland's resurrection, but virtually—the figure of Piłsudski. Scholars were pouring out endless streams of idolatrous, mystic-messianistic-nationalistic exegeses on the thoughts of Wyspiański—the new Mickiewicz. Witkacy, however, admired Wyspiański on a purely formal level, quite soberly aware of his literary weaknesses. 'For me', he would write years later in his essay *The Pure Form in Wyspiański's Theatre* ("Studio", 1937, nos. 10-12), 'Wyspiański was above all a theatre writer in the sphere of Pure Form, a playwright par excellence, with a preponderance of the visual element, and not at all a great author as such, or a painter; those elements of his nature, by themselves, were weak, but they served him extremely well as a stage artist.' Moreover, he was contemptuous of the Fourth Seer's ideology; for example, the 'national peasants' in *The Shoemakers,* who arrive 'with the bare-footed girl and Mr. Wyspiański's mulch, whose ideology even fascists would want to make the metaphysical-national basis of their joyous knowledge of how to use life' etc.

These are not superficial sneers; they run deeper. In *The New Deliverance*[3] there is a mock-paraphrase of the story line of Wyspiański's *Deliverance*. Instead of the powerless Konrad from Mickiewicz's *Forefathers' Eve,* Shakespeare's Richard III rages, immobilized by a pillar, while on a nearby settee, the assembled company chatter, drinking their tea. Instead of the Masks, the hero is surrounded by ordinary assassins with drawn daggers, and later, instead of the Erynyes, six ruffians rush on the stage, led by Someone; and the finale is not modelled on ancient tragedy, but taken straight from Kafka. What was for Wyspiański tragic, for Witkacy becomes nightmarish and grotesque: the Konrads are powerless not because of national torpor or because they are overcome by the 'poetry of the tombs,' but because they are rendered helpless by the new anonymous forces, which sweep them off the stage, together with the tea-drinking society. The whole concept of the artist-leader, of the gigantic personality, of the super-man, becomes anachronistic, just as does Richard's sword and armour.

Witkacy was influenced by Miciński in an altogether different way than he was by Wyspiański. He is no longer derivative: in fact of all Wyspiański's successors in drama (including Karol Hubert Rostworowski) Witkacy alone is not derivative. His work is rebellious, sneering, polemical with regard to the 'seer' and his advocator. At the same time it is not limited to matters of form, as Witkacy the essayist assures us: he is as bitter as Wyspiański about the powerlessness of spiritual Titans, of the little quasi-Konrads constantly reappearing, each of whom 'surpasses everyone else so much that he becomes almost nobody.' Yet even in matters of form, Witkacy is greatly indebted to Wyspiański: in the intermingling of contemporary and historical characters, in visual inventiveness and sensitivity to colour, in bringing to life figures from portraits (Julius II in *The Cuttlefish*, dressed 'as in Titian'), in the phantoms who mislay some prop—like the character in Wyspiański's *Wedding* who loses a golden horseshoe, for instance, or the hand of the Knight in *Matthew Korbova*. But even these small allusions have an altogether different tone. They are totally devoid of symbolism: they mean as much as they mean.

The third name to come to mind is that of Przybyszewski. Their affinity was commented on long ago. 'Just as for Przybyszewski the meta-word was a manifestation of the naked soul, so for Witkiewicz, pure form is a symbol of the unity in plurality' wrote Irzykowski in his *Fight for Substance.* 'They both cultivate what I call the *philosophy of the lost paradise:* they regard art as a means of momentarily patching up metaphysical and cultural holes. As poets, they both envy music. They are both, to a certain extent, rooted in the philosophy of Schopenhauer.' To this one has to add the most striking similarity: the demonic turn-of-the century eroticism. Richest in Witkacy, it is—almost as in Przybyszewski—rhetorical, expressed openly rather than through situations, or through psychological characterisation. Because of the use of words, the eroticism in both playwrights tends paradoxically, not to be sensual. Both tend to fan the flames with hyperbolic adjectives—perfidious, hideous, terrible, satanic, monstrous, violent, wild, unbridled, orgiastic—such that the audience can experience the 'metaphysical shiver.' Compared to Witkacy though, Przybyszewski is rather shy in his obscenities: he would not dare to describe most of Witkiewicz's 'perversions,' particularly those in the novels, the plays being comparatively innocent. More significantly, Przybyszewski's 'lusts' are conveyed with deadly seriousness, with sullen conviction, while in

Witkacy they are mockingly ambiguous, always turning into parody,
self-irony or sneering grotesque.

It was Wedekind who pioneered this kind of eroticism. Wedekind's
demonic Lulu (in *Erdgeist*, 1895 and *Die Büchse der Pandora*, 1901)—
tantalising with her ostensible wish to be subdued, and turning the most
magnificent males into lifeless rags—was the prototype of the modernist
femme fatale, and also the mother of all the 'wildly alluring' drawing-
room lionesses in Witkacy. Both authors also handle males similarly. It is in
Wedekind that the Przybyszewskian seriousness suddenly breaks into the
grotesque grimace. The first three acts of *Erdgeist* are a conventional
middle-class drama, but the fourth could have been written by Witkacy.
Lulu murders her jealous lover with five pistol shots, throws herself on
her knees before him, tries to save him with champagne, then seduces his
son, while another lover of hers—an acrobat, and a school boy (also in
love with her) and a Lesbian countess—pry on them from under the table
and behind the screens, interfering at the most dramatic moments. It all
ends with the school boy sobbing: 'Now they're bound to chuck me out
of school.'

There is still a certain inconsistency between the two conventions; the
change seems artificial and puzzling, even today. No wonder Wedekind's
plays caused so many scandals and the critics attacked him for unfairly
deceiving the audience, or with the inability to write 'a true tragedy.'
But some of them understood his intention even then. After the first
night of *Erdgeist* at the Berlin Kleines Theater in 1902, Friedrich
Kayssler wrote to Wedekind: 'Do you know what you accomplished
today? You have strangled the naturalistic beast of probability, and
introduced the element of play on the stage. May you live long for us.'
What made it easier to understand was Wedekind's own, hysterical and
spontaneous acting, almost like cabaret in its grotesque exaggeration.
The fact that Wedekind was both the author and cabaret actor was
significant. His plays are full-scale demonic, modernist *sur-cabaret*.

It was Boy-Zeleński who used the word 'sub-cabaret' to describe
Witkacy's plays, and it accounts for the enthusiasm Boy-Zeleński had
for Witkiewicz. Wedekind's sur-cabaret was the sphere where their
tastes converged.

There is, however, yet another modernist sur-cabaret, with which
Witkacy has much in common—Alfred Jarry and his *Ubu Roi* (1896).
Echoes of Jarry are present in Witkacy's brutalisation of language and
in his tendency to introduce consciously 'sordid' situations or
characters, sometimes even signified by their names. The pure nonsense
style is also common to both: Witkiewicz's steam rhinoceros and
steam Napoleon belong to the same family as Jarry's 'financial horse.'
And it is from *Ubu Roi* that the vision of history as a bloody and
absurd slaughter is taken, particularly in Witkacy's *Janulka*; so, too,
his succession of awesome and grotesque tyrants, leaders, dictators,
headed by foaming-at-the-mouth *Gyubal Wahazar*. The model of
Pére Ubu is given by Witkacy a new twentieth-century reality, at the

same time helping to neutralise the Nietzschean Superman (Witkacy called Nietzsche a 'monstrous intellectual impotent'). In that respect it is unlike the little quasi-Konrads taken from Wyspiański.

This completes the list of Witkacy's sources of literary inspiration. One could add some other names for instance Andreyev, and the late Strindberg. But it is the nature of the group itself which is significant—modernists all, but of a peculiar, expressionist kind, with a blend of other tendencies such as the symbolism so strong in Miciński and Wyspiański. It is worth mentioning, too, the monumental contempt he felt for Maeterlinck, of whose *L'Oiseau Bleu* he says that one has to 'remember all the time that it is not a bird that flies round the stage but Love, with a capital L.' Thus, of the modernist trends he cultivates not symbolism, but the most avant-garde tendency, that will come to full fruition only in the years of the First World War and immediately after, and then in Poland.

Witkacy remains faithful to expressionist inclinations in the theatre even when he has written all his plays, except *The Shoemakers*. In a letter dated 26 August 1927 Witkacy advises Edmund Wierciński, who has just broken with the Reduta Company and who has a passion for the avant-garde, what it is worth taking interest in among new works. 'As for the Polish authors, there are very few', he writes, and mentions only the now forgotten plays of Andrzej Rybicki and a handful of avant—garde poets. 'As far as foreign authors are concerned, above all Strindberg's *Ghost Sonata*. . . I know little of foreign literature. But among the Germans, Goll Iwan, Hasenclever, Kaiser, Unruh, Bronnen, Paul Kornfeld (Vienna).' He throws in Synge ('I have one thing by Goll and one by Synge translated, but not authorized'), O'Neill ('I don't know him, but they say he's very good') and, of course, *Ubu Roi*, with a now amusing confession: 'I have forgotten the author.'

This list needs no comment. But the conclusions one might draw from it would only be partially true. Witkacy was an expressionist—and he was not. But could he really be an expressionist in Poland between the two wars? The difficulty he had in recommending to Wierciński an expressionist Polish play of the period is indicative. What could he recommend? Graphomaniacs from 'Zdrój'? Effective but reactionary plays, like Rostworowski's *Compassion?* The naïve pacifism of Wandurski's *Death on a Pear-Tree*, a pale echo of German pacifism, which in Poland did not—for abvious reasons—open any bleeding wound?

From the tangle that is Witkacy, a new thread emerges.

III

Imagine quite a big country somewhere in the middle of Europe which, after several centuries of glorious past, ceases to exist as a nation and, for over a hundred years, goes into hibernation. Flat fields, thatched cottages, a peasant cart on muddy roads; small dreamy towns, cobble-stones in the market square, black Jewish gaberdines, and the parson's cassock; fields again, a herd of cows, poplars overlooking a pond, a small white manor house among trees. In the house, dark, moustached portraits on the walls: great-grandfather—a Napoleonic officer; grandfather—an insurgent of 1830; father—an insurgent of 1863. By the oil lamp a young man with flushed cheeks is reading the last sentences of Sienkiewicz's novel, to the effect that there is no predicament from which, with God's help, one cannot extricate oneself. In the West middle-class fortunes flourish and fall; the stock exchange, industry and commerce are the topics of the day. Here, in the capital city, gentlemen in frock coats argue in Lours's café that one ought to develop industry, spread education, begin work from the very foundations, but they still treat with contempt those who try to develop trade on a European scale. In another big city, abounding with noble monuments and national relics, a pale intellectual marries a peasant woman and puts on peasant attire, while journalists and artists come to the cottage for the wedding in order to fraternize with the people. This it is necessary to do, we were undone by dissent; the only miracle to happen is to unite the Polish peasants with the Polish gentry. Horse's hooves are heard beyond the windows: can it be a signal for the new uprising? That 'scene' from Wyspiański's *Wedding* prefigures the action of *Ubu Roi* which is being played out in this country. 'In Poland, and that means nowhere. . .' From the persepective of France or Germany, Jarry's 'nowhere' was fully justified: the country seemed slightly mad, wild, oriental. Moreover, it did not exist on the map.

This is, of course, a partial and prejudiced picture; but it does explain something. It makes it possible, for instance, to understand why naturalism hardly touched Poland: it had to remain frail and short-lived in a country which did not have either a strong middle-class, or the monstrous proletarian poverty of the industrial metropolis, or the Darwinian jungle of the big capitalist cities. The picture also explains something else: the early start of Polish expressionism. A cry of despair and revolt, more intuitive than intellectual, the feeling of tragedy and powerlessness, the bitterness, irony and pathos—for all these things there were favourable conditions. It consisted of the memory of lost uprisings, characterized by the feeling of disillusionment and destabilisation of the post-gentry intelligentsia, by economic stagnation and backwardness, by the strong—but no worse than in Germany—background of Romantic drama, and by the fervent dreams of national liberation. In the early phase of the development of expressionism, then, Poland kept pace easily with Europe, and was even ahead in the scope of the problems it encompassed. The Strindberg and Wedekind phase in the West was in Poland covered by Wyspiański, Miciński, Przybyszewski. The revolt of the foreign writers, however, was directed mainly against the middle class, and did not encompass the moral issues. In Wedekind there are sarcastic attacks on Wilhelminian militarism, imperialism, colonialism, police and censorship, but not in his plays, only in his satiric poems from *Simplizissimus*. In Polish drama national, political, and social problems erupted at the same time: they were there in Wyspiański's *Curse* and *Wedding*, while the year 1905 was echoed in two pre-expressionist dramas—Miciński's *Prince Potemkin* and Zeromski's *Rose*. Poland anticipated, in a sense, the second, peak phase of the development of expressionism which in Germany happened in the years of the First World War and in the twenties. For it was then that the great themes of that movement appeared: war and revolution, militarism and pacifism, the army and the proletariat, the crowd and the individual, unemployment and exploitation. The crisis of 1929, for example, was immediately and dramatically reflected in Brecht's *Mahagonny* and *St. Joan of the Stockyards.* A fierce clash of political views was taking place, from the pre-Hitlerian nationalism of Johst to the entire social-democratic and communist left, headed by Toller and Piscator. And then came a rich eruption of new forms of expression—spontaneous and growing out of the turbulent substance of the theatre.

In Poland on the other hand the second phase of expressionism in drama never happened. The few sporadic attempts after 1918 were decidedly derivative, barren and empty. Why did this happen, after such a promising start? A literary analysis leads nowhere; the answer lies in the situation of the country. It was a paradox. Unlike Germany, Poland did not experience the shock of a lost war, the collapse of the empire, the revolution suppressed by the forces of the right, the murder of Liebknecht, the equally fierce struggle between the social democrats and the communists, the chaos of the Weimar republic, the spectre of famine, the unemployment and uncertainty. Unlike Russia, Poland did not experience two revolutions, the overthrow of Tsardom, civil war, foreign intervention, the horrible years of starvation, typhoid, blood-shed and deprivation, which gave birth in early Soviet art to avant-garde experiment akin to expressionism. Poland experienced only the miracle for which generations had prayed throughout the nineteenth century: regained independence. And thanks to the pattern of international relations this happened with a minimum of effort, though Poles believed it was through their armed struggle. Instead of a polarization of attitudes, everything was drowned in a feeling of blissful solidarity. And Wyspiański, who in the *Wedding* sneered at its futility, was declared its patron.

It was believed that the traditional patriotic struggle for

liberation had come to an end: heralding an idyll, normal life in a normal nation, where one could enjoy the spring, love, street traffic, 'the city—mass—machine.' This was the sentiment of the Skamander group, and the futurists, and the so-called Cracow avant-garde, and others. Almosty nobody—with the possible exception of Zeromski—could see that Pulsudski's Poland was a creature on straw legs, that it was doubtful whether her fate would be decided on Polish territory, that, with the Russian Revolution and Italian Fascism, a page of history had turned.

The nineteenth century was over. To accept the situation would have required a modern political consciousness of the entire society. How was this possible against a background of superstition, in a country run by remnants of the gentry, priests and Pilsudski's legionaries; a country where a weak attempt at agrarian reform—described as bolshevik—fell through; where until 1939 the pride of the army was its cavalry; where the press denounced the wretched Boy-Zeleński as a corrupter of morals, because he demanded the right to divorce; where with great conviction the slogan 'Sea and colonies are the road to Poland's might' was proclaimed. Colonies, indeed!

Anyone who was aware of all this, would be socially so isolated that a not unreasonable response would be cynicism conveyed in the form of wild grotesque, disguised as 'futurist' fantasy. 'Nothing could shake our country from its heroic defence of the idea of nationality in the old, almost pre-historic nineteenth-century style, even against the tide of the Fifth, or Sixth [the oldest people did not remember which] Internationale. Syndicalism—whether workers' or sorelian, or American-fascist-intellectual—was not easy to establish. How much time has elapsed since those days: Poland, as always, was the 'redeemer', the 'bulwark', the 'mainstay'. That, after all, had been her historic mission for centuries. In herself she was nothing.' The contempt was to become a shout of protest, a shout of despair from the 'last individualist': 'I have no intention of being a manufacturer of tonic injections for the dying national sentiments, or the degenerating social instincts, those dying worms on the remains of the carrion of that splendid beast of past ages;' Eventually something even more tragic was to emerge—self-mockery: 'Oh, how abominable was the average Polsih intellectual of those days. Even upper class scoundrels, even the crowd in whose mass lurked the sinister, relentless future, were better than he.'

Only some of this Witkacy can be found in the plays, seen fully only in his last works—*The Shoemakers* and *Insatiability*. But this is the greatest Witkacy, the one the 'moderns' overlook when searching for the ingredients of the avant-garde: Witkacy with the raised visor, the only Polish expressionist of the 'second phase' rivaling his European contemporaries in the sharpness of his vision, and surpassing them in philosophical perspective, in awareness of the sociological and political processes which were to follow.

The crooked mirror of *Insatiability* shows Poland between the two wars. The work was somehow done, but what it was *au fonds des fonds,* nobody knew. The idea of statehood as such (and the illusions it produced) had long ago ceased to be sufficient motivation for even the simplest sacrifices or for giving up individual greed. And yet everything went on through a paradoxical and mysterious inertia, whose sources the ideologies of the ostensible ruling party— the Syndicate of National Salvation—were trying in vain to discover. Everything happened by *appearances*—that was the essence of the period. . . Apparent people, apparent work, apparent country. 'The political background of all this was, for the moment, too remote. But something was creeping out from the dark mountains of the unknown, like a glacier. Small, quick avalanches were occurring at the sides, but nobody took any notice. Statesmen of all parties, which had lost their old identity in the general, *artificial,* pseudo-fascists, non-ideological *au fond* prosperity, adopted a hitherto unknown broadness of view and unconcern, bordering on jolly idiocy. . . All in all, apart from Poland nobody talked about nations any more. And the latest discoveries of anthropology supported this, for that matter.'

That vision of a stultified society, with everything based on appearances, nobody realising what the realities of the situation were—the Vision of 1927—is that presented in *The Wedding.* And for that reason in *The Shoemakers* allusions to *The Wedding* recur, even in Pugnatsy Jawbloatski's last song where it is easy to perceive a parody of the Hetman in *The Wedding:*

> 'I wear red boots and a plumed cap,
> My sabre frightens everyone,
> My wild popeyes can really snap
> That's what I'll be and what I am'[4]

Witkacy however, surpasses the author of *The Wedding* in his acute awareness of how the idyll will end. 'The time came when the island of happiness shrank strangely, if not materially for the time being, then morally. Although the country did not grow smaller by an inch, it seemed to be an ever smaller patch, surrounded by red hot magma. The Syndicate members burnt their feet, but they held on. In the name of what? Nobody knew—there was nowhere they could escape to, if the worst happened.'

To call Witkacy the Fifth Seer would do him an injustice, for he had no such ambitions. But his national prophecies came true in September 1939. Only during the German occupation did the people realize that the fantastic story of the Quatermaster General Kocmoluchowicz had suddenly become reality.

IV

Where, though, did Witkacy get the mercilessly objective vision of the outsider? His intellectual background was extensive and exceptionally modern. He studied Whitehead and Russell, Husserl, Carnap; he admired Picasso and Stravinsky; he read Spengler and Freud; he was a friend of Malinowski, Chwistek, Szymanowski, Kotarbiński, Cornelius; he travelled widely before the First World War. But none of this is sufficient explanation. And from where did his expressionism stem, since the atmosphere in Poland in the twenties was not ripe for it. The answer lies in the Russian chapter of Witkiewicz's biography.

It was in Russia that Witkacy happened by chance to see the new face of the twentieth century. When the war broke out he returned to Petersburg from Australia where he had accompanied Malinowski on a scientific expedition. He reported for military service; as he was a Russian subject he considered it his duty. He graduated from the officers' school and, on his uncle's recommendation, was admitted to the guard regiment with its 'white' aristocracy. The life of the regiment—with its drunken sexual orgies, with its 'après nous le déluge' attitude, and the great Russian decadence, whose size and nature were virtually unknown in Poland—was to leave its mark on all his work. Somewhere here literary tradition ends and Witkacy begins.

Superimposed now on the literary inspiration of Miciński, Przybyszewski and Wedekind, on the innocent carousing of the Young Poland boheme of Cracow and Zakopane were the writer's new, catastrophic and monstrous experiences. It wasn't only from literature that Witkacy drew the duchess Ticonderoga's evenings, the preverse Persy Zverzhontkowskaya, the extermination of the boyars in *Janulka,* the atmosphere of *Matthew Korbova,* the philosophical discussions mingled with orgies, the orgies of drink and drugs, the use of Russian phrases and idioms. And Witkiewicz's fascination was all the greater because he had been brought up in the God-fearing Austrian part of Poland, and because—in the atmosphere of raging war and seething revolution—the state of dissolution and 'couldn't care less' attitude was even more pronounced. Jerzy Rytard recalls that Witkacy would go back in his mind to the Russian period as to an inexhaustible mine of adventures and anecdotes. These included the famous cuckoo game, the shooting at mirrors, and the collective sexual assault on a 'magnificent aristocratic broad,' who seemed to enjoy it immensely. But the shock experienced by Witkacy was not only of a moral nature; it was also historio-sophical, catastrophic and class-conscious. All those people were, more or less consciously, living through their 'last days of Pompei.' Hence the grotesque in Witkacy's decadentism. 'Experiences of a gang of degenerate "ex-human beings" against the background of life becoming mechanical': this is how he later described the theme of his first play *Matthew Korbova*.

And that was only the overture, the beginning of his Russian experience. The tsarist officer was then enveloped by the revolution he had sensed coming. 'From his accounts of what was for him a macabre period,' Rytard writes 'I learned that those were the two most difficult and terrible years in his life, full of constant hiding, evading the death which lurked round every corner.'

Rytard does not mention another fact; perhaps because Witkacy did not like to talk about it. Some time after the outbreak of the Revolution the soldiers of Witkiewicz's regiment elected him their political commissar. (According to another version, he was only made commander of a military unit. One thing seems clear, though: both versions relate to the February not the October Revolution.) The proof of trust given him by the mass of the soldiers was not, of course, a guarantee of safety: in the heat of rebellion even the 'white' ex-officers in such posts, were threatened by mob law. It was for this reason that Lenin issued a special decree in 1919 ensuring relative safety for the officers as 'war experts.' But the trust that was put in him left Witkiewicz more influenced than he might have wished to acknowledge. The man who returned to Poland in 1918 was not a communist. But neither was he an ordinary tsarist officer, saved from the holocaust.

Witkacy now saw the world from an entirely new perspective, alien to the Polish and French avant-garde of those years. This was partly the result of his first-hand experience of revolution and counter-revolution, with perceiving certain laws governing the political and social processes. But not entirely. Nor was it entirely connected with his language, often echoing the political jargon of the then left; or with the subjects discussed by his characters— with syndicalism, anarchism, fascism, liberalism, democracy; or with the grotesque Witkacy types, often deliberately given class characteristics—bourgeois, capitalist, proletarian, decadent aristocrat— in a way similar to that in which the young Soviet avant-garde was portraying them at that time. For that matter Witkacy showed similarities, in expressionist style with Pilnyak's *Naked Year*, with the early Erenburg, and with Mayakovsky's *Bathhouse* and *Bedbug*. And his theories of theatre and art theories were influenced by the Russian constructivists.

Witkacy believed that after the revolution artists would receive protection and patronage from the state. For an avant-gardist in Poland, surrounded, as Witkacy often said, with bitterness, by misapprehension, disrespect or mockery—this was undoubtedly an

argument for the Revolution. Furthermore it was an argument
confirmed by practice, a fact that Witkiewicz did nothing to conceal. Of
Tenger the ultra-modern musician of genius, in *Insatiability*—a
monstrous cross between Pére Ubu and Karol Szymanowski—Witkiewicz
says that 'all the music circles in the country were against him. . . they made
it impossible for him to establish official contacts with the bolshevik
countries where he could have found recognition in his life-time.' All this,
however, is marginal.

More important is the fact that for Witkiewicz Revolution was
inevitable. More than that it was necessary, and at the same time,
catastrophic, because by speeding the mechanization of society it meant
the end of great individualities. Speeding, not *causing* this is worth stressing.
Witkiewicz's analysis was deeper; revolution was, for him, only one stage
in a much more general process.

To discuss Witkiewicz's political views in their entirety would require
a separate dissertation. And it is too difficult right now: it will probably
be left for the next generation to do. And one can be quite sure that
Witkacy will feed several generations of researchers. To understand his
plays (where the political tissue is weaker and less essential than in his
novels) it is sufficient to be aware of Witkiewicz's inner political split:
knowing the necessity and doubting its sense. 'Only you are men now,
everyone knows this,' he addresses the Apprentices in *The Shoemakers.*
'But, on the other hand, I do not believe any more in that new life which
you are to create—this is my tragedy in a nutshell.' To this he adds in his
novel *Farewell to Autumn:* 'On the one hand, I cannot bear the lies of
today's democracy, with its equal start for all, parliamentarianism,
pseudo-equality before the law, and so on; but one the other hand, I am
not at all concerned with the fate of the working classes and their fight
beginning now against the dying democracy.' But is he really so
unconcerned, since in his theory of art, philosophy, and his theories of
Pure Form he is so anxious to escape the diseases of democracy?

Witkacy cannot always be taken at his word—though he constantly
interprets himself, refers to and comments on his ideas, thoughts,
feelings and mostly with amazing accuracy. Somewhere between full
self-awareness and half-conscious self-deception, between unmasking
reality and constructing an artificial paradise, between revolt and
escape lies all of Witkiewicz's work. In scenes from his plays or novels
one can see quite clearly—though in grotesquely demonic dimensions—
what sort of world is perishing, rotting, degenerating: 'bourgeois
formation,' 'ex-human being,' the aristocracy, financiers, diplomats,
artistic-intellectual bohemians, giving themselves up to 'satanic'
orgies while waiting for the deluge. In Witkiewicz's theory of art and
historiology this culminates in an annihilation of *all* culture.

To live through such a psychosis is not easy. Witkacy transformed
his own inner anxiety and feelings of inadequacy into the theory of
metaphysical insatiability. He looked for 'metaphysical shocks' which

would make him forget the world and enable him to experience in a
sudden flash—directly, almost mystically—the individual Mystery of
Being. Once this was the kind of experience induced by religion. Today
they can only be got by art, sex, drugs—and even that will not last
long, because with the growth of civilization the possibility of
metaphysical emotions vanishes. Witkacy elevated that tarnished
decadentism to the dignity of a confession of faith, then ridiculing
it both from the point of view of the decadents, and of the coming
'masses.' At the same time, he earnestly endeavoured to elevate the
whole concept of Experiencing the Mystery of Being as Unity in
Plurality, to the status of the absolute, to 'theorise' about it
philosophically and aesthetically. Then by putting whole chunks
of discourse—in discursive, theoretical language—into his novels and
plays he created a unique product. Various elements constantly
contradict one another: the drama unmasks the philosophy and the
philosophy cancels out the drama. The contradictions grow into
a monstrous grotesque world from which there is no escape.

And here are the roots of Witkacy's expressionism. But what
was he to do with it in the Poland of the twenties, where the
joie de vivre made it unintelligible even to the avant-garde?
Constructivism and futurism were most akin to his world views:
one had to build the resurrected state, 'demolish the museums' of
tradition, as Marinetti would have it, construct machines, cities,
glass buildings, the new poetry of labour. This tendency can be
found in Tadeusz Peiper and the early work of Julian Przyboś.
It was a tendency that contained the trap of intellectualism, and
Witkacy tended anyway to over-intellectualise. Even his own
expressionism was usually framed with irony, and his theory was
soberly formulated. He also admired logic, physics, mathematics,
and valued highly philosophical speculation and conceptual
thinking. In *Insatiability* before Tenger stuns Genezyp with the
hurricane of 'monstrous' music, the latter protests: 'But I must
know this in *concepts,* and this is an altogether different matter.'

The tendency to escape from reality into the sphere of
abstract constructions, into the theory of Pure Form, also
appeared. For that matter in the twenties the words 'expressionism,'
'formism,' 'futurism,', and 'constructivism,' were often inter-
changeable. They simply meant the avant-garde—new art.
Different directions were still in the melting pot; their advocates
often argued bitterly, but usually overlooked essential
contradictions. It is only with hindsight that one can see the
absurdity of the Cracow formists who called themselves 'Polish
expressionists'—a total confusion of different concepts.

Witkacy betrayed expressionism in favour of the Cracow formism.
He joined that group shortly after his return to Poland, and became
its foremost theoretician and representative. The union seemed a
happy one too, for those years were the peak of his creative activity.

Between 1918 and 1926 he produced over thirty plays, three theoretical books on painting and the theatre of Pure Form. He also painted, debated, lectured, engaged in polemic with Rostworowski and Stern, Irzykowski and Kleiner, Boy-Zeleński and Breiter, Chwistek and Slonimski. He was surrounded by a whirl of argument, hate, admiration, scandal and gossip, and lived to the full with his nervous, over-sensitive nature..He achieved a considerable popularity, which began to wane immediately the formist ferment died out.

It was a rather superficial popularity to be sure: formal, connected with new styles, not new substance. Hardly anyone at that time took any notice of substance. On the other hand, Witkacy was attacked for having too much substance in relation to his theory of Pure Form for the difference between his theory and his practice, for his barren doctrinairism, for his contradictions. The contradiction between theory and practice was an undoubted fact: Witkacy's formist theories seemed artificially self-imposed by the artist, whose spontaneous creative instincts had an altogether different tendency. Witkacy defended his Pure Form vehemently; but the very vehemency of his self-defence suggest that he was protesting too much—to evade uncertainty.

And then, about 1926, the formist chains broke. Was it because the heroic period of Cracow formism was nearly over? Or because dark clouds were gathering over the Polish idyll? There was Pilsudski's coup d'etat in May, the gathering wave of the Great Depression leading up to 1929, threatening to end the 'artificial prosperity' based on American credit. There were certainly also other more complicated reasons. Witkacy virtually abandoned theatre and painting at that time, though he still painted portraits to earn money. He abandoned the very art he had defended so strongly with his theory of Pure Form.

He turned to the novel. In 1925 he began to write *Farewell to Autumn*, published in 1927, and then went on to *Insatiability*. In this area, he simply by-passed the theory of Pure Art. He declared that it was not valid for the novel, because a novel is too long and does not have the direct impact of a play, a painting, or a poem. It did not occur to him that one could write a *short* novel, no longer than a play.

The absence of this simple observation suggests that the explanation was an excuse. But that was what Witkacy needed: to reject the ballast of his own aesthetics; to argue that the novel was not a work of art, so that it could be anything—'beginning with a non-psychological adventure, presented from outside, and leading to something bordering on a philosophical or social treatise.' Then, rid of the shackles of Pure Form, what Witkacy really wanted to say could break out: the wild, expressionist socio-political grotesque, the catastrophic treatise, the crooked mirror of morals. In the novel, he would confess quite openly, 'the main thing is the content, not the form.'

The betrayal seems childishly naïve. All the more so because Witkacy also wrote *The Shoemakers* at that time, in a style similar to that of the novels. Though he still maintained: 'I have not at all changed my aesthetic and philosophical views. On the contrary, I have developed them.' (*Reply and confession*, 'Linia' no. 3, 1931) But the betrayal was also heroic. It was an act of determination; it meant that he had found himself. It meant that the escape into the artificial paradise of formism did not pass the test. It did not stifle fear, or revolt against reality, though it attempted to do both. It achieved only what dreams do: it created, as Freud would say, vicarious gratification.

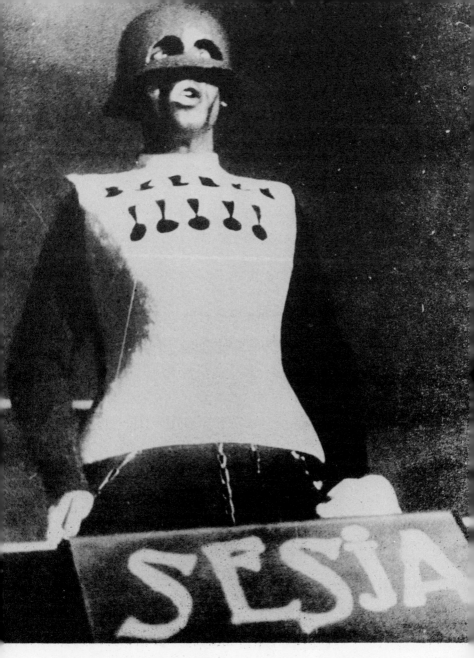

Above. From *The Cuttlefish*, directed by Tadeusz Kantor, 1956.
Cricot 2, Cracow.

Opposite. Stanislaw Ignacy Witkiewicz: a self-portrait.

From *The Cuttlefish*, at the National Theatre, Warsaw 1966.
Directed by Wanda Laskowska, designed by Zofia Pietrusinska.
Photo: Fr. Myszkowski

From *The Cuttlefish*, directed by Tadeusz Kantor, 1956
Cricot 2, Cracow.

V

Nearly all Witkiewicz's plays were written in the formist period of 1918-1926. He aimed high: it was an attempt—like his painting—to regenerate the vanishing metaphysical emotions in art by striving at Pure Form. According to the degree of his success in attaining that ideal, Witkacy marked his plays with an asterisk, or a cross. He treated them in a somewhat doctrinaire manner, almost as exemplifications of the validity of his theoretical theses. With unfortunate consequences sometimes for the plays themselves, giving them an aura of artificiality, gracelessness and—paradoxically—a formal roughness.

A detailed examination of Witkacy's theory would lead to a dissertation on the aesthetics of the avant-garde, on the similarities between the theory of Pure Form and certain ideas of Tairov and Artaud, on its—now obvious—misconceptions, and on the equally obvious break-through from the naturalist and psychological fossilisation in the theatre that the theory allowed.

The theory of Pure Art had its origins in the plastic arts. Witkacy built the theory on the ground of painting, and only later transferred it to poetry and theatre, still using arguments taken from painting as examples. Witkacy the painter was not, however, more of a formist than Witkacy the writer. Indeed, his painting and his literature were homogeneous. Soft linear curves, inherited from art nouveau were combined with expressionist deformity of shape and fantastic colours, and with the aura of 'metaphysical' eeriness, sometimes dangerously akin to Podkowiński's *Frenzy*. He was also a representational painter with no marked tendency towards the geometric abstraction one might reasonably expect from a formist. In his theoretical works Witkiewicz was against 'visceral' painting and stressed the importance of composition, the interplay of colour and form, the flatness of the canvas, the total indifference of the subject and detailed thematic elements which only serve the purpose of 'directional stresses.' In short, as Mieczyslaw Wallis rightly observed, 'Witkiewicz sketched an artistic oeuvre most akin to the painting of Gaugin, Matisse and the early Picasso.'

But the work itself, when looked at closely, betrays a crypto-expressionism. It was significant that Witkacy did not attempt to postulate pure abstraction: 'this factor, of compositional mass becoming similar to such and such a subject, involves the entire psyche of an artist, all his remembered experiences, the whole world of his imaginings and emotions; it is his psyche—irrespective of his capacity to transpose his vision into reality—that makes him, and not other Particular Beings, what he is, a being of such and such character and psychic attributes.' To express that psyche is the fundamental task of an artist. Matisse and Picasso would shrug their shoulders at such a requirement. Witkacy was aware of that, so he tried to marry fire with ice. 'A work of art,' he would say in *New Forms in Painting,* 'must come into being, passez-moi l'expression grotesque, out of the most essential viscera of a given individual, and as a result must be altogether free from that particular "viscerality". That is the recipe—but how difficult it is to effect it.' Exactly! The purpose of a work of art is to evoke in the recipient a metaphysical shiver, his own, individual experience of the Mystery of Being.

The theory of Pure Form in the theatre is analogous. Here too Pure Form is the construction of the total work, the composition and the formal harmony of its elements. The author warns that 'the concept of Pure Form as the composition of the work has nothing in common with the concept of form as a vehicle for the content: the form to express thought or emotion, or the form of the subject in painting.' Only the 'directional stresses' now change into temporal-spatial 'dynamic stresses' and the difficulties of effecting it in practice will be increased. 'If we can imagine a painting as consisting of totally abstract forms which, without a clear auto-suggestion in this direction' will not evoke any association with objects from the external world, we cannot even think of such a stage play, because pure 'becoming in time' is only possible in the sphere of sounds. And a theatre without the actions of some persons, no matter how wild and improbably they might be, is unacceptable, becuase theatre is a complex art, without its own *homogeneous* elements, like the pure arts: Painting and Music.' But in spite of the basic impurity of theatre, Witkacy thinks that Pure Art can be achieved, with a certain compromise: 'Just as the emergence in painting of a new pure, abstract form, without a direct religious basis, came about at the price of distorting the vision of the external world, so it is possible for Pure Form in the theatre to emerge at the price of distorting the psychology and action. Such a play can be imagined with absolutely all options open, from the viewpoint of life, with immense cohesion and elaboration in the twists of its action.'

The formula is clear enough. But the clarity is superficial. It is hard to say, for instance, of what the immense cohesion and elaboration in the twists of *action* ought to consist, since the action is to have all options open, as far as 'life' is concerned. Criteria are lacking, or to be precise, there are two, totally subjective criteria: the arbitrary decisions of the author and the metaphysical experience of the spectator. This is not much of a theory of art, but Witkacy does not seem to be worried by this. Maybe he would have worried more, had he noticed the lack of logic between the 'distortion of psychology and action,' and 'all options open'— there is quite a serious difference. Witkiewicz explains that by 'distortion' in theatre he means 'a lack of sense in the statements and actions of any individual,' but he stresses that 'our aim is not programmatic nonsense, but an extension of compositional possibilities by not holding on to life's consistencies in art,'

When arguments are not sufficiently precise, examples may be helpful. To a certain extent all Witkacy's plays may serve as examples, rather more often of 'distortion of psychology and action' than 'absolutely all options open'. Some, however, like *Metaphysics of the*

Two-Headed Calf, are 'open', but these are usually the weakest plays, with excessive disruption of cause-and-effect structure. It is difficult to grasp the rules of the game; and as everything is permitted, nothing evokes any interest.

Witkiewicz's intentions are best demonstrated by another example, which he himself gives in his book *Theatre*: 'And so: three persons dressed in red come on and bow—it is not clear to whom. One of them recites a poem (it ought to give the impression of something necessary at just that moment). A gentle old man comes in, with a cat on a lead. All this happens against the background of a black curtain. The curtain is then pulled open and an Italian landscape can be seen. Organ music is heard. The old man says something to the other characters, which must help to create an atmosphere suited to everything that happened before. A glass falls off a table. They all fall to their knees and weep. The old man turns from a gentle creature into an enraged beast, and murders a little girl, who has just crawled from stage left. A beautiful youth rushes in and thanks the old man for this murder, and the characters in red sing and dance. Afterwards the youth cries over the girl's corpse and says very joyous things, and the old man again turns into a gentle and good creature, and laughs in a corner declaiming in lofty and clear sentences. The clothes can be any style—period or fantastic; some parts can be accompanied my music. Is it a madhouse then? Or rather the brain of a madman on stage? Possibly yes, but we can say that, using this method, one can, *writing a serious play and staging it properly, create things of hitherto unknown beauty;* it can be a drama, a tragedy, a farce, or a grotesque, all in the same style, not recalling anything hitherto written. Leaving the theatre a man must be under the impression that he has just awakened from a strange dream in which even the most common things had a strange, unfathomable charm, characteristic of dreams, not to be compared with anything.'

This is Witkacy's ideal of the theatre of Pure Form. Witkacy's practice fortunately differs greatly from that ideal; reality in his plays is more often condensed than rendered totally unreal. But something very essential in his playwriting is clarified in his example. From the clash between the grotesquely hyperbolic, violently committed expressionism of Witkacy the novelist, and the escapist and aesthetizing formism of Witkacy the theoretician of painting, there emerges in his theatre an unexpected result: surrealism. Unexpected, because not planned, emerging from the inner contradictions of the artist; unexpected also, because sincere and—at least in the episode of the gentle old man, in the poetics of the strange dream, and in the madman's dream on stage—almost discovered by the author himself.

Witkacy was the first and only Polish surrealist in the theatre who has passed the test of time. Ironically, a surrealist by chance. Not, of course, in all his plays. The first two were very much under the influence of Miciński; *Tropical Madness* and *The Independence of Triangles* are not far removed from Wedekind's Lulu-Dramen;

John Matthew Charles Hellcat is almost an ordinary realist play; *The Crazy Locomotive* breaks out in the direction of futurism, *The Anonymous Work* and *The Shoemakers*—in the direction of expressionism. But most of the plays are within the poetics of surrealism. There are the dreams with their absurd fantastic characteristics, their seemingly illogical sequence of events, the restrained, often disguised expression of the conscious and unconscious in the author's psyche. On this level, surrealism was quite close to expressionists. But unlike Witkacy's expressionist novels, his aim in the theatre was not so much to mock reality with all its political confusion, not so much to present the catastrophic philosphy of history and theory of culture, but to reveal the very 'Strangeness of Existence,' creating a separate, autonomous sur-reality, which is the basis of must surrealist poetry.

His fantasies are wonderfully strange: at one moment rapid in the flow of events, then suspending the action for philosophical discourse; at one moment sharply pointed, then with endings blurred, like a phantom dissolving into nothingness. They are also more cheerful than in the novels. Even brutality and sex seem less sullen here. At the same time, they are—as in dreams—immensely *optic* visions, where the colour, shape, movement have a strong and memorable impact. Witkacy, the painter, creates the colours not only of the sets and costumes but also the thinness or obesity of the characters, the colour of hair, moustaches, beards and bald patches, the green fire in the chimney, the dark-red earth on which strange flowers grow, and in which grave-diggers dig a grave in *The Anonymous Work*.[5] In *The Mother* everything is black-and-white, even make-up: the faces are cadaverous white, 'black lips, darkly flushed cheeks.' The only gaudily coloured thing is the Mother's knitting and later . . . the face of Sophia, when that modest girl gives herself for money. Even the number of people present on the stage has a plastic sense, and sometimes also expresses, as in a dream. Freudian subconscious states: in *Sluts and Butterflies* the demonic Sophia is followed by—apart from her principal admirers—*forty* Mandelbaums, who lust for her. And when at last they throw themselves on her with a roar, Sophia disappears quite literally under the heap of bodies. When they disperse, only her dressing gown and slippers remain on the floor.

The impression of surrealism is further emphasised by the dialogue, without a particular 'lack of the sense of conceptual links': normal, logical, full of temperament, not without longueurs, but also sharp and witty, sometimes enriched by fantastic pure-nonsense neologisms, particularly when it comes to the invention of verbal abuse—but in general quite ordinary. All the characters talk the same careless, and quite expressive language—the language of the author. In effect, the dialogue is in a fixed key: it sounds like drawing room conversation in the circles of intellectual boheme. Because the key does not change— though historic and fantastic characters may invade the action, people murder and rape one another, split in two, die, resurrect, none of which makes any impression on those present—all this increases the feeling of weirdness in this genre of black comedy.

Like the key of the dialogue, certain fixed types recur in Witkacy's plays: the titanic leader, the tyrant, the artist or scientist, the perverse upper class courtesan, the sweet young girl with an ambiguously naive expression. Several obsessional themes also recur. These themes may be unimportant to Witkacy the theoretician—and used as pretexts (which explains the phenomenon of his prolific playwriting), but they are quite 'realistic,' connected with the author's entire life experience and intellectual equipment. Rockoffer in *The Cuttlefish,* when trying to persuade the other characters to leave for Hyrcania, says: 'I'll create a really cosy little nook in the Infinity of the world. Art, philosophy, love, science, society—one huge mishmash.'[6] Those are the basic Witkacy themes.

One could add three more, slightly less frequent: drug addiction, madness and the tropics—exotic reminiscences of his stay in Australia and the expedition undertaken with Malinowski to Malaya. The latter themes have often attracted surrealists like Artaud, who were also drawn to literary parody, common in Witkacy, and sometimes even performing the function of narrative structure: the parody of Wyspiański in *The New Deliverance,* of Tadeusz Rittner in *In the Small Mansion,* or of Ibsen's *Ghosts* in *The Mother.*

But there are even deeper affinities with surrealism. They can be seen in Witkacy's distortion of the laws of physics and biology, in the mockery of the empiricism and narrow 'common sense' of the naturalists. Not to mention the live mummy and the Masculette in *The Pragmatists,* the numerous resurrections, or the situation in *The Madman and the Nun,* where the hero appears well and happy on the stage where his corpse is still hanging. In Witkacy's plays there are effects, whose bravura surpasses the entire European drama of the time, and is unsurpassed to this day, either by Ionesco, or by N.F. Simpson, though both these writers are consciously within the surrealist tradition.

In the epilogue to *The Mother,* when the old Mother is lying on the catafalque, and her son, Leon, mourns over her, lost in thought, the same Mother enters, aged 23, accompanied by the Aunt. Mother is pregnant with Leon, but she engages in conversation with Leon, who is on the stage. The Aunt comments thus on the situation: 'Physical doubling plus displacement in time—no, that's going too far. We've been raised on Einstein, but we can't take a hoax like that seriously, even as an intellectual experiment.' Witkacy draws even more hellish 'conclusions' from Einstein in *Janulka,* where the theory of relativity is applied not to biological, but to historical time: history in Lithuania 'has turned its back to its front,' and all epochs are muddled up. This is the measure not only of Witkacy's black humour, but also of his philosophical imagination, of the perverse intellectualism of his plays.

The most amusing thing is that Witkiewicz did not appreciate the surrealists. He protested strongly when he was compared to them. He charged them with using the absurd for 'real' purposes, not for Pure

Form; he astutely accused them of disguised naturalism and indifference to 'formal beauty.' But his own plays have much more 'real' sense than he supposed. And, of course, surrealism had several variants. The main current was characterised by the aim to destroy tradition and bourgeois common sense; it was deliberately anti-aesthetic, because 'beauty' is also a reflection of habits and tradition, a stereotype of imagination. The source of that main stream was in the provocative anti-aesthetism of the dadaists, clearly stated by Ribemont-Dessaignes in his *Histoire de Dada* (1931): 'The aim is a new, abstract world, composed of elements borrowed from concrete reality, but being outside any formal values.' There were, however, in French surrealism also classicist tendencies, growing not so much from the Dada movement, as from Cubism (Jacob, Reverdy), stressing the necessity of formal composition, construction, a new structure.

Even Breton, who propogated *écriture mécanique* and scorned any 'arranging of verses,' sometimes reverted to the concept of 'beauty.' 'One begins with the fact that the intellect has not observed anything consciously. From a change coming together of two elements of reality a light has flashed, *the light of an image,* to which we are particularly sensitive. The value of the image depends on the beauty of the obtained spark.' (*Manifeste du Surréalisme,* 1924). Witkacy the theoretician would subscribe to this formula. And if the 'image' resulted not from a coming together of words, as Breton would have it, but from a coming together of actions, characters and scenic situations, Breton's formula would indeed fit, if not in full, Witkiewicz's playwriting.

Another fragment of the same *Manifeste* applies even better to Witkiewicz's plays: 'The innumerable number of types of surrealist images require classification, which I do not intend to do now. . . . I will not conceal the fact that for me the strongest is the one containing the largest dose of free options, the one that is most difficult to translate into practical language, either because one of the elements of the image has been somehow lost on the way, or because, while having been most promising, it comes suddenly to a very weak solution (like the suddenly folding arms of compasses), or because it evolves of itself an unimportant *formal* justification, or because it is hallucinatory, or because it puts the concrete mask on the abstract, or the other way round, or because it assumes the negation of a fundamental physical property, or because it evokes laughter.' All these types of surrealist image can be found in Witkacy's plays. Not a single one is missing.

There are differences only in the themes. And they are, on occasion, striking. The French surrealists of the twenties could not foresee either Witkiewicz's experiences, or the philosophical, political and social problems troubling him. Even in the suppressed form in which they appeared in Witkiewicz's plays, they were apparent only in Central Europe, not in the West.

Many of them grew from specifically Polish soil: from the national situation, from the cynical polemics against the traditions of 'antemurale christianitatis,' from the profound connections with Polish literary tradition. And this is where the originality of Witkacy's philosophising surrealism lies. It could also have been a deliberate opposition to French surrealist tendencies as he knew them that saved Witkacy from imitation, that nightmare of Polish avant-garde movements. His surrealism was entirely his own, distinct, authentic, only chronologically parallel to the French, as with the second wave of expressionism in Germany and Russia. It was still firmly rooted in modernism. But the amusing thing is that even the turn-of-the century elements of his theatre (in the negative sense of the phrase) have now a surrealist impact, thanks to associations with the paintings of Salvador Dali or Felix Labisse, where, with naturalist literality, elements of art-nouveau fashion, sculpture and architecture were introduced into the composition. Why not then elements of literature, ideas, language?

The reply to the question 'epigone or precursor?' now seems clear. And yet Witkacy's innovations do not end with his surrealism. This is only one of the strange discoveries of that writer—and not the most important.

VI

One is inclined to treat catastrophists, decadents, prophets of fear and uncertainty of all kinds with contemptuous forbearance. If they are not reproved for being so unconstructive—for not constructing foundations for the glorious future—they are treated as buffoons. But in times of historical cataclysm, war, revolution, political upheaval—those hysterical buffoons sometimes see and know more than the vigorous, optimistic rationalists.

Witkacy saw the end of the old Poland in the perspective that, in the twenties, could perhaps only be sensed by Zeromski. But he went further: he saw the disintegration—final, as he felt—of a certain civilisation—the European civilization. *Farewell to Autumn* even included this observation in the title. It had a deeper, and wider, meaning than just the ever recurring statements about the end of the bourgeois era. A sense of catastrophe certainly, but also ambiguity: metaphysics and art would perish, life after the holocaust would be grey. But at the end of Witkiewicz's two main novels (he wrote four in all) the heroes, free from metaphysical feelings, are at last, in some measure, happy.

There are echoes of Spengler however partial and relative: from *Untergang des Abendlandes* Witkacy took mainly the thesis, which is even now still worth consideration. The present pattern of political forces in the world, the vitality of two young civilizations (the American and the Soviet), the growing importance of the peoples of Asia and Africa, and the shrinking importance of the European nations—all this gives reason to suppose that an era of syncretism is coming, that the Christian culture of the West will soon lose its centuries-old monopoly. Those were the suppositions of the turn-of-the century decadents.

Miciński had similar thoughts. But today they are more difficult to ignore than half a century ago.

Even Witkacy's 'decadentism' is no simple matter. Irzykowski, and Stawar after him, made things too easy for themselves, aware only of the mechanical relicts of modernism. It is significant that this decadentism always appears in the inverted commas of mockery or in grotesque hyperbole. There is always as much fascination as contempt. On a purely intellectual level, in the philosophical discourses, one often encounters Witkacy's obvious arguments against certain tenets of decadentism, quite open polemics in fact, beginning with attacks on Nietzsche and Bergson, and ending with those on Spengler. Some of the dialogue from *The Mother* illustrates this:

LEON. What the hell! If we really possess the intellect which Spengler says is a symptom of the decline, we must have it for some purpose, and not just be conscious of the decline and nothing else. This same intellect can become something creative and avert the final catastrophe.
SOPHIA. Those are just hollow promises. You don't have any idea how to go about it.
LEON. I know how to begin. First of all, not hide our heads in the sand, but look the truth straight in the face, and with the help of this intellect which is so scorned nowadays, resist the historical truth that is rushing at us: universal greyness, mechanization, a foul swamp of social perfection. Just because the intellect has turned out to be a symptom of decadence, why become an anti-intellectual, a synthetic simpleton, a practical joker à la Bergson? Oh, no. Just the reverse: all the more reason to become aware of all this oneself, to the highest possible degree, and not only yourself, but to make others aware of it, too. A damn difficult assignment: to make the masses aware that spontaneous, natural social development threatens us with annihiliation.[7]

This is the intellectualist, anti-decadent credo of Witkacy. Someone might argue that statements made by characters in plays must not be credited to the author. All the more so as Witkacy himself asserts in the introduction to *Tumour Brainard* that he does not attribute objective meaning to any of his characters. But one can find in his theoretical works the same theses and arguments as those put forward in *The Mother*, and Witkacy included whole chunks of them in his plays, almost in total. The dialogue quoted above is important for many reasons: it defines the frontiers not only of Witkiewicz's decadentism, but of his catastrophism.

The greyness, mechanization, end of great personalities, vanishing of metaphysical feelings, thoughtless happiness of well-fed animals which 'free social development' would bring about all this, says Witkiewicz, is *probably* inevitable, but it is not *absolutely* inevitable. If societies realized the sad reality of this perspective, one could begin counter-action, just as by creating art in Pure Form one can attempt to save metaphysical feelings. It is a frail hope, but nonetheless, it exists. Leon goes on to say: 'Only the entire human race, alerted to the danger, can create the sort of social atmosphere in which individuals of a new type can arise. It may be claptrap, too, but it's the only kind still worth trying. In any case, where we're headed now, where blind social forces are dragging us, that is, toward total mechanization and imbecility, there's absolutely nothing in store for us.'[8]

Here again is something worth pondering: is what Witkacy warns against just a gloomy figment of his imagination? An unusual figment, though, compared with the naïve technological enthusiasm of the futurists, and given the Polish reality of the twenties.

For Witkacy's contemporary this could have been taken as just one more fantasy. The warning was one of the first of that kind in twentieth-century literature: the quotation from *The Mother* (1924) was seven years earlier than Huxley's *Brave New World,* and Witkacy had fully formulated this thesis as early as 1918. Now, however, it is no longer a fantasy. 'Prophecies uttered in 1931 are being fulfilled much faster than I supposed', declared Huxley later in *Brave New World Revisited.* He has now been echoed by a whole galaxy of sociologists and psychologists in the West: the problem of the 'civilization of the ant-hill' is beginning to be a crucial issue of the very near future in the highly industrialized countries. It has not been fully encountered yet, but in the United States for instance, it is something now provoking open concern. 'Thanks to specialization and the mechanisation of work,' says the outstanding American 'sociologist' of mass culture, Van der Haag, 'the majority of the people have become standardised; there are no variations; the patterns and rhythms are fixed by the machine, leaving smaller scope to individual intelligence. Organised production, feeding the machine and being fed by the machine, depends on a bureaucratic system and requires from the worker only small actions, repeated ad infinitum. Monotony is all the more unpleasant because the dimensions of the production system loosen the worker's bond with the final product, and in general with production as a process that can be embraced . . . Life falls into two parts: work is the means, and enjoyment—the end. The burden of entertainment and personal experience is shifted to the ever longer part of life free from work. But the longest period of time devoted to one single occupation is still used for work. The stultifying effect of a purposeless outlet of energy remains, and influences the kind of experiences looked for in enjoyment. Although people are condemned to pleasure, they very often feel themselves prisoners on parole, trying to forget, going absentmindedly from entertainment to entertainment. Monotony hurts people psychically, stifles and irritates them . . . Leisure often becomes a chase after something exciting, even though it may be a substitute to balance the monotony of work and give the feeling that one "lives".'

People are now caught in the middle of the modern problem of alienation, frustration, mass neurosis, the 'diseases of civilization.' It is not easy to say how Witkacy sensed and foresaw all this. He may have been helped by his decadent over-sensitivity, or by the early—still antitechnological—Russian futurism, by 'taylorism' (scientific efficiency of labour), or by the gloomy expressionist visions of the society of robots (like Capek's *R.U.R.*, or Spengler's violent aversion to cities). But Witkacy's analysis in this area allows one to minimise the surrealist discoveries made by his stage imagination. And if one wants to talk about Witkacy's affinities with Ionesco, their surrealist humour is less important than their identical vision of contemporary alienation: Ionesco's three-nosed Roberta is less important than 'the last individualist' Beranger in *A Stroll in the Air (Le Piéton de l'Air)* and the ideal, terrifying, modern city in *The Killer (Tueur sans gages)*, and the social uniformity spreading like fire in *The Rhinoceros*. And if one wants to compare Witkiewicz with Beckett, the latter's pessimism is far less important than his great dramatic study of loneliness and *boredom*.

These feelings of frustration pervade all Witkacy's work. They are not so perfectly expressed through form, as Beckett has done. They are mostly—just like his eroticism—related and analysed in the statements of his characters. But they are also apparent in Witkacy's long discourses which lead nowhere; in the constant lack of contact between the people talking to one another; in the climaxes which dissolve into nothing much; in the stage rhythm; while in *The Shoemakers*, the entire actionless construction deliberately aims to shock through boredom. The dialogues themselves are unambiguous: they provide ever-new analyses of these feelings of frustration, build them up on purpose in perverse variations and complications. Boredom is Witkiewicz's principal hero; boredom, insatiability, nausea and loneliness. All four emotions constitute a deliberate and delicate system of inter-relations, with a theoretical, ontological background. Loneliness, for instance, is for Witkiewicz the fundamental loneliness of Particular Being, very much like Heidegger's 'Geworfenheit', 'throwing' every human being into the void. 'Artistic creation,' he writes in *New Forms in Painting* (1918) 'is the direct confirmation of the law of loneliness as the price for which existence is possible at all; the confirmation not only for oneself but for other Particular Beings, just as lonely: it is the confirmation of Existence in its metaphysical horror.' This is very close to Sartre's ideas in *La Nausée*.

This is another area in which Witkacy was a precursor: his existentialism. It defines Witkiewicz's general attitude to the question pertaining to individual existence, rather than detailed philosophical constructions.

More interesting, however, is the question: where did Witkiewicz's existentialism come from? Polish philosophical tradition, with Józef Hoene-Wronski, Bronislaw Trentowski and Wincenty Lutoslawski on the one hand, and the then flourishing 'Lwów School' and the 'Warsaw School' on the other, was alien to existentialist philosophies; it certainly did not produce a Pascal, or a Kierkegaard. Kierkegaard's writings were known to the 'Young Poland' intellectuals through translations by Lack and Bienenstock. It is not known, though, whether they played a significant role then, or whether Witkacy knew them. He did not know Heidegger, but he knew Husserl, and valued him highly. He avidly read *Logische Untersuchungen*, and out of Husserl grew both Heidegger and Sartre and Merleau-Ponty. Witkacy's inspiration by phenomenologists. though, is too mechanical an explanation. It makes sense only when placed in the specific climate of the twenties: the climate of expressionism.

Not nearly enough attention has been paid to the closeness between existentialism and the philosophy of expressionism. A return to the foundations of metaphysics, the stress put on *expressing* personality, self, the loneliness of existence, and awareness of the loneliness of others, the wish to 'be oneself' and the impossibility of achieving that state, the problems of alter ego, non-existence, nothingness, despair, rebellion against one's situation—this is the trend of thought in which both movements meet. The closeness is not accidental: as a matter of fact, Heidegger and Sartre are to expressionism what Schelling and Hegel are to German Romanticism. One often tends to forget that existentialism— that most *literary* of the philosophies of our age—was born not in France, but in the expressionist Germany of the twenties. It was in the late twenties that the fundamental works of Heidegger and Jaspers appeared, and the darkly poetic stylistics of Jaspers does not leave any doubt as to its expressionist affiliation. Nor does Sartre. I have already mentioned that the prose of *Les Chemins de la Liberté* strangely recalls *Insatiability*. One could add that Sartre's first play, *Flies*, updated the Greek myth in a way that was closer to the German expressionists, than to the sceptical-aesthetising French trend of Giraudoux, Cocteau, Gide, even though that particular movement was fashionable then in Paris. One should also bear in mind that existentialism as a cultural trend became extremely popular in France immediately after the Second World War, just as expressionism had been in vogue in Germany immediately after the First World War. The psychological and social situation was similar in both cases, at least within the scope of what Durkheim called 'anomy'— a sharp split between social strivings and desires, and the slender possibilities of their achievement. This was accompanied by the feeling of danger, uncertainty, the threat of a new war, and the shock caused by the Nazi occupation to the previously stable, cheerful ideals of the French bourgeoisie. An analogous shock had once been experienced by the expressionists.

Viewed from this perspective, Witkacy's existentialism becomes somewhat less mysterious. This philosophy had been expressed not only by Witkacy. A little earlier it had been sensed, in a more general way, by another loner from the frontiers of expressionism, Kafka. Though Witkiewicz's existentialism does not lose any of its lustre.

And now a final thread in Witkacy.

VII

Witkiewicz's best works evoke in us today a bitterness, similar to the best works of Stanislaw Brzozowski. Hovering over them is the tragi-comedy of the Polish intelligentsia: when it chances on truly new European ideas, they usually come at the wrong time. If Witkacy had written in another language —the naïve for example—he would be famous now all over Europe. In the twenties, attempts were made to translate Witkiewicz's plays into French, German and English. Boy-Zelenski wrote his enthusiastic article on Witkacy in French for *La Pologne Littéraire*. It was in vain. The reason goes deep. For the German expressionists these plays were, perhaps, too surrealist and too turn-of-the century, not committed enough to the struggles they themselves were waging. For the French, or the English, Witkacy's problems were still quite unintelligible.

It was only in the years between 1947-1950 that Witkacy could have begun to conquer Europe. Only during the Second World War and the occupation did the West experience fully the collapse of values, the unsettling of middle-class order and nineteenth-century political concepts, the terror, hunger, the paroxysm of fear and despair, experienced by Witkacy a quarter of a century earlier. It was only the early post-war years, with growing international tension, the beginnings of the cold war, that evoked in Western countries the psychosis of frustration and fear, that black bottomless pit, into which Witkacy had once peered. Sartre's fame would now begin, Camus's philosophy of the absurd would appear, Kafka would be discovered, Ionesco would make his debut. The problems of revolution, mechanization, 'civilisation of the anthill' would loom large. During those years the French intellectuals would become aware of the fact that they were not the hub of the universe, that not only did they not decide its fate, but even the fate of France would be decided without them. Simone de Beauvoir stated this openly in her *Mandarines*. The end of the hegemony of the West in the sphere of culture would return as a real prognosis; Spengler's old thesis would be taken up, though more cautiously, by the disciples of Toynbee. More and more eyes would turn in the direction of Central and Eastern Europe and a conviction would grow that it was here that the history of the century had faced its first testing range. Such a state of mid was necessary, if Witkacy was to make an impact.

He did not find it during his lifetime—neither in the West, nor in Poland. His loneliness was complete—both intellectual and artistic. He knew it. 'As for the void "being created around me",' he wrote in 1931, 'I cannot recall a period when I would not feel quite isolated in our society.' Surrounded by the indifferent forces of native reaction, he remained misunderstood, waiting for the holocaust, looking powerless as all his predictions came true, one after the other. He could perform, as Leon Chwistek wrote about him, 'a great role in the history of Polish theatre.' But he felt he would not be able to play any role, that his words were the voice of Cassandra in Toytown. 'I am like a highly explosive missile, lying quietly in a meadow. But there is no cannon as yet and no one to fire me. And I cannot fire myself, I must have people.' A fascinating man, an impossible megalomaniac, a charming madman—his friends used to say.

Compared to newer, artistically more sophisticated works, Witkacy's plays may now seem sketchy, stylistically untidy, rhetorical. These plays, full of invention, of marvellous flashes of theatrical imagination, absurd humour, rapacious analyses and hypotheses, distorted observation, may be considered by some as 'embryos of works.' But that is usually the fate of the artistic avant-garde. Its task is not to produce perfect works. Its tasks are much more modest and much more heroic: to destroy fossils of prejudices, to reveal new perspectives, to revolutionise awareness, to pose drastic questions to its time, and not to shirk from any answers, even false ones.

These tasks were Witkacy's passion. He was an authentic avant-garde writer. In Polish drama he definitely closed the 'Young Poland' period, and its inter-war developments; he revealed in modernism the seeds of other, more important possibilities; he put his tongue out at the epigones of bourgeois realism; he opened the new era, the one in which we now live. The rest is up to us.

From *The Cuttlefish,* a Sigma Student Theatre production, Warsaw 1966. *Photo:* Jerzy Wojciewski

Translator's notes

[1] Now available in English as *Insatiability*, A novel in two parts by Stanislaw Ignacy Witkiewicz, translated, with an Introduction and Commentary by Louis Iribarne, University of Illinois Press, Urbana-Chicago-London, 1977.

[2] For an English translation, see Stanislaw Ignacy Witkiewicz, *Tropical Madness*, four plays translated by Daniel and Eleanor Gerould, introduction by Martin Esslin, Winter House, New York, 1972. (Contains: *The Pragmatists, Mr. Price, or Tropical Madness, Gyubal Wahazar, or Along the Cliffs of the Absurd, Metaphysics of a Two-Headed Calf, 'Witkacy'* by Daniel Gerould.)

[3] For an English translation, see Stanislaw Ignacy Witkiewicz, *The New Deliverance*, translated by Daniel Gerould and Jadwiga Kosicka, *The Polish Review*, New York, Vol.XVIII, No.1–2, 1973; republished in *New Directions 29*.

[4] Stanislaw Ignacy Witkiewicz, *The Shoemakers*, in: *The Madman and the Nun and Other Plays*, translated and edited by Daniel C. Gerould and C.S. Durer, with a Foreword by Jan Kott, University of Washington Press, Seattle and London, 1968, p.278. (This edition also contains *The Madman and the Nun, The Water Hen, The Crazy Locomotive, The Mother, They.)*

[5] For an English translation see *Twentieth-Century Polish Avant-Garde Drama*, Plays, Scenarios, Critical Documents, edited, with an introduction by Daniel Gerould, translated by Daniel Gerould in collaboration with Eleanor Gerould, Cornell University Press, Ithaca and London, 1977. (Contains i.a. Stanislaw Ignacy Witkiewicz, *The Anonymous Work   Four Acts of a Rather Nasty Nightmare*, pp.97-152.)

[6] Stanislaw Ignacy Witkiewicz, *The Cuttlefish, or The Hyrcanian Worldview*, translated by Daniel C. and Eleanor S. Gerould, in: *A Treasure of the Theatre*, ed. by John Gassner, revised by Bernard Dukore, vol.II, Holt, Rinehart & Winston, vol.II, 1971.

[7] *The Mother*, in: *Madman and the Nun. . .* , pp.131-132.

[8] *Ibid.* p.133.

HOLIDAY OR HOLINESS?
A critical revaluation of Grotowski
Jan Blonski
Translated by Boleslaw Taborski

There are books one thinks about all through one's life. As time
passes, one has new observations, or reservations, often as incoherent
as thoughts about people one knows intimately, even in memory or in
the imagination. It is like this with Grotowski's Theatre—or Institute—
Laboratory.

I must confess that I have not taken part in the meetings, or
'holidays' organised in recent years; more by chance than an
unwillingness to do so. I have reflected, though, on the statements
of the Laboratory's founders, and it might be useful to put down some
of the thoughts that have occurred to me. The 'wordless' experiments
which are the core of the Laboratory's work hardly lend themselves to
rationalization. Grotowski himself stresses this by saying that the truly
essential questions today do not have 'any answer at all in words'. But
even earlier he must have thought that the intellect divides more than
it unites: the need to understand was thus always subordinate to the
desire of experiencing together. However fragmentary and imprecise
the Laboratory's *Texts*[1] might be, one can say with absolute certainty
that even if I did not gain anything by participating in a 'beehive,' or
'holiday,' my insensibility could not constitute a critical argument,
because I cannot consider myself the measure of all things. The
Laboratory is sufficiently important to study from the perspective of
art history, or the history of culture, just as one can study masonic
rites or *cours d'amour* rituals one has never seen.

One can ask first why *Apocalypsis cum Figuris* has been—and
most probably will remain—Grotowski's last theatrical undertaking.
He says today that he has found himself beyond theatre, or beyond
art . . . and presents his break with theatre as a spiritual breakthrough.
We must believe him. That decision, or revelation, was already
imprinted, like a watermark in hand-made paper, in the doctrine of
Poor Theatre which he proclaimed ten years ago. That Theatre—
denuded of lighting, sets, music, even literature—was to put the actor
and the spectator face to face, so they could recognise each other and
unite. The axis of the union was then the gesture of giving—sacrifice—
performed by the actor.

67

For the gesture to be effective, and the revelation perfect, the actor had to transform himself from a sinner into a holy man. He who wants to be admired must pretend, and pretending—the essence of all acting—inevitably creates stereotypes. By the same token sincerity and spontaneity disappear. If, however, the actor—by strenuous effort—rids himself of stereotypes, he will reach the truth of myth, archetype, collective imagery, dormant in every body, every soul. The shout and the sign, spontaneity and discipline will then be one! The effort of identification is in the suffering of a victim: the actor must get rid of his fear of his neighbour—the fear that breeds false signs, distorts gestures, warps behaviour. As in the Garden of Eden, so in the theatre men ought to face one another—naked. The 'act of theatre' is a sublimation of the act of love in which there is no shame. Sublimation? Yes. And also transcendence, as there is no pleasure derived except the happiness of giving and sacrifice.

And yet Grotowski has abandoned his theory and his theatre—both very beautiful. He says that even in 1966 he understood that the success and failure of an artist are nothing more than creating and then destroying an idol. 'Passes the charm, and flimsy is the beauty . . . ' Why then climb the steps of the Odeon? To come to understand that fame is but the taste of ash in the mouth of the artist? For this is precisely what the lives of artists reveal—from Michaelangelo and Rembrandt to Mickiewicz and Proust. The artist finds truth and consolation in his work: *pereat ego, fiat opus*—or, as the poet declares with perverse simplicity, 'small are men, great their works.'

An actor's work is also an aesthetic 'object': it has no vehicle but the body, and it evaporates as the audience's applause dies out. It can only last in the spectator; and then only if it is imprinted sufficiently deeply to make him repeat the actor's inner patterns of behaviour. One can, of course, love like Valentino, clown like Chaplin; but that only involves an exchange of stereotypes. In the beginning, therefore, Grotowski tried to place the audience in an archetypal situation, revealed in the performance. Later, unsatisfied, he began to 'offend' the audience, by limiting the number of spectators, or by enclosing them behind a stockade, where they could safely watch the martyrdom of the Constant Prince. The insult was intended to be a warning and a shock which, paradoxically, compelled them to participate. But even the insult became a theatrical effect. Throughout his theatre work Grotowski maintained a profound conviction: of the need to transform the spectator, by offering him the actor's human truth (and indirectly his own). However, in order genuinely to transform the spectator, one had to persuade him to repeat the gesture of giving or sacrifice; otherwise he would be only a voyeur. The consummation of communication is impossible without visible, enacted reciprocity.

In short, only two people can meet. 'There is a point,' says Grotowski, 'at which one discovers that it is possible to reduce oneself to the man as he is; not to his mask, not to the role he plays, not to his game, not to his evasions, not to his image of himself, not to his clothing—only to himself. This reduction to the essential man is possible only in relation to an existence other than himself.' This is an inversion of what one is accustomed to think—that the presence of our neighbour—no matter how friendly—makes one play a role. Someone's look inclines one to goodness, scholarship, challenge, humility. It determines actions and shapes associations. Only God, before whom one cannot pretend or lie, sorts the wheat from the chaff, and sees through the heart's intentions. Thus Christian tradition has often salvaged the substance of personality. Among men, on the other hand (to recall Gombrowicz), it is 'form' that holds sway and relentlessly determines response and behaviour. For Gombrowicz, it is the neighbour who turns man into an actor. The question is how to regain, even momentarily, one's freedom and distinct features? The answer: by removing labels, by destroying form, by fighting. The human world is a battlefield of ceaseless psychological war, and those who argue to the contrary, lie. For Grotowski, it is the other way round: loneliness arouses fear in the individual and compels people to put on masks. In Arcadia people were not afraid of one another, nor even of animals.

So if the partner—'brother'—accepts my humanity, I shall be able to rid myself of the roles and images with which I protect myself! It is one's neighbour who turns the actor into a man'. On condition, though, that the assent will be mutual. If I do not recognise the partner, he will not be able to recognise me either, except as a master, or as a slave. 'One thing is certain, that in order to select one another democratically, one has to select one another mutually.' The romantic theory of love echoes here, however faintly. And what does the word 'democratically' mean? Simply: without pressure and compulsion, no matter how discreet and friendly. Nobody will 'guide' the actor in the theatre any more. For there will be no actor.

Nor will there be any more theatre! Grotowski was once a strict adherent of theatre discipline. But with the passing of time, he came to stress the strictness of actors' rules less and less, until he finally abandoned all 'repressiveness'. But the truth is that all work in the theatre is 'repressive'. Action, characters and plot—all that is 'performed'—is the norm to which the actor has to adjust. Or at least to relate to. It is surely a matter of indifference whether the norm is 'policed' by the writer, the director, or the actor's colleagues! 'Coercion' in this sense cannot be divorced from the process of theatre. Take the stage, and put on it an actor who plays Romeo. Why does 'he' evoke joy, concern, compassion? Precisely because 'he' has ceased to be an actor, has become a 'symbol', directed intentionally towards the audience, which constructs his 'sense' with him, following the directions gradually revealed by the structure of the symbol. Assume now that the actor falls out of his part: madly in love, he wants to offer everything—even his life— to the young lady he has invited to the manager's box. So it is in front of the box, instead of in the tomb that he commits suicide.

At this point theatre ends and scandal begins; the understanding with the audience ends, though it no doubt establishes itself quite strongly with the lady.

Not a very serious example, but it demonstrates that the distance from the actor to Romeo is precisely the same as that from Romeo to the spectator. The distances are symmetrical and interdependent, because a symbol cannot be 'nearer', but, at most, fuller, richer, more precise. One can, indeed should, look at the theatre as a process of communication. But it is a process of complex mediation. The utopia of union is reduced to the utopia of mediation: 'what had seemed an interest in acting turned out . . . to be a search for, and finding of, partnership. Someone, some other, whom . . . in the process of work, in those years, I defined with words usually used to define God. I thought then—son of man. Every thing became different, it could be dramatic, painful. A certain rapacity did not disappear . . . But it was already something quite different.' Certainly something very different from theatre!

At this point really difficult questions arise. First: is it really possible to 'undress' from playing a role or pretending, and take off a mask? After all, any inter-human relationship presumes selection and self-limitation. Even in the smallest community—between two people say—there are relations of dependence, imitation and (vaguely mutual) subordination, which spontaneously create the patterns of behaviour which become 'masks'—the kind of masks that cause such concern to the Laboratory's founders. In small groups, such pressures are usually even stronger, because they are more deeply embedded within each individual, and more self-protectively concealed.[2]

What would Grotowski reply to that? Nothing perhaps, because he does not consider himself to be a theoretician, or philosopher, but one invites people to a holiday, to human co-existence, to be together. But at a guess for Grotowski the words 'mask, role, dodging' have two meanings. One cannot altogether abandon one's social role, unless one leaves the community. But one can strongly limit its activity, as evidenced by the rules of religious orders connected with the prohibition of speech, something equally as rare as it is significant. Not by chance is the Laboratory reminiscent of a monastery. It keeps its door open, does not refuse shelter to anyone. At the same time, however, it professes to guard 'the mountain of flame'; the mountain which 'carries distance in it, but from which one returns.' A flame burns there 'of something which has not died out.'

The mystical vocabulary is as old as mankind. But 'role' also means a lack of psychic authenticity, alienation, a psychic compulsion which paralyses free spontaneity. Does one thus have to abandon all discipline and give way to chance impulse? Not really, because a freely chosen discipline changes its quality; conscious, inner, necessity becomes freedom. And freedom—always desired, never fully attained—is not just a whim, but involves values. This is no doubt Grotowski's view when he says that freedom is associated for him with the 'principal temptation.'[3]

Yet if there are degrees of temptation, there must also be a hierarchy of behaviour. One cannot become free and perfect all at once. There will at least remain the relation of the master and the disciple. Will that disappear during and after initiation. For the sake of argument, assume that it will.

For the time has now come to ask what it really means to say: 'reduce oneself to the man'? Perhaps the idea of 'reduction' is not the most appropriate: perhaps better 'creation', 'growth'. But the Laboratory has always aimed at pure qualities: pure theatre, pure acting, pure humanity. To get to the core, the centre, the essence. Perhaps this ambition is arrogant? Does it really matter that man's cognitive, technical and political activity condemns him to evasion and pretending? Not all 'masks' distance us equally from our neighbours, and not all values are born from loving acceptance. It would be easy to draw quietist conclusions from Grotowski's statements. But neither he, nor anyone else, is obliged to know everything, nor to suffer for how others interpret his experiments. 'To reduce oneself to the man' means to ask about the philosophers' stone, about the *substantia prima*, the essence of humanity.

It is not difficult to find the answer in Grotowski. At the Laboratory— or on the Mountain—'there ought to happen what is simplest, most elementary, confident among beings'; and it must be 'based on such things as the fact of recognising someone, as dividing substances, sharing elements . . . meetings connected with the wind, with the tree, with the earth, with the water, with the fire, with the grass—with the Animal.' Elsewhere he 'explains' by analogy: 'games, frolics, life, our kind, ducking, flight, man-bird, man-colt . . . man-brother.' All this contains 'the likeness of God,' man giving. Man as he is, whole, so unable to hide himself; man who *lives* and that means—*not everyone.* 'Body and blood—this is brother, that's where "God" is: it is the bare foot and the naked skin, in which there is brother. This, too, is a holiday, to be in the holiday, to be the holiday.' The access to the Mountain, though open, is not, alas, possible for everyone. Only those 'who live' will come there. That means those who can mutually recognise one another as particles of nature, particles, through which flows 'something which has not died out.' Moments of recognition bring great happiness, irradiating from then to the entirety of human life. These moments are also the proper justification of the present activity of the Laboratory. They cause the past and future (that 'which could be') to give way to the present, which fills man with . . . How to define such moments? 'To be "looked at"' (yes, "looked at", and not "seen"); to be looked at, like a tree, a flower, a river, the fish in that river.' We are all fish in the river of life . . . but greedy, grasping. The aim and also the problem is to 'be looked at' disinterestedly.

Labels reduce the new to the familiar and inevitably diminish profound experiments. The activities of the Laboratory have been wide ranging. Some have been quite simple, as 'when people from all over the world sang sad songs, composed in the Theatre, which were soul-tearing in a quite slavonic manner, and there was present that spirit of indefinable melancholy, as well as nostalgia for some great unity and reconciliation.'[4] Basically the ordinary brotherhood of man around the universal camp fire. Some have been quite traditional, such as the 'purification by word' which made the participants talk about 'their devil.' Those adventures had their reference in half-forgotten rituals: recognising newcomers by the light of a match recalls masonic initiations. All such exercises renew people through concentration and friendliness, releasing them from their different 'burdens', as Grotowski calls them, and above all from the burden of recurring triviality. How much the participants gain depends on their personal contribution: but it has been known for a long time that it will be given to those who have already come to possess much. Participation in 'beehives' or 'holidays' obviously does not force on people a particular outlook on life. The source of the Laboratory's most original experiments is in the tradition of pantheistic mysticism.

Grotowski says: 'I have felt—though this may be mythologising—that at the roots of the road is the combination of two desires: freedom, with which I envelop my own skin—carrying oneself, alone. Secondly, the desire for Something/Someone, other, third, someone with whom one is together on the wave. Not only a man; not that I have in mind some spirits, beings from the beyond. I am talking about what is seen, live. Wind lives and air can be seen. A plant is a being, a creature, is also in movement. This is discovered later but only in action.' Beautifully said! Grotowski stresses the moment of surrender ('carrying'), the extinguishing of individuality, and then the elation and regeneration involved in recognising 'another' reality, unobtainable in everyday life. The dialectics of renunciation and regeneration recalls, of course, the alternation of subordination and enlightenment, renunciation and grace, characteristic of all mystic experience. The sense of holiness seems inseparable from humanity: but only within the 'sacred' experience—trans-historic perhaps—does mysticism flourish in 'philosophical' religions.

Mystic experiences, sensations, communions with the Holy and the Incomprehensible must be as numerous as there are human beings. It is difficult, however, to imagine a history of mysticism. At most, a history of mystic *doctrines*: conceptualisation depends on the intellectual capacities in any given epoch. That is why labels are dangerous. Convenient perhaps, but saying little about the inner content of the Laboratory's experiments. In the luminous darkness the frontiers between different kinds of human experiences are obscured. In the mysticism of nature there must have been more of a quest for the transcendental God than is usually assumed. And conversely, in theistic mysticism, the desire to dissolve in cosmic unity has appeared more frequently than one might judge from theological doctrines.

One hears occasionally of the Laboratory's oriental inspiration, which looms large, even for a layman. But perhaps they are too obvious to be true? Oriental mysticism undermines Western tradition and at the same time alters its meaning and direction. The activities of a physicist or a biologist, exploring (dreaming? creating?) life or the cosmos are rooted in isolated contemplation, freely derived from many different traditions. Not necessarily Christian, nor Asiatic. Mystics of nature have always done without companions. Grotowski on the other hand lays stress on partnership and feels committed to what might be described as missionary activity. What is more, he seems to think that the presence of another person constitutes a condition of success for the Laboratory's experiments! This is perhaps the Christian aspect of his attitudes.

In Grotowski's and Flaszen's statements in recent years one can find ideas taken from Master Eckhardt, St. John of the Cross, Paracelsus, Mickiewicz, Swedenborg, Boehme and Angelus Silesius (who deserves a street-name in his native city)—all concerned with the world soul theory. And the Laboratory's founders could be described as descendants of romanticism. There are also half-or-unconscious echoes of Rousseau. Grotowski calls Che Guevara his idol . . . and at the same time climbs the Mountain of Flame! Those are the precise contradictions of the 'social contract'! Rousseau's theory almost demands antagonist conclusions: there is no *tertium datur* between escape and revolution, between total abandonment of society and its constant transformation.[5]

'Reduction to humanity' means for Grotowski reducing (return, identification) to the state of nature, and assumes a consequent weakening of interest in or indifference to social roles. In other words, one reaches 'God' (the inverted commas are Grotowski's) insofar as one recognises man's first substance, and that is basically the substance of the cosmos. God is immanent in nature and in man; but the latter, in order to become a part of God, must be seen (excuse me: looked at) by the partner as a particle of nature. This echoes Schulz's mythology of archetype. And from Schulz it is not far to Jung, from Jung, to German romanticism. We have come full circle.

Has Grotowski—in deciding to end the Laboratory experiments— really found himself outside art? It must depend on what is meant by this word. One can, of course, regard the theological, artistic and philosophical discourses as homogeneous, though custom and common sense prefer to differentiate between them. I would suggest that Grotowski rightly evaluated the road he has taken—more so, perhaps, than his friends and admirers, who act as if the Laboratory's activities are still an introduction to theatre, however elaborate and esoteric. It is sufficient to read what Brook, Barrault, or Chaikin have said on the subject. And it is understandable that such men of the theatre search for inspiration. But the Laboratory's work leads as equally to shoemaking as to theatre.

These experiments are perhaps even further removed from theatre than from anything else. Theatre assumes a knowledge of the symbols it invokes. In its magnificent origins, theatre was born of already established religions, and was not a 'preliminary' quest for the sacred. The Greek audience knew well the fate of Oedipus and Heracles; the medieval audience had heard the story of Christ's passion many times. Grotowski on the other hand, clearly wants to go back, to an earlier epoch: to the moment when ritual first occurs and then almost immediately disappears.

In other words, one is concerned with half-inspired, half-improvised activities common to a group of already skilled people. In the course of these activities, they invent, and frequently paraphrase archetypes, momentary, almost instantly obliterated. Nothing is preserved, not even in the memory of the participants, because every gesture, to be authentic, has, of necessity, to begin, to be born, anew. The whole technique of 'holidays' or 'beehives' aims at the recurrent renewal of symbols. But, Grotowski tells us, nothing is really born, nothing begins; rather it 'reduces', goes back to the common, the original, the homogeneous.

Grotowski rejects the epithet 'religious' to describe the Laboratory's activities. He says that an exceptional moment in the history of mankind has come, 'even if we look at a certain singular phenomenon which occurred two thousand years ago on the peripheries of the huge empire encompassing the entire Western world, as it then was. Some men walked in the wilderness and searched for truth. They searched in accord with the character of those times which, unlike that of ours, was religious. I do not see the possibility of being religious today. This is how it is with me, at least, and I think with many of you, as well.' What does Grotowski propose instead? A quest for holiness! He says that for him 'the appearance of the mass of the Sun' is a sacral, not an astronomic, fact. Also other natural phenomena and activities, particularly those that make it possible to associate with the elements, or which seem appropriate to man as a particle of nature (flight, being washed, house, road). What then does Grotowski consider religious? Only that which emerges from the already established religions. He himself by contrast wants to explore, arouse, recognise the pure sense of holiness, more primary, if not richer, because it embraces the fear of the holy snake, as well as the ecstasy of St. Francis. It is doubtful whether one can build theatre—any theatre—on a "neutral" sense of the sacred, particularly if it is to be revealed through actions 'simpler than rites!' Even etymologically, religion binds man to a Deity, the cosmos, community, even the unconscious. Religion organises such bonds, strengthens them, makes them intelligible and makes them accessible through parables, rites, sacraments. In short, it develops by constructing a system of signs, symbols, rituals. The theatre may originally have been based on that system, as far as its primary patterns of activity were concerned. But it is a different sense of the sacred—constituting the condition and material of established religions.

Abandoning theatre requires courage. There is a street in Seville, named after an actress who had so deeply experienced her part that on leaving the stage after a performance she knocked at a convent gate. Grotowski has done something similar, though he found himself in a different sort of monastery. Making a sacrifice, visualised devotion was for years a common denominator of the Laboratory's performances. That is why Grotowski was able to renew so profoundly the perception of tragedy. The theme of the sacrifice almost always betrayed its Christian origin: it functioned as a model which, freely and perversely transformed, made it possible to cultivate theatre in the conventional sense of the word. This was true of *Faustus*, of *Acropolis*, of *The Constant Prince*, in all their great performances.[6] But in *Apocalypsis*? Much has been written about that production, but it is all timid. Certainly, no performance can be a treatise. But should not critics, nevertheless, offer their interpretation? Should they not say how they understand the message of *Apocalypsis*? My impressions the twice I saw *Apocalypsis* were contradictory: I was moved, shaken, revolted, but also bored and tired. The overall effect was vague and blurred. Perhaps the production was deliberately, provocatively conceived to prevent analysis and criticism.

Apocalypsis ended with the final words spoken by the Grand Inquisitor to Christ: 'Go and come back no more!'. Dostoyevsky's Grand Inquisitor is well known. So there is a tendency to interpret this exclamation as a painful irony, stimulating sympathy for the Simpleton (a Christ-like character). But what does Simpleton want? Salvation—or the gaining of some higher value—is not the object of his goodness, sacrifice, devotion. They are more a means of enabling him to establish contact (attachment, understanding?) with people. These half erotic endeavours end in failure.

Apocalypsis would thus seem to be not so much a tragedy of sacrifice, as a drama (*not* tragedy) of communication, ending with a confession that this is not possible. Simpleton, like Grotowski, searches for 'partnership . . . Someone, different'. And he searches without success. After *Apocalypsis* the obtrusiveness of sacrifice disappears from Grotowski's statements, and has taken as its toll the theatre. There is something very moving in such an end to the Laboratory as theatre. European theatre began with the mystery play. In the end, surely we could go without theatre, just as Christianity went without for ten centuries. But how to go without Christ? Grotowski no longer seeks for understanding through sacrifice or brotherhood through action or assent.

'I am with you not because I am doing something for you, but because you look at me and I too am looking at you, and together we are looked at like flower, river, fish in that river . . . We have no other role to play for ourselves, except our common finding of ourselves in nature. But it will inevitably be a "reduction" because, when meeting, we always retreat to the beginning; we emerge from the beginning only to return to it.' This is neither like the Gospels, nor—in spite of appearances to the contrary—like Plato, when he wrote that 'the beginning is like God who, for as long as he lives among us, illumines all things . . . '

Author's Notes

1 *Institute Laboratory: Texts,* Wroclaw 1975 and *Document Mountain of Flame,* Wroclaw, 1975. Actor's Institute Theatre Laboratory. These publications consist mainly of interviews and statements by the Institute's founders, published in Poland and abroad.

2 Cf. I. Wojtczak, 'Why the University of Explorations?' *Dialog,* No. 11, 1975. 'It is often surprising how certain permissible areas of behaviour have been perpetuated in the Institute's work up to now. To take out a newspaper, or to come up to the window when everyone else sits in silence, is already considered tactless, even though it might be my spontaneous true impulese . . . The whole area of permissible and less permissible behaviour, a group's style, is recognised very quickly and, taking into account one's own individual interest, the most proper behaviour would be that based on an early subordination to the group, in order to be like them and not to expose oneself.' (p.100) Miss Wojtczak —an enthusiast of the Laboratory, a point I am stressing to avoid misunderstandings—realises full well that it cannot be otherwise, since the Laboratory's activities oscillate between the Scylla of disorder and Charybdis of pseudo-exaltation.

3 The difficulty of understanding Grotowski often boils down to the fact that he systematically reverses religious vocabulary. 'Temptation' is traditionally associated with 'sin'. Here, on the contrary, it means the inner necessity of seeking the principal value. Why not? After all, we are not watchdogs of definitions.

4 Wojtczak, op. cit., p.99. My next examples have also been derived from pp.99, 102.

5 Cf, e.g. B. Baczko, *Rousseau: samotność i wspólnota (Rousseau: Loneliness and Community),* Warsaw, 1964, pp.515-533, or V.Goldschmidt, *Anthropologie et politique. Les principes du systeme de Rousseau,* Paris 1974, pp. 780-781.

6 About models of sacrifice, tragedy and Christian inspiration cf. J. Bloński, 'Teatr Laboratorium' *(Theatre Laboratory),* *Dialog,* No. 10, 1969. A detailed description—and a somewhat vacillating commentary—of the Laboratory's last production was given by M. Dzieduszycka, *Apocalypsis cum figuris. Opis spektaklu* (description of performance), Kraków, 1974.

THEATRE VERSUS FILM an interview with
Andrzej Wajda
Teresa Krzemién
Translated by Boleslaw Taborski

KRZEMIEŃ. What satisfaction have you had from your work in the theatre?

WAJDA. Behind your question lurks another: is it worth doing anything at all? Because I take the view that it is worth doing something, I can only reply that my work in the theatre has brought me a few successes and a few failures.

KRZEMIEŃ. Does your theatrical success satisfy your need to do something socially useful to the same degree as your film success?

WAJDA. The view that a larger audience is worth more than a smaller audience is profoundly alien to me. I am often asked why I direct in the theatre for thousands, when I can make films for millions. This is an obvious misconception—what has one to do with the other?

Firstly, I am convinced that theatre has a deeper impact on a person than film. Films may provide strong experiences, but for the most part they are more superficial. One rarely returns to a film. Yes, a film may be brilliant and dazzling, but it is theatre that remains with us somewhere deep. It is more durable. Also, in relating to a smaller audience I have different duties; not smaller or greater, simply different.

The theatre is, perhaps, the last place where a live dialogue is still continuing. This kind of dialogue is infringed on in our daily life, diminished by the fact that we either work, or drive the car, or watch television. Everything we do makes conversation impossible. And these few half-hours we spend at home, or with other people, do not always provide us with a subject for conversation either. Conversation between people generally dies out: this is somehow a social problem. So the theatre becomes really the last place where one hears the dialogue of man with man.

Secondly, the theatre requires a more disciplined way of thinking than film. A film is valuable when it succeeds in creating an illusion of life: it is alive, it justifies itself. In the theatre, to create something which is an illusion of life is only the beginning. I do not want to say that it is more difficult to create a stage production than to make a film, but I want to make it clear that theatre requires a greater discipline from the director.

KRZEMIEŃ. You have said that a film is quickly forgotten. But this can be prevented by the very fact that film is preserved on tape.

WAJDA. I am not convinced that preserving films is of value in itself. Many excellent kinds of art disappear: the art of great actors has disappeared, of great singers who were not recorded. Does this mean that they were inferior to today's artists? Spoken poetry has also almost completely disappeared. The fact that someone, or something, has been preserved on celluloid does not increase his, or its, importance. On the contrary, the whole beauty of theatre is in its once-only nature, in its transiency, its disappearance even. It is as beautiful as the candle burning out: this is commonly agreed, and I am not at all sure whether it would be the same if that burning out were filmed. Everything we do in the theatre is addressed to people now, to ourselves and to people like us. I do not think about posterity: I want to speak to the audience sitting in the theatre, or in the cinema, now. It must have been the same for Chekhov, Shakespeare and Stanislavsky, certainly for Grotowski. The decisive factor is that the spectator shares the same problems, dramas and miseries as the artist, that he knows and understands them.

Sometimes it happens, of course, that a film does not date and we can watch it years later. This is very nice too, but it is not healthy to think about this while working on it. I repeat: the greatness and splendour of theatre consists in its being a once-only affair. If you don't come and watch, you will miss it. It is a gift, offered from those who act on stage to those who come to see it. I have seen a few great actors in my life and that gift is what I have taken out of the theatre: it is my property. There is also a disinterestedness, a self-realization inherent in theatre which determines its nobility: this fascinates me most.

KRZEMIEŃ. All this is true, but what does it mean today to watch, for instance, your films with Cybulski, if there is no possibility of returning to the original emotions, equally noble and disinterested, already lost, and yet—alive?

WAJDA. Yes, but you see, what remains of a film, what moves us still, even after many years, is always either a magnificient, marvellous discovery which happens only once in a lifetime—something like *Battleship Potemkin, Citizen Kane,* or *Rome, Open City* or else something which happens more often (though this is a rarity too) when an actor does not date. I recently saw a film on television made in the fifties, with Marlon Brando. Once I had learned my directing craft on that film. Today everything in it is old and ridiculous, except for Brando who has been untouched by time. Watching him one has the impression that it is all happening just now, at this moment, before our eyes. This, I think is what has remained of Cybulski in *Ashes and Diamonds.* His eccentric behaviour and artificial acting have ironically turned out to be the film's greatest strength.

KRZEMIEŃ. The undiminshed strength of *Ashes and Diamonds* surely lies in its tackling of problems imbued with national, general and authentic emotions.

WAJDA. Yes, it's true that Jerzy Andrzejewski's scenario showed us the way, gave us wings.

KRZEMIEŃ. So, the flickering candle flame has been preserved?

WAJDA. This happens in films, but it is not something one ought to strive for. Zbyszek did not act so he could be watched in twenty years. He simply expressed himself as he was at that particular point in time. He also expressed the young people at that particular time, who would go to the cinema to see him. And the young people saw him, and accepted him as he was, because he had simply anticipated them by a fraction of time: they did not know yet how to behave, and saw it on the screen. 'Ah, this is what we are like! We shall now go home and be bold'. And then they knew. James Dean anticipated us, made us bold: me as a director, Zbyszek as an actor. But even when something 'live' has been preserved in a film, we are still dissatisfied with other things in it that we also have to watch: the unfashionable cut of trousers and hair styles, unfashionable camera work, a way of directing which is not acceptable any more. When, however, I recall a theatre performance, my memory brings me only things that are beautiful, great, moving. This is the strength of theatre—that our experience goes deeper, compared to film and its functional verifiability.

KRZEMIEŃ. You are declaring yourself almost as an opponent of film . . . Do you also deprecate that advantage of film, that it is a record of reality, of a certain period, its atmosphere and morals? Synthetic and somewhat artificial, perhaps, but still a record . . .

WAJDA. This is a matter for historians who, when examining a certain period, take film into consideration as well as other documents, always realising that it reflects reality through a filter, and that it is never a true reality, even in a documentary.

KRZEMIEŃ. Why do you so often direct abroad? Do you find it easier to work on Polish plays in a foreign theatre and language, and with foreign actors?

WAJDA. I direct abroad because it is difficult. It gives me no relief. I have to rely only on what I really know. I have to be more clear, intelligible. It is not necessary for me to be a director in the West because if I wanted that, I would simply stay there for good. No, it is necessary for me here, at home, when I return. During my stay in Brazil I realized why their footballers are so good. On the beach I saw a crowd of boys from the suburbs who played football ankle deep in the sand. This requires a tremendous effort. But when they later come to play on a hard field, they literally fly in the air.
For me, directing abroad is a similar kind of exercise. I do it

in order not to have the feeling that something is only intelligible because one speaks the same language as the audience. There is a language of the theatre, and the spoken language is only part of it.

KRZEMIEŃ. Does this mean that you regard directing as an ordinary profession requiring professional training, experience and craft?

WAJDA. Of course, it's a profession, madam! In our country to be a director is to be considered as acting under inspiration, having a mission, and other such things. But few people look at it as a real profession. One must know the road one is taking well, if one wants to achieve results. I am learning this. Still. Also in my experience abroad.

KRZEMIEŃ. On the Polish repertory?

WAJDA. Yes, because this is my strength. Polish repertory is what I know and understand best. There is also another consideration: to expose Polish art to foreigners somewhere. This is important. Różewicz's *White Marriage*, seen at the Yale Repertory Theatre drew attention to the play for example. All the reviews said it was excellent and that nobody would write such a play in America.

I shall soon be directing another play abroad—Witkiewicz's *They* at Bochum in West Germany. This will be difficult, because I had wanted to do it in Warsaw, and already had an ideal cast for it in my mind. I cannot accept the idea that someone else can, and must, play it. But I shall have to wait, because these actors are very busy. And after my experience at Bochum I shall be better than I am now.

KRZEMIEŃ. What is the greatest difficulty you encounter working abroad?

WAJDA. The fact, alas, that I know so few people. This causes me the greatest fear and concern. It makes of everything a question mark. The success of a film or theatre production is decided much earlier than when rehearsals begin, from the moment when it is known what play or scenario will be tackled and what people are going to do it. Not only actors but all the others as well. In Poland I know everything and everyone exactly. I know why I direct a play at the Stary Theatre in Cracow; I likewise know why I do a play with Tadeusz Lomnicki at the Wola Theatre, or with Zygmunt Hübner at the Powszechny Theatre Warsaw. I know what I can expect when I make a film with such and such people, and I know—depending on which people are selected—what sort of film this can be.

Abroad, on the other hand, everything is a matter of chance: I do not know those people! I did not see the actors in their diploma performances. Hence the fear and the misery. But there is nothing to be done about it. If one only occasionally works abroad—this is how it must be. And the audience! This is even more fearful. There is no amount of money or fame worth that kind of fear!

KRZEMIEŃ. With regard to your films, you often say about yourself: 'I am a Polish director.' Does this apply to the theatre? Does the description 'Polish director' mean something too? And if so—what?

WAJDA. There are aspects of Polish art in everything I do. I am somehow different, and I suppose I stress it more clearly than others.

KRZEMIEŃ. What are you going to direct in the near future here in Poland?

WAJDA. I still have no clear idea as far as feature films are concerned. I would like to do something soon, begin this year, because so far in 1977 since *Man of Marble* I have not been able to work on anything.

As far as theatre is concerned, I am going back to the Stary in Cracow, if one can actually say that about a man who really only lives permanently in Cracow, who feels lost in the capital. I will begin with a venture about which I have been dreaming for a long time. The Stary Theatre, which is so Cracovian in its character, and has actors who are typical Cracovians, does not produce anything from the Cracow repertory—the plays written in and about that city. And there are so many of them. It is a pity, of course, that they are not about Cracow as it is today. They are plays from the nineteenth Century. Joanna Ronikier is preparing their—adaptation? collage? extract? I don't know what to call it. Having read these plays we came to the conclusion that there is something which connects the characters and enables us to relate the stories of the people over a period of many years. We will start with a play by Michal Balucki and finish with a fragment of Juliusz Kaden-Bandrowski's novel *The Arch*. Within that framework we will perform almost all the works by August Kisielewski, two fragments from Gabriela Zapolska's *The Morals of Mrs. Dulska,* and a play unperformed for a long time, *Kalina's Drama.* Many Cracow characters will also appear. In short, we are preparing a surprise.

KRZEMIEŃ. Is this medley going to be a rest after your stormy encounter with Dostoyevsky, Przybyszewski and Wyspianski?

WAJDA. No. The action will last for hours—I think it will have to be six or seven hours, and it is going to be performed like that. The very fatigue of the audience must lead to something which is not there in those brilliant and excellent plays, but which ought to appear in our performance. We are not going to rework the plays, but simply use the material in a different way. The effect ought to come close to what one looks for in the theatre today: a new, different relationship between stage and audience.

KRZEMIEŃ. What you are looking for is a new form?

WAJDA. No! My reason is the desire to show the life which flows through the stage for a long time. The duration of that performance —all those hours—will not be an exercise in form, but in its most essential content. Similar to a writer making a decision to write a short story, or a three-volume novel. Everything depends on that decision. Those plays can be joined together because their style is similar: there is no butchery involved, no artificiality. From that flow of time a surprise can be born. I want to believe in this; this is my whole intention. One more thing: on the stage there ought to appear the soul of the city, of old Cracow, where there has always been too many people with more aspirations than there have been possibilities of their fulfilment.

KZREMIEŃ. How do you regard modern Polish plays? So far you have produced only one in Poland: Mrozek's *Emigrés*.

WAJDA. I know I ought to produce them foremost. And this is what I have been doing lately. When I have a choice, I select the Polish repertory.

KRZEMIEŃ. Do you intend to attempt ancient tragedy and Shakespeare— as the supreme test?

WAJDA. Yes. I would like to produce *Antigone*—somewhere in the street with amateurs, with an obscure group. And I know a few actors who could perform Shakespeare.

KZREMIEŃ. After you had produced *The Devils*, did anything change in your view of the theatre?

WAJDA. Only in so far as the success of my production caused actors to have more confidence in me. As a result, we can now undertake more risky ventures.

KZREMIEŃ. What did you think of the success of *Nastasya Philipovna* abroad, at the Helsinki Festival?

WAJDA. I realised once more that Dostoyevsky is more intelligible than Wyspiański. But this gives me little joy! And I think I came closer to Dostoyevsky. This lasts, of course, like an acquaintance with an unusual person, regardless of whether one likes or hates him.

KRZEMIEŃ. Do you think that having a talent means one owes something to society—morally?

WAJDA. You must be joking! I do not think that talent commits one to anything. It can remain buried in oneself; one can use it only for oneself and not give any of it to others. There is after all no duty to love others. One can, of course, assume duties voluntarily. I give what I have.

KRZEMIEŃ. What do you think about the young generation of Polish theatre directors? What are their weaknesses, their strengths?

WAJDA. To put it in one sentence: too much of their work does not succeed. And there are too few of them. If there were more, things would be easier: a normal market situation would emerge. Instead, statistics have been worked out: how many theatres there are in Poland, how many directors, and—on that basis—how many more directors are needed. But things ought to be altogether different: the greatest possible number should be trained, and then—let life eliminate those who cannot be directors. This is the most natural and the healthiest way.

I think also, judging by the results they have achieved, there are too many conflicts: with the company, with the plays worked on, with the text. Almost every venture by a young director is a tremendous shock for the theatre concerned, but a shock not resulting in enlivening the actors, in a dazzling flash of theatre art, but, unfortunately, usually ending with yet another conflict.

KRZEMIEŃ. Do you read press reviews?

WAJDA. I am glad you have asked me that! Because recently several persons have regularly attacked the theatre: it distorts the classics, says Putrament; performances of Shakespeare are dead, says Redlinski, talking to you; a Commission for the Protection of Directors should be established, says a lady, to whom Hübner has replied in *Dialog*. But the reason is simple: there are no theatre critics who will say: this is good, this is bad, and why. It is better with films: I believe Kalużyński in *Polityka*, though he does not always believe me. Most theatre reviews make no value judgements, do not state clearly whether it is worth going to the theatre to see the particular play which is being reviewed. The places of Boy-Zeleński and Karol Irzykowski have not been filled with critics of similar quality; and though there are many serious and profound deliberations about theatre, there is no one whom one would wish to read. This is the reason why those who have gone to the theatre by chance and then noticed with some surprise that something is not quite in order, are beginning to write now!

KRZEMIEŃ. Could you, end by revealing some of your professional ambitions?

WAJDA. There are many. Too many—decidedly too many. But, alas not everything that I want to do depends on me alone.

Witkacy adapted from the plays of Witkiewicz by Jozef Szajna and directed by Szajna at the Teatr Studio, Warsaw, 1972.
Photo: Wojciech Plewinski

Dante, directed by Szajna at the Teatr Studio, Warsaw, 1974.
Photo: Stefan Okolowicz

SZAJNA FROM MOUNT SINAI an interview with
Jozef Szajna
Maria Czanerle
Translated by Boleslaw Taborski

CZANERLE.   I would like our conversation to be concerned with
general, fundamental matters. Since your theatre has now become
known throughout the world, it would be helpful to explain it as a
phenomenon. This is an opportune time, for it seems that you are
a master of the post-war avant-garde who has produced many
imitators, particularly among students. And for a couple of years
now, you seem to have been tending, consciously or not towards a
classicism in your art. This is a natural process: the avant-garde which
lasts and influences others, in time becomes classic. In ageing it does
not die but acquires dignity and permanence.

So let us begin with a basic problem, with your great theme—
the tragedy of man in the modern world. I think that you explore
this tragedy—as illustrated by the victims of Hitler's concentration
camps—in many different areas and layers of world literature. This
is the substance of your recent productions: *Faust, Witkacy, Dante,
Cervantes* and *Gulgutiere*. It is a universal theme—man and the world.

SZAJNA.   In the context of 'man and the world,' I am concerned with
finding a way out of the situation which has been imposed on man,
and which conditions him. I am opposed to the pattern of the world
and to man's tragedy. Beckett is the modern Sophocles, and
Replique is an ancient tragedy. Not long ago in Paris, Louis Barrault
and Madeleine Renaud said that I ought to produce Beckett. I
told them that Beckett came too late for me. I move from darkness
into light, and Beckett does the opposite: moves us into darkness.
All of this really relates to Aeschylus and Sophocles. I am looking
for a way out of tragedy.

CZANERLE.   You have been described in a foreign journal as a
greater 'catastrophist' than Kafka.

SZAJNA.   That is a great compliment. Because my 'catastrophism' is
optimistic. I warn—but actively. Kafka fought the myth of law and
unmasked it. I oppose myths.

CZANERLE.   Unmasking is also a form of opposition, of fight. Kafka did
it much less agressively, though, and more intelligibly. But only had
words at his disposal.

Gulgutière by M. Czanerle and Jozef Szajna at the Teatr Studio,
Warsaw, 1973. *Photo:* Wojciech Plewinski

SZAJNA. For me theatre begins where literature ends. Let's leave aside
closet drama; let's be faithful to the art of theatre. Theatre is image,
and literature is word. My theatre is closer to film than literature. As a
man of the theatre, I feel entitled to the same freedom and technique
as Fellini or Bergman. Even when working on *Gulgutière*, I thought in
terms of performance, rather than in terms of the text, though I was a
co-author of the scenario. My theatre defies convention. It enlarges
reality. That is why I think I avoid the categories critics usually operate
within.
CZANERLE. It would be useful then, if you defined yourself, your
work . . . .

Gulgutière by M. Czanerle and Jozef Szajna, directed by
Szajna, at the Teatr Studio, Warsaw, 1973. *Photo:* Wojciech
Plewinski

SZAJNA. I look for an exit from the theatre into art. I call this process
   'open theatre.' Art is an open concept, unlike theatre, which is
   'closed' even when it is situated out of doors. I am concerned
   with the theatre of living, direct confrontation, not with a dead
   theatre concerned with historical relationships or topical subjects.
   Mine is a theatre of stylisation.
CZANERLE. But that does not define its essence. It seems to me
   that whether you produce 'open' or 'closed' theatre in the Palace
   of Culture, it is most significant that your theatre is aggressive—
   that it attacks the audience with images.
SZAJNA. That is because the 'language' of my theatre is 'plastic'
   narration. That doesn't mean that I am a painter in the
   conventional sense. I do not make a painted decor, like that of

87

Wyspianski, Drabik or Potworowski. In 1957 and 1958 I was reproached for not cultivating classic stage design. Andrzej Pronaszko once said about me: 'I put solids on the floor, and that man—meaning me—hangs them on strings.'

CZANERLE. But that was said with admiration for a man who could hang solids from string . . .

SZAJMA. I have never used silk, or lace or tulle as in opera or conventional theatre. This has irritated the aesthetes. I have made costumes out of sacks; I have prepared jute and burnt plastic—invariably with the assistance of the upholsterer, not the master tailor. What I did was then called 'stage design,' which was something inferior to 'decor', as the word was then generally in use. I avoided the facade — architectural stage design—and instead used sculpted objects and forms filling space.

CZANERLE. You have even made the actor into an object and called it 'the connection of man with the prop, his partner in the acting.' So the actor animates the object, and the object dominates man. This would seem to be done to discredit the civilisation which, by mechanizing man, destroys his personality and takes away the character and pride which he used to have in the past.

SZAJNA. Man in my theatre—he who experienced the war as well as he who lives today—is only a victim of civilisation. If I belong to the avant-garde, it is a post-industrial avant-garde, which reflects life as precarious, in a state of dissolution, unstable in its process of coming into being and of dying. In this world, the fundamental content and concepts connected with morals and ethics—such as religion, patriotism, family, and honour—have been devalued. For Dante treason was a sin; we have betrayed everything. Modern man has been uprooted from his background, tradition, faith . . .

CZANERLE. Total catastrophism, then?

SZAJNA. I was born into a tragic community or 'commune' where people lived for people. They shared not only the smokes and potato peel; they shared solidarity, the mutual offering of one to another. This was not loyalty, but the solidarity of a commune—a tragic human love going back to the concentration camp crematoria ovens. A great, tragic commune of people, a great idea.

CZANERLE. And now?

SZAJNA. Today we live in loneliness—in a world disintegrating and full of threatening danger to which we react by a feeling of overwhelming helplessness. Something has happened to man: the contemporary world has fallen from his hands. We have been driven away from the time which made us and which ought to be our time—hence our passivity, lack of direction. Under so much pressure, man is unable to find himself. Lost, he attempts to save himself, by protesting, contesting, accusing the State of impending threat, his human agony (as in *Replique*).

CZANERLE. So the world is accused in the name of man. But in

Replique written and directed by Jozef Szajna at the Teatr
Studio, Warsaw, 1973. *Photo:* Wojciech Plewinski

showing man in the modern world you seem to have no compassion
for that degraded, ill-treated man. You treat him symbolically—as a
dehumanised object, a rag, a remnant of what he once was. You often
say that 'man has neglected himself.' You defend your anti-
aestheticism with man's ugliness, his poverty, lack of ideals or reason
for living, his inner desolation. You do not seem to like man, though
perhaps you would wish to help him.

SZAJNA. In art, aesthetic revaluations took place long ago, but theatre
lags behind and does not take them into account. This is partly
because of the difference in the mode of expression. My art is created
from and by my own experience, lived authentically—and not from
borrowed literary experience. I would say that my art is both
constructive and destructive.

Cervantes written and directed by Jozef Szajna, at the Teatr
Studio, Warsaw, 1976. *Photo:* Stefan Okolowicz

To become beautiful, one must have a moral imperative. Man can
become slave or God, but to be God he would have to struggle to
secure autonomy for himself. By showing violence, the aggression of
evil, I intend to unmask the new danger—the uniformity of man who
becomes smaller and smaller, more anonymous. That is why the
positive hero has become banal, I am trying to discover man in the
tragic hero—Faust, Dante, Cervantes.
CZANERLE. All this classification seems to indicate again that you are

Cervantes written and directed by Jozef Szajna, at the Teatr
Studio, Warsaw, 1976. *Photo:* Stefan Okolowicz

becoming a 'classic.' There is evidence of this in what you say, in
what you do, in your past development and future plans. You have
become a moralist.

SZAJNA.   I am absolutely appalled by the banality of today's world . A
morality play arms for the ultimate matters which will protect man
from banality.

CZANERLE. With your sense of artistic and historic duty, you have
lost your sense of humour?

SZAJNA. I lived out the war honestly, as a member of a particular
generation. Now it is the more universal problems found in the
classics that seem to me important.

CZANERLE. But this seems to support your classic tendencies: moving
away from the roots of creative inspiration—which for you were the

91

concentration camp and war experiences—in search of more general or modern problems. In the early period of your independent work as a director (in the theatres of Nowa Huta and Cracow), you mainly produced famous literary works—*The Government Inspector, Don Quixote*, Mayakovsky's *The Bath House,* Kafka's *Castle* and O'Casey's *Purple Dust.* The last work in that series was Goethe's *Faust* which you directed at the Polski Theatre in Warsaw. Later, after becoming artistic director of the Classic Theatre in Warsaw, you seemed to prefer the older and nobler classics, produced in toto, synthetically, one could say, and you called those productions by the names of their authors: *Witkacy, Dante, Cervantes.* Those titles seem to be indicative of your ambitions and interests, even despite the fact that you changed the name of the Classic Theatre to the rather more modest 'Studio'. You also attempt to find support for what you do in your own theory, composed, it would seem, to justify your theatre practice.

SZAJNA. I try, whenever possible, to lessen the distance in art which divides what has been consciously perceived from the unconscious. I consider the tendency in theatre to illustration to be tautology, something which diminishes the thematic scope of the work. I produce 'open' theatre with universal themes. The word is a commentary, an impulse which stimulates and directs the action. In a theatre of events and confrontations, where elements of collective play are integrated, the word becomes a metaphor. Today facts are blurred; only meanings remain.

CZANERLE. You have mentioned in passing an important matter: the role of words, of literature in your theatre. So far, you have only once omitted the text altogether—in *Replique.* Your attitude to literature seems to be that of a painter to his material and to the colours he uses to create his picture. He does what he wants with them, what inspiration guides him to do. This would be a natural process, if the literary material of your 'plastic' compositions were not the great world classics. Great titles and their authors' great names make special demands and raise certain expectations. *Gulgutiere* was one exception—and the recent *Cervantes,* where you presented yourself as the author of a work on a classic theme.

SZAJNA. For me words have become a whisper aiming at a great silence. I am concerned with one thing in the theatre: that word should become image. Words have failed us, so I can only talk about visual theatre. In *Replique* I cultivate claustrophobia—people do not see, do not hear, do not have a shape, and do not talk. They animate the object-puppet and are reduced to object-puppets.

CZANERLE. Your props are a basic part of your productions. You use a whole arsenal of objects: they are the instruments of torture with which you beset man. Your loyalty to the same props in the changing world is remarkable, even touching, though some reproach you for it. I shall not forget the goat from *The Government*

Replique written and directed by Jozef Szajna at the Teatr Studio, Warsaw, 1973. *Photo:* Wojciech Plewinski

Replique written and directed by Jozef Szajna, at the Teatr
Studio, Warsaw, 1973. *Photo:* Wojciech Plewinski

Inspector which has followed you like a faithful domestic animal. Though it was originally only a prop, like your mannikins, ladders, wheelbarrows, or wheels . . .

SZAJNA. Man moves among forms which have been imposed on him. The absence of ideas, tradition and religion has created the hegemony of objects. In the beginning was the word, but in our endgame there is a theatre of collective life which has pushed man into selfishness and degeneration. That is why I have given him those object-symbols— for assistance. A ladder directed at the empty heaven, or fast-turning wheels, or abandoned shoes, dummies—all these objects function as instruments of voluntary torture. Their meanings are, I think, clear: man imprisoned among the forms which have been imposed on him. The ladder signifies the tower of Babel; a ladder directed at the empty heaven means the proximity of God, man's aspiration for the absolute, or—maybe—the atom bomb?

In the ancient world the wheel was a form of perfection. Somewhere I have used four joined small wheels instead of one wheel, that is to say, instead of perfection . . .

CZANERLE. A small car?

SZAJNA. Those wheels have become a new camp bunker, symbolic terror of a too-fast imagination—our new Odyssey. A ladder aiming at the sky and the wheels running on earth are an attempt to maintain contact with two planets—heaven and earth, superior laws and earthly laws. Man belongs biologically to earth, unites himself with elements like fire and water, looks for purification and the way out.

CZANERLE. You have created at least five models, only taking into account the productions of your Warsaw period: *Faust, Gulgutiere, Dante, Replique, Cervantes.* Which of these models seems to you to best express the style and sense of production you have aimed for?

SZAJNA. I will reply to this with a story. When, a few years ago, I had an exhibition of my 'plastic composition'—Reminiscences— painters said it was not plastic art but theatre, while men of the theatre saw it only as plastic art. At the Venice Biennale in 1970 I exhibited that same 'stage production' without action, without movement and without actors—as a menacing world of silence, a world in which the 'literature' was created by the visitors to the exhibition. This was a theatre of questions asked by the spectators themselves. In the art of concrete objects, there are no unambiguous answers. In an arranged situation, embracing a new reality, composed of suitable selected elements (like shoes, ladders, easels, outlines of human remnants, shreds of civilization) we try to create a new world from the multiplicity surrounding man.

CZANERLE. So, yours is an art of symbols and meanings, of accusation and warning, of optimism and catastrophism, an art of words (of which there are often too many, though in theory they are superfluous), and of the image (which is the most important element, though supported by the word). Yours is an art which repudiates man in order to defend him; an art thirsting for love, though so cold; an art of raging imagination, not of sentiment or heart; an art of talent and intuition, not of intellect and theory.

THE THEATRE OF DEATH A Manifesto
Tadeusz Kantor
Translated by Vog T. and Margaret Stelmaszynski

1. Craig's Postulate: to bring back the marionette. Eliminate the live actor. Man—a creature of nature—is a foreign intrusion into the abstract structure of a work of art.

According to Gordon Craig, somewhere along the banks of the Ganges two women forced their way into the shrine of the Divine Marionette, which was jealously hiding the secrets of the true THEATRE. They envied the ROLE of this Perfect Being in illuminating human intellect with the sacred feeling of the existence of God, its GLORY; they spied on its Movements and Gestures, its sumptuous attire and, by cheap parody, began to satisfy the vulgar taste of the mob. At the moment when they finally ordered a similar monument built for themselves—the modern theatre, as we know it only too well and as it has lasted to this day, was born. A clamorous Public Service Institute. With it appeared the ACTOR. In defence of his theory Craig cites the opinion of Eleanor Duse: 'to save the theatre, it must be destroyed, it is necessary for all actors and actresses to die of plague. . . for it is they who render art impossible. . . .'

2. Craig's Version: Man—the actor ousts the marionette, takes its place, thereby causing the demise of the theatre.

There is something very impressive in the stand taken by the great Utopian, when he says: 'In all seriousness I demand the return to the theatre of the imagination of the super-marionette. . . and when it appears people will again, as before, be able to worship the happiness of Existence, and render divine and jubilant homage to DEATH. . . ' Craig, inspired by the aesthetics of SYMBOLISM, considered man to be subject to unpredictable emotions, passions, and consequently to chance as an element completely foreign to the homogenous nature and structure of a work of art, which destroys its principal trait; cohesion.

Not only Craig's idea but also that whole elaborate programme of symbolism—impressive in its own time—had in the 19th century the support of isolated and unique phenomena announcing a new era and

97

new art: Heinrich von Kleist, Ernst Theodor Amadeus Hoffman. Edgar Allan Poe. . . . One hundred years earlier, Kleist for the same reasons as Craig, demanded the substitution of the actor by the marionette: he regarded the human organism, which is subject to the laws of NATURE, as a foreign intrusion into Artistic Fiction, based on the principle of Construction and Intellect. This accounts for his reproaches stressing the limited capabilities of man and charges of an incessantly controlling consciousness, which excludes the concepts of grace and beauty.

3. From the romantic mysticism of mannequins and the artificial creations of man in the XIX century – to the rationalism of XX century abstract thought.

On what seemed to be the safe road traversed by the man of Enlightenment and Rationalism there appears out of the darkness, suddenly and in increasingly greater numbers, DOUBLES, MANNEQUINS, AUTOMATONS, HOMUNCULI. Artificial creations, a mockery of the creatures of NATURE, bearers of absolute degradation, ALL human dreams, DEATH, Horror and Terror. There is born a faith in the unknown powers of MECHANICAL MOVEMENT, a maniacal passion for the invention of a MECHANISM surpassing in pefection and severity the human organism and all its weaknesses.

And all this with an aura of demonism, on the brink of charlatanism, illegal practices, magic, transgression and nightmare. This was the SCIENCE FICTION of those days, in which the demonic human brain created ARTIFICAL MAN.

At the same time all of this signified an abrupt loss of faith in NATURE and in that realm of man's activity which was closely tied with nature. Paradoxically, from these extremely romantic and diabolical efforts to take away nature's right of creation – there evolved a movement increasingly independent and more and more dangerously distant from NATURE – A RATIONALISTIC, even MATERIALISTIC MOVEMENT of a 'WORLD OF ABSTRACTION', CONSTRUCTIVISM, FUNCTIONALISM, MACHINISM, ABSTRACTION, finally PURIST VISUALISM, recognising only the 'physical presence' of a work of art. This risky hypothesis, whose origin is none too attractive for an age of technology and scientism. I take upon my conscience and for my personal satisfaction.

4. Dadaism, introducing 'ready-made.' elements of life, destroys the concepts of homogeneity and cohesion in a work of art, as postulated by symbolism. Art Nouveau and Craig.

But let us return to Craig's marionette. Craig's idea of replacing the live actor with a mannequin – an artificial and mechanical creation – for the sake of preserving perfect cohesion in a work of art, is today invalid.

Later experience destroyed the unity of structure in a work of art by introducing FOREIGN elements in collages and assemblages; the

acceptance of 'ready-made' reality, full recognition of the role of
CHANCE, and the placing of a work of art on the sharp borderline
between the REALITY OF LIFE AND ARTISTIC FICTION—
made irrelevant those scruples from the beginning of this century,
from the period of Symbolism and Art Nouveau. The two possible
solutions—either autonomous art and intellectual structure, or
naturalism—ceased to be the ONLY ones. When the theatre, in its
moments of weakness, submitted to the live organism of man and
his laws—it automatically and logically agreed to the form or
imitation of life, its presentation and re-creation. In the opposite
circumstances, when the theatre was strong and independent enough
to free itself from the pressure of life and man, it created artificial
equivalents to life which turned out to be more alive, because they
submitted easily to the abstractions of space and time and were
capable of achieving absolute unity.

Today these possibilities are neither appropriate nor valid
alternatives. For a new situation and new conditions have arisen in
art. The appearance of the concept of READY-MADE REALITY,
extracted from life—and the possibilities of ANNEXING it,
INTEGRATING it into a work of art through DECISION,
GESTURE or RITUAL—has become a fascination much stronger
than (artificially) CONSTRUED reality, than the creation of
ABSTRACTION, or the surrealistic world, than Breton's
MIRACULOUSNESS. Happenings, Events and Environments
with their colossal momentum, have achieved the rehabilitation of
whole regions of REALITY, disdained until this time, cleansing it
of the ballast of life's intentions.

This 'DECALAGE' of life's reality, its derailment from life's
practices, moved the human imagination more strongly than the
surrealistic reality of dreams. As a result, fears of direct intervention
by life and man in the scheme of art—became irrelevant.

5. *From the 'Ready-Made Reality' of the happening—to the
   dematerialization of the elements of a work of art.*

However, as with all fascination, so too this one, after a time,
was transformed into a convention practised universally, senselessly
and in a vulgar manner. These almost ritualistic manipulations of
Reality, connected as they are with the contestation of
ARTISTIC STATUS and the PLACE reserved for art, gradually
started to acquire different sense and meaning. The material,
physical PRESENCE of an object and PRESENT TIME, the only
possible context for activity and action—turned out to be too burden-
some, had reached their limits. The TRANSGRESSION signified:
depriving these conditions of the material and functional
IMPORTANCE, that is, of their COMMUNICATIVENESS. Because
this is the latest period, still current and not yet closed, the

observations which follow derive from and are tied with my own creativity.

The object (*The Chair,* Oslo, 1970) became *empty,* deprived of *expression, connections, references,* characteristics of programmed *communication,* its *'message'* directed 'nowhere,' it changed into a *dummy.*

Situations and activities were locked into their own CIRCUMFERENCE: the ENIGMATIC (theatre of the impossible, 1973), in my manifesto entitled 'Cambriollage', followed the unlawful INTRUSION into that terrain where tangible reality was transformed into its INVISIBLE EXTENSIONS. The role of THOUGHT, memory and TIME becomes increasingly clear.

6. The rejection of the orthodoxy of conceptualism and the 'Official Avant-garde of the Masses.'

The certitude which impressed itself upon me more and more strongly that the concept of LIFE can be vindicated in art only through the ABSENCE OF LIFE in its conventional sense (again Craig and the Symbolists!), this process of DEMATERIALIZATION SETTLED on a path which circumvented in my creative work the whole orthodoxy of linguistics and conceptualism. This was probably caused in part by the colossal throng which arose on this already official course and which will unfortunately become the latest installment of the DADAIST current with its slogans of TOTAL ART, EVERYTHING IS ART, ALL ARE ARTISTS, ART IS IN THE MIND, etc.

I hate crowds. In 1973 I wrote a draft of a new manifesto which takes into consideration this false situation. This is its beginning:

'From the time of Verdun, Voltaire's Cabaret and Marcel Duchamp's Water-Closet, when the "status of art" was drowned out by the roar of Fat Bertha—DECISION became the only remaining human possibility, the reliance on something that was or is unthinkable, functioning as the first stimulant of creativity, conditioning and defining art. Lately thousands of mediocre individuals have been making decisions, without scruples or any hesitation whatever. We are witnesses of the banalization and conventionalization of decision. This once dangerous path has become a comfortable freeway with improved safety measures and information. Guides, maps, orientation tables, directional signs, signals, centres, Art Co-operatives guarantee the excellence of the functioning of creativity. We are witnesses of the GENERAL MOVEMENT of artist-commandos, street fighters, artist-mediators, artist-mailmen, epistologs, pedlars, street magicians, proprietors of Office and Agencies. Movements on this already official freeway, which threatens with a flood of graphomania and deeds of minimal significance, increases with each passing day. It is necessary to leave it as quickly as possible. This is not easily done. Particularly

at the apogee of the UNIVERSAL AVANT-GARDE—blind and
favoured with the highest prestige of the INTELLECT, which
protects both the wise and the stupid.'

7. On the side streets of the official avant-garde, Mannequins appear.

My deliberate rejection of the solutions of conceptualism, despite
the fact that they seemed to be the only way out from the path upon
which I had embarked, resulted in my placing the above-mentioned
facts of the latest stage of my creativity and attempts to describe
them, on side streets which left me more open to the UNKNOWN!!!
    I have more confidence in such a situation. Any new era always
begins with actions of little apparent significance and little note,
incidents having little in common with the recognised trend, actions
that are private, intimate, I would even say—shameful. Vague.
And difficult! These are the most fascinating and essential moments
of creativity.

> *All of a sudden I became interested in the nature of
> MANNEQUINS.*

The mannequin in my production of THE WATER HEN *1967
and the mannequins in* THE SHOEMAKERS *1970, had a very
specific role: they were like a non-material extension, a kind of
ADDITIONAL ORGAN for the actor, who was their 'master.'
The mannequins already widely used in my production of
Slowacki's* Balladyna *were DOUBLES of live characters, somehow
endowed with a higher CONSCIOUSNESS, attained 'after the
completion of their lives.'*

These mannequins were already clearly stamped with the sign of DEATH.

*8. The mannequin as manifestation of 'REALITY OF THE LOWEST
ORDER.'*
    The mannequin as dealings of TRANSGRESSION.
    The mannequin as EMPTY object. The DUMMY. A message of
DEATH. A model for the actor.
    The mannequin I used in 1967 at the Cricot 2 Theatre (*The Water
Hen*) was a successor to the 'Eternal Wanderer' and 'Human
Ambellages,' one which appeared naturally in my 'Collections' as yet
another phenomenon consistent with my long-held conviction that
only the reality of the lowest order, the poorest and least prestigious
objects are capable of revealing their full objectivity in a work of art.
    Mannequins and Wax Figures have always existed on the peripheries
of sanctioned Culture. They were not admitted further; they occupied
places in FAIR BOOTHS, suspicious MAGICIANS' CHAMBERS, far
from the splendid shrines of art, treated condescendingly as
CURIOSITIES intended for the tastes of the masses. For precisely
this reason it was they, and not academic, museum creations, which

caused the curtain to move at the blink of an eye.

MANNEQUINS also have their own version of TRANSGRESSION. The existence of these creatures, shaped in man's image, almost 'godlessly,' in an illegal fashion, is the result of heretical dealings, a manifestation of the Dark, Nocturnal, Rebellious side of human activity. Of Crimes and Traces of Death as sources of recognition. The vague and inexplicable feeling that through this entity so similar to a living human being but deprived of consciousness and purpose there is transmitted to us a terrifying message of Death and Nothingness— precisely this feeling becomes the cause—simultaneously—of that transgression, repudiation and attraction. Of accusation and fascination. All arguments have been exhausted in accusations. The very mechanism of action called their attention to itself, that mechanism which, if taken as the purpose, could easily be relegated to the lower forms of creativity! *IMITATION AND DECEPTIVE SIMILARITY,* which serve the conjurer in setting his *TRAPS* and fooling the viewer, the use of 'unsophisticated' means, evading the concepts of aesthetics, the abuse and fraudulent deception of APPEARANCES, practices from the realm of charlatans.

To make matters complete, the entire proceedings were accompanied by a philosophical world-view which, from the time of Plato to this day, often regards as the purpose of art the unmasking of Being and a Spiritual Sense of Existence and not involvement in the Material Shell of the world, in that faking of appearances which are the lowest stage of being.

I do not share the belief that the MANNEQUIN (or a WAX FIGURE) could replace the LIVE ACTOR, as Kleist and Craig wanted. This would be too simple and naive. I am trying to delineate the motives and intent of this unusual creature which has suddenly appeared in my thoughts and ideas. Its appearance complies with my ever-deepening conviction that it is possible to express *life* in art only through the *absence of life,* through an appeal to DEATH, through APPEARANCES, through EMPTINESS and the lack of a MESSAGE.

The MANNEQUIN in my theatre must become a MODEL, through which pass a strong sense of DEATH and the conditions of the DEAD. A model for the live ACTOR.

9. *My elucidation of the situation described by Craig. The appearance of the LIVE ACTOR as a revolutionary moment. The discovery of the IMAGE OF MAN.*

I derive my observations from the domain of the theatre, but they are relevant to all current art. We can suppose that Craig's suggestively-depicted and disastrously-incriminating picture of the circumstances surrounding the appearance of the Actor— was composed for his own use, as a point of departure for his idea of the 'SUPER-MARIONETTE.' Despite the fact that I remain an admirer of Craig's magnificent contempt and passionate accusations (especially since I see before me the absolute

102

downfall of today's theatre) and then only after my full acceptance of the first part of his Credo, in which he denies the institutionalised theatre any reason for artistic existence—I dissociate myself from his renowned decisions on the fate of the ACTOR.

For the moment of the ACTOR'S first appearance before the HOUSE (to use current terminology) seems to me, on the contrary: *revolutionary* and *avant-garde*. I will even try to compile and 'ascribe to History' a completely different picture, in which the course of events will have a meaning quite the opposite. . .! From the common realm of customary and religious rituals, common ceremonies and common people's activities advanced SOMEONE, who made the risky decision to BREAK with the ritualistic Community. He was not driven by conceit (as in Craig) to become an object of universal attention. This would have been too simplistic. Rather it must have been a rebellious mind, sceptical, heretical, free and tragic, daring to remain alone with Fate and Destiny. If we also add 'with its ROLE,' we will then have before us the ACTOR. This revolt took place in the realm of art. Said event, or rather manifestation, probably caused much confusion of thought and clashing of opinions. This ACT was undoubtedly seen as a disloyalty to the old ritualistic traditions and practices, as secular arrogance, as atheism, as dangerous subversive tendencies, as scandal, as amorality, as indecency; people must have seen in it elements of clownery, buffoonery, exhibitionism and deviation. The author himself, set apart from society, gained for himself not only implacable enemies, but also fanatical admirers. Condemnation and glory simultaneously. It would be guilty of a ludicrous and shallow formalism to interpret this act of SEVERANCE (RUPTURE) as egotism, as a lust for glory or latent inclinations toward acting. It must have implied something much greater, a MESSAGE of extraordinary import. We will try to illustrate this fascinating situation: OPPOSITE those who remained on this side there stood a MAN DECEPTIVELY SIMILAR to them, yet (by some secret and ingenious 'operation') infinitely DISTANT, shockingly FOREIGN, as if DEAD, cut off by an invisible BARRIER— no less horrible and inconceivable, whose real meaning and THREAT appears to us only in DREAMS. As though in a blinding flash of lightning, they suddenly perceived a glaring, tragically circus-like IMAGE OF MAN, as if they had seen him FOR THE FIRST TIME, as if they had seen THEIR VERY SELVES. This was certainly a shock—a meta-physical shock, we might even say. The live effigy of MAN emerging out of the shadows, as if constantly walking ahead of himself, was the dominant MESSAGE of its new HUMAN CONDITION, only HUMAN, with its RESPONSIBILITY, its tragic CONSCIOUSNESS, measuring its FATE on an inexorable and final scale, the *scale* of *DEATH*. This revelatory MESSAGE, which was transmitted from the realm of DEATH, evoked in the VIEWERS (let us now call them by our own term) a metaphysical shock. And the

reference to DEATH, to its tragic and MENACING beauty, were the
means and art of that ACTOR (also according to our own terminology).

It is necessary to re-establish the essential meaning of the relationship:
VIEWER and ACTOR.

IT IS NECESSARY TO RECOVER THE PRIMEVAL FORCE OF THE
SHOCK TAKING PLACE AT THE MOMENT WHEN OPPOSITE A MAN
(THE VIEWER) THERE STOOD FOR THE FIRST TIME A MAN (THE
ACTOR) DECEPTIVELY SIMILAR TO US YET AT THE SAME TIME
INFINITELY FOREIGN, BEYOND AN IMPASSABLE BARRIER.

10.   RECAPITULATION

Despite the fact that we may be suspected and even accused
of a certain scrupulousness, inappropriate under the circumstances,
in destroying inborn prejudices and fears,
for the sake of a more precise picture
and possible conclusions
let us establish the limits of that boundary, which has the name:
THE CONDITION OF DEATH
for it represents the most extreme point of reference,
no longer threatened by any conformity,
FOR THE CONDITION OF THE ARTIST AND ART

. . . this specific relationship
terrifying
but at the same time compelling
the relationship of *the living to the dead*
who not long ago, while still alive, gave not the slightest
reason for the unforseen spectacle
for creating unnecessary separation and confusion:
they did not distinguish themselves
did not place themselves above others
and as a result of this seemingly banal
but, as would later become evident, rather essential
and valuable attribute
they were simply, normally
in no way transgressing universal laws
unremarkable
and now suddenly
on the other side
opposite
they astound us
as though we
were seeing them for the first time
set on display
in an ambiguous ceremony:
pointless
and at the same time repudiated,

irrevocably different
and infinitely foreign
and more: somehow deprived of all meaning
of no account
without the meanest hope of occupying some position
in our 'full' life relationships
which to us alone are accessible, familiar
comprehensible
but for them meaningless.
If we agree that a trait
of living people
is the ease and ability
with which they enter into mutual and manifold
life relationships
only then
with regard to the dead
is there born in us a sudden and startling
realisation of the fact that
this basic trait of the living
is brought out and made possible by
their complete
lack of differentiation
by their
indistinguishability
by their universal *similarity*
mercilessly abolishing all other opposing delusions
common
consistent
all-binding.
Only then do the *dead*
become (for the living)
noteworthy
for that highest price
achieving
their individuality
distinction
their CHARACTER
glaring
and almost
circus-like.

THE DEAD CLASS SCENE BY SCENE
Jan Klassowicz
Translated by Karol Jakubowicz

The Dead Class—A Dramatic Seance is a composition made up of both
Tadeusz Kantor's own texts and those of three leading Polish
avant-garde writers of the 1930's: Stanislaw I. Witkiewicz, Witold
Gombrowicz and Bruno Schulz. A few of the characters, snatches of
dialogue, the structure of some scenes and some monologues are taken
from Witkiewicz's play *Tumour Brainard.* As for Gombrowicz,
Kantor has drawn on his work for the symbolic treatment of objects
and parts of the human body, growing huge and alienating themselves
from it ('heel', finger', 'backside', the making of faces), as well as for
the atmosphere of schoolboyish jokes and antics. Finally, Bruno
Schulz's short story *The Pensioner,* whose hero returns in his last days
to his old school room, suggested the overall idea of the piece. Another
thing that Kantor takes from Schulz's writings is the setting and
distinctive local colour of a small town in south eastern Poland as it
was in those days, with a sizeable Jewish population and with
memories and traditions of the pre-1918 Austrian occupation still
fresh. Schulz, who illustrated his own works, also inspired the visual
style of the play; its combination of naturalism and expressionism and
the deformed figures populating the school room owe much to
Schulz's drawings.

Generally speaking, the spoken text is just one of many elements
that go into the making of *The Dead Class,* alongside mime, gesture,
music and motion. A written documentation like this also tends to
make quotations from the text seem more important than they are in
the performance itself.

In my opinion it is not possible to do justice to the show in a written
description. To adequately and faithfully describe *The Dead Class* one
would have to translate the 'language' of the visual spectacle into the
'language' of prose. In other words, to write a short story that would
equal the style and imaginative power of those of Kafka or Schulz.
Hence, this effort should be viewed as an account of stage business
in which sometimes a more subjective and metaphorical presentation
is also attempted.

In terms of composition, *The Dead Class,* which takes about 90
minutes to play, is divided into three parts, but the show actually
has no intervals. The setting is an old-fashioned school room. The

students are not young but old, and are played not by professional actors (though some are), but by people whose own lives and dreams are interwoven through the piece. The teacher—who remains on stage throughout conducting (in the musical sense) the pace, length and direction of this dream play—is Kantor himself. It should also be noted that all the material here described is not always played and what is played is not always done in this order. *The Dead Class,* therefore, like one's own perception of reality, is constantly changing and is different from night to night.

Tadeusz Kantor (right) as the teacher conductor of *The Dead Class. Photo:* Gallery 'Foksal' Archives

PART I

A WAXWORKS TABLEAU

The rectangular playing area has been roped off to form a narrow, long
rectangle, with the spectators sitting along its base and the right side.
The longer left side runs along a wall, and at the back, the actors enter
from behind a dark curtain. Inside this rectangle there is another one,
made up of four rows of wooden, dark grey, almost black school desks
that have been nailed together. Kantor calls them 'the wreck'. To the
side, a village privy—the loo 'where one got one's first taste of freedom'—
knocked together from similar boards as the desks. Beside it, sitting on
a chair, there is a dummy with a waxen face, dressed in black—the
Beadle. It's quite dark in the hall, but the playing area is well lit with
a clear white light. There are no lighting changes throughout.

The general impression is of a small-town school room, only everything
is grey and black, and the books and copy books seem on the point
of crumbling into dust. The Beadle's dummy reinforces the impression
that the black school room is but an imitation, the external shell of
something whose real existence is long a thing of the past.

Twelve old people stand behind the desks. All are dressed in black
funeral garb and bowlers; their old-fashioned clothes are rumpled and
baggy; figures twisted and bent. White and greyish faces, staring
straight ahead with unseeing eyes. Silence.

SITTING DOWN. SILENT REQUESTS.
HANDS.

Inside the rope which surrounds the school room stands Kantor,
wearing his 'private' black clothes. He looks at the old people, turns
his long face away, then—like a conductor—raises his hand. The oldsters
sit behind their desks. Silence. Another sign from the conductor.
One of the old people puts his hand up. Then another, yet another,
more and more, quicker and quicker. Finally, they have all put their
hands up to show they have a question to ask; they get up and lean in
one direction, towards the spot where the teacher normally stands
in a school room.

This group of old people, frozen behind school desks, in the pose
of urgently and eagerly wanting to ask a question, look like an unknown
drawing by Bruno Schulz. And such, indeed, is the style of the
entire spectacle, both in its 'external,' as well as 'visual' and 'literary'
aspects.

SUDDEN DEPARTURE

A sign from the conductor and the oldsters jump up from their desks
and, one after another, quickly disappear behind the curtain. Only the
Absent Old Man From the First Desk remains in the empty school room.
After a while the Old Man Exhibitionist comes back and pulls him away. Pause.

The Dead Class, Part One, 'Hands'. *Photo:* Gallery 'Foksal'
Archives

GRANDE ENTREE. PARADE.
DEAD CHILDHOOD.
RETURN TO THE WRECK.

The Old People reappear suddenly in the entrance. They all carry dummies seemingly growing out of their bodies, effigies of themselves, pupils in black school uniforms with the white faces of children. They stand motionless for a moment then move rapidly forward, staging a parade around the desks. And suddenly, the strangely powerful and magnificent second phrase of the *Waltz Francois* can be heard. They walk with gusto, but they are still bent, awkward, rickety, carrying their own childhoods on their backs. They hobble, their movements are jerky, clumsy. They go round the room three times before sitting down at their desks. They freeze, and beside each of them there is an effigy with a child's face.

LESSON ABOUT SOLOMON

The first to speak is the Stranger (Green) from *Tumour Brainard:* 'What do we know about King Solomon?' The others repeat the question. Further questions and answers follow:

> What do we know about King Solomon? *(repeated)*
> King Solomon . . .
> loved . . .
> who did King Solomon love?
> many . . .
> strange women
> what women were they?
> the moa . . . bites

Meanwhile, two oldsters drag the Old Man Exhibitionist to the corner, and put him in the loo.

Then they pull his trousers down. Old Man Exhibitionist bends down and bares his backside, remaining like that for the duration of the lesson.

THE CHEDER

Everybody is back at their desks.

Questions and answers come in every quicker succession. They grow into shouting and general commotion. The oldsters wave their hands and shout:

> Ammo . . . nites
> Edo . . . mites
> Hit . . . tites
> Zidonians
> Ammonites, Zidonians, Edomites, Moabites

A sign from the conductor. Speech slows down. Two quieter lines:

> King David . . .
> What did King David do?

111

And again the Oldster Pupils shout among the silent dummies:
>King David . . .
>oompah, oompah
>shit
>on your pa,
>King David's grown old
>David's crown
>Absalom cursed David!!!
>Where is the Ark, where is the Ark?
>Because of Cedron, because of Jordan
>Absalom cursed David

There is renewed hubbub and commotion. They shout out the
Hebrew alphabet.

THE LAST ILLUSION.
A GRAND TOAST.

Their recitation of the alphabet gradually changes into a group chant,
accompanied by wialing coming from the loudspeaker. The oldsters go
into a trance. They sway at their desks, then they all rise and their
wailing grows ever louder and more frenzied, as if they hoped to keep
death away with their singing or shouting.

A NIGHT LESSON

A sign from the conductor. The loudspeaker goes dead and they all
calm down. From the crowd there now begin to emerge distinct
characters and individuals. A white-haired Old Man leaves his desk
and goes into the privy—he's the Old Man in the Loo and Tumour
Brainard at the same time. He sits on the toilet in his rumpled funeral
suit and speaks lines from *Tumour Brainard,* the play.

He is answered by the Somnambulist Prostitute (also Izia from the
same play). She 'walks the street' in her dishevelled black dress, baring
her breasts and showing her thighs:
>Mommy says to ask if you need anything?
>*Old man in the Loo:*
>I need a bull, a chariot, boundless fields
>and your blue eyes, Izia.
>*The Somnambulist Prostitute:*
>Calm down
>I know a lot . . .

All the time, the Old Man With a Bike (Tumour's Father) circles
silently round Brainard in the loo and the Somnambulist Prostitute who
is still showing her breasts. Small and stooping, he drags behind him a
child's bicycle put together the wrong way, looking very much like
un objet trouvé from the garbage dump. As the dialogue grows faster
and faster, and the Somnambulist Prostitute's gestures and behaviour
more and more vulgar, the Old Man With a Bike goes into a trot around

112

the school room dragging the heap of metal with him. At the same
time, the Woman Behind the Window comes forward from the crowd.
Wearing a black dress with puffed sleeves, her long hair down, she
holds a window frame up in front of her face at all times. She looks
out through the glass which separates her from the others in both
the physical and symbolic sense. At first she moves slowly, smoothly,
gracefully in a way that seems to suggest astonishment and uncertainty.
Later, her movements become successively more violent and jerky
and finally she starts shouting from behind her window what sounds
like abuse and curses. (The Woman Behind the Window is also Balantyne
Fermor from *Tumour Brainard.)*

DRIFTING TO SLEEP

Gradually, everybody's movements slow down and become sluggish,
the class calms down and everybody returns back to their places
beside the dummies.

HISTORICAL DELIRIUM

At first drowsily, but then ever more loudly and rapidly, the oldsters
shout sayings and phrases remembered from history and Latin lessons:
> What year was Capet's head . . . ?
> What year was Capet's head . . . ???
> Queen Anne is dead!!!
> And the geese which saved the capitol?
> And the geese which saved the capitol???
> *Hannibal ante portas!!!*
> THE IDES OF MARCH
Meanwhile, two Old Men-Pupils, who previously left unnoticed,
return carrying two dirty eiderdowns. They are followed by the
Old Man Repeater (led on long reins by another Old Man) who comes
in front of the first row of desks.

Terrible disorder ensues. Polish and Latin quotations drown one
another out until nothing but gibberish is heard. The eiderdowns
are thrown around, they run around the desks, screaming, pushing
and shoving. The Woman Behind the Window keeps walking around
on the sidelines, looking on through her window frame. A sign from
the conductor. Everybody returns to their desks. They sit down
by the dummies. Silence.

A GRAMMAR LESSON

The Repeater stands in front of the class. He says:
> Various things happen in the mouth when you speak. Lips
> take different positions to articulate A or E, and quite
> different ones for U!!! For B or P, they come together to
> completely close the air channel, and this is followed by a
> sudden release resulting in an audible explosion.
Gradually his speech slurs into incoherent gabbling.

PHONETIC BLOTS

The Old People, who have so far been sitting quietly by their dummies, begin fidgeting. The mood of unrest heightens.

The Dead Class, Part One, 'Faces'. *Photo:* Gallery 'Foksal' Archives

They seem physically aroused by the description of the speech organs and they begin using their own, producing a dissonant vocal composition with a shaky, broken rhythm and a jarringly cocophonous tune (the very opposite, it seems, of the sweet *Wlatz François* which was heard earlier):

vyst rr bzirk FUMTSEKAKA
vyst rr brk FUMTSEKAKA
bistri virk FUM TSE KA KA
str brk . . .

This sound composition slowly begins to be accompanied by gestures. Then the voices die down.

FACES

The Old People begin making faces at one another. They puff out their cheeks, contort their faces, squint, turn their noses up with their fingers, aping one another in the process (this is an important quotation from Gombrowicz—as was the Old Man-Exhibitionist's backside. It also seems to symbolise their return to childish immaturity. But all this time, there are the frozen, children's faces of the dummies among the clowning dotards).

THE WAR LESSON.
NAMES.

The mimicking faces gradually animate their whole bodies and draw them into play. Finally, the little group, thrashing about and waving their arms at their desks, looks as if it were floundering in its sinking 'wreck' among ever stormier seas. They begin screaming:

oompah
oompah
shit on your pa
oompah
oompah . . .

Seconds before the 'wreck' is to go under, there is a sign (a school bell) from the conductor (Kantor) and everybody runs out (in the commotion, the Beadle's dummy is taken away and an actor appears in its place). They disappear behind the curtain. Only the children-dummies stay in place, staring straight ahead with unseeing eyes. Pause.

THE CHARWOMAN'S ENTREE

The Charwoman rises from the corner where she has so far sat unnoticed. She is a big, skinny woman (played by a man), wearing a rag-like black dress and a hat—a cross between a bonnet and military shako—hanging to the side. She begins cleaning up. This consists in throwing the decaying readers and copy books around, thus advancing the disintegration of this

classroom of the dead. She also puts the dummies in order. Some
of them which have been lying on the floor to the left she sits behind
the desks. Then she sweeps the floor, raising a cloud of dust as she
pushes paper and litter around. Finally, the charwoman sits comfortably
at a desk, produces a 1914 newspaper and begins reading:

> Konstanty Wisniewski, the chemist, recommends tablets
> of his own prescription.
> Cheap meals for the unemployed.
> In the streets of Sarajevo, the capital of Bosnia,
> a Serbian named Gavrilo Princip
> has assassinated the Crown Prince,
> the Archduke Francis Ferdinand and his wife . . .
> Kaiser Wilhelm II has ordered a general mobilisation
> of the German Empire . . .
> Well, there's going to be a war . . .

The Beadle jumps up from his chair, stands to attention, salutes and
sings the Austrian national anthem, wailing like a beggar by the church
door:

> Gott erhalte,
> Gott beschütze
> Unsern Kaiser, unser Land!
> Mächtig durch des Glaubens Stütze
> Fuhr' Er uns mit weiser Hand!
> Lass uns Seiner Väter Krone
> schiren wider jeden Feind:
> Innig bleibt mit Hapsburgs Throne
> Oesterreichs Geschick vereint!

Singing the anthem, the Beadle exits. The Charwoman runs after him,
to return a while later with his dummy, which she puts on the chair.
'The Historical Delirium' can now be heard from the loudspeaker. The
Charwoman flees.

THE FAMILY MACHINE. BIRTH.
THE MECHANICAL CRADLE.

The Old People return to the school room. This time, they no longer
form a group. Some of them (Podophyllinic, the Stranger, and The
Ordinary Old Man) drag in The Old Man in the Loo (Tumour Brainard),
put him in the privy and start tormenting him. Old Man Tumour writhes
and tosses as if being tortured. The Old Man with a Bike (Tumour's
Father) says to him:

> 'Uber transfinite Funktionen im alef—dimensionalen Raume,
> Professor Tumour von Brainard. Oh, how clever you are, my
> son!'

The Old Man in the Loo answers, writhing in pain:

> 'I've never had time for anything, not even for love. But then,
> what is love to me?'

116

Another group of Old People now pulls in the Family Machine—a strange contraption looking like a cross between a gynaecologist's couch and an instrument of torture. The third group of Old People begins to chase the Woman with a Mechanical Cradle (Rozhulantyna) who is finally caught and put on the machine. The accompanying dialogue is taken from Act I of *Tumour Brainard* and Rozhulantyna's words: '. . . when I think about it, all I want is to explode into some magma from another world' are a cue for the machine to start operating. It spreads her legs and draws them up; in the meantime, the Charwoman brings on the Mechanical Cradle. It is a wooden box whose shape brings to mind, if anything, a child's coffin. With every move of the cradle, which keeps time with the Family Machine, the two wooden balls inside the cradle-coffin collide, giving off a mournful clatter. The movements of the Old Woman with the Mechanical Cradle stretched out on the Machine grow quicker and more violent—birth and death, birth and death, birth and death.

A GREAT CLEANING UP.

The Charwoman, now playing Death, re-enters the school room, holding a broom-scythe. She begins sweeping the floor with wide-ranging movements and one of the Old People falls with every move. The wooden balls in the cradle-coffin keep rattling. Old People grouped around the Machine and the loo scatter in panic. Death goes on a rampage. With every move of the broom-scythe. Old People drop. Others flee around the desks. One of the Old People speaks Maurycy's lines from Act I of *Tumour Brainard:* 'Papa writes poems, you know . . . Recite one for us, Izia.' The Somnambulist Prostitute (Izia) recites a poem from Witkiewicz's play which is an ironic paraphrase of a nursey rhyme about a foetus that was eaten by a kitten. She keeps up a staccato rhythm, repeating some phrases and pausing now and then, all the time evading the broom-scythe of Charwoman-Death. Finally, having said the last words, she falls, joining all the other Old People lying on the floor. A pause. A sign from the conductor and one of them raises his head and speaks Alfred's lines from Act 1 of *Tumour Brainard.* Then follows the 'family quarrel' between the Old Man Alfred and the Prostitute on the one hand, and Tumour in the Loo and Rozhulantyna on the Machine on the other. Finally, all the Old People get up and sit down at their desks.

LESSON ABOUT PROMETHEUS

The dummies and the Old People are at their desks. One of the Old People goes to the front of the class, assuming the role of teacher. He calls upon a pupil with a gesture. The pupil gets up and is questioned, with the other pupils prompting him.

117

OLD MAN-TEACHER. Prometheus. *(Silence. Fear.*
Gently but with confidence.) Prometheus. *(Still*
confident of getting a reply.) Prometheus! *(He points*
impatiently.) Prometheus!!! *(The Old Man-Pupil is*
at a loss.) Pro-me-theus.

OTHER OLD PEOPLE *(prompting).* Liver. *(The word*
comes from various directions.) Liver, liver, li-ver!!
Go on, Prometheus and his liver!!!

OLD MAN-PUPIL *(automatically).* Prometheus and his
liver . . . *(Reverses the order.)* The liver of Prometheus . . .
(He sits down furtively.)

Pause. Silence.

OLD MAN-TEACHER *(gives up waiting for further*
information and asks another question). Now,
Cleopatra's nose . . . *(Expectantly.)* Cleopatra.
(Emphatically.) Cle-o-pa-tra.

OLD MAN-PUPIL *(panics).* What about Cleopatra's nose?
(Looks around for help.) C'mon, fellers, what about it?

THE OTHERS *(trying to help, they make signs, point to*
their noses, shout). The nose, the no-o-se, her no-o-o-se.
Cleopatra's nose!!!

OLD MAN-PUPIL *(tries to do the best he can).* It's the
nose of Cleopatra, her no-o-ose . . . *(He sits down quickly.)*

OLD MAN-TEACHER *(tireless when it comes to finding*
topics). And the foot of a mountain? . . . *(He is clearly*
on the point of losing self-control.) Well, the foot of a
mountain?

OLD MAN-PUPIL *(stammers, scared stiff, he looks at*
Old Man-Teacher *with dog-like devotion, but draws back*
to be as far from him as possible. He speaks with assurance).
Foot. *(Retreats.)* Foot. *(He tries to look as if he had the*
answer at the tip of the tongue.) Foot. *(He feels secure*
enough, but is still unable to stand the tension and screams
hysterically.) Foot, foot, foot. *(As if in an epileptic fit, he*
throws himself down on the floor.) Foot, foot, foot, foo . . .
(And then returns calmly and peacefully to his desk.)

OLD MAN-TEACHER *(realising it's going to be a long haul).*
And what about Achilles' heel? Quickly. *Vite! Vite! (Now*
he gets carried away and comes out with a stream of questions,
as if reading from an encyclopedia.) Achilles' heel, Adam's
rib, and what about the ear, or the finger, or the eye, or a
hair, a hair! Heel, heel . . .

As in Gombrowicz's works the heel now becomes real for the Old Man-
Teacher, a thing of flesh and blood, it grows, swells.

118

The Dead Class, Part One, 'About Prometheus'. *Photo:* Wojciech
Szperl

The Dead Class, Part One, 'Lesson About Prometheus'.
Photo: Wojciech Szperl

OLD MAN-TEACHER *(screams)*.   Heel! Heel!!!

The Old Man-Pupil also gets carried away by the Old Man-Teacher's excitement. It's like the Revelation, or the Ascension, of the heel.

OLD MAN-PUPIL.   Heel! Heel!!!

Screaming, he takes off his shoe and shows a bare heel all around. A general obsession with the heel sets in. They flap around with great agitation.

OLD PEOPLE *(screaming)*.   Heel, heel, heel, heel . . .
OLD MAN *(suddenly sobers down and asks)*. But why
    precisely a heel?
ANOTHER OLD MAN.   And why Achilles' heel? Why a
    heel and not the whole leg?

There is general consternation and they all calm down.

OLD MAN-TEACHER *(the pendant and sadist that he is,*
    begins his questioning anew.)
    Adam's rib. Well?
    And the finger?
    And what about the eye?
    The eye!!! *(Screams.)*
    OUT!!! *(He shows to Old Man-Pupil that he is to go into the*
    corner and he obediently goes and stands there.)
    OUT!!! *(He screams, pointing at another Old Man, who also*
    goes to the corner.)

The remaining Old People begin prompting.

OLD PEOPLE.   Of a needle
                The eye of a needle . . .
                Through the eye of a needle . . .

OLD MAN-PUPIL *(a complete blockhead)*.   But who?
OLD PEOPLE *(prompting)*.   A camel. A camel!!!
OLD MAN-PUPIL *(still can't catch on)*.   But who's supposed
    to go through it?
OLD PEOPLE *(prompting)*.   A camel. Camels!! *(They start*
    shouting.) The de-se-e-ert!!! Through the eye!
OLD MAN-PUPIL *(repeat frantically)*.   The camel, of a camel, by a
    camel *(Screams.)* Camels!!

They all start shouting now and general disorder ensues.

OLD PEOPLE *(at the top of their voices)*. O, camels!
    by camels! on camels! O, camels!

The Dead Class, Part One, 'Lesson About Prometheus',
Photo: Wojciech Szperl

The word 'camel' is thus declined in all possible ways and this
gradually changes into tearful wailing, moans and plaintive cries.
The Old People-Pupils seem to be praying—avidly and desperately
at the same time. The Old Man-Teacher tries to regain control over
the situation. He assumes the pose of an inquisitor, then a judge.
He raises his hand, pronouncing a sentence. He straightens a finger,
and then suddenly cries out: 'But let's get back to the finger!!!'
then repeats 'Finger finger!!!' His raised finger becomes a separate
autonomous entity of its own (as in Grombrowicz in whose play

The Wedding, finger-related symbols play a particularly important role), and seems to grow and tower above the class. The Old Man-Teacher repeats in his trance: 'Finger. Whose finger? Just one finger, or more?'

His excitement infects everyone. The Old People at the desks begin chanting:

> He touched him with a finger . . .
> Sheer madness. Touched him with a finger!
> From a finger, under a finger,
> at the finger, between fingers,
> in the finger!! With a finger . . .
> Finger, finger, finger, finger . . .

They all jump up and raise a cry, like a toast. The *Waltz François* resounds form the loudspeaker. The conductor signals to turn it up. The silly waltz swells to become truly magnificent. The Stranger (Green) tears himself away from the crowd shouting 'Another moment and it will be too late' and runs to the privy. The Charwoman follows him and tries to drag him out of there by his hair. The Stranger begins speaking, but shutters and falters like a scratched record. He delivers his 'Grand speech' (that is, Green's monologue from Act I of *Tumour Brainard*) frequently stuttering and repeating the same words:

> Madam, you must, Madam, Madam, you must, must choose,
> the whole universe, you must, it cannot, it can, it . . .
> THE OLD PEOPLE *(interrupting)*
> We have been through all this
> we are running around in circles
> we can bear it no longer
> we are in a bad state

And again the stuttering soloist:

> Madam, you must, in the interest of culture as a whole
> he can, he cannot
> to please the fancy of that wench
> he can do everything

And The Old People in reply:

> We can bear it no longer
> we are in a bad state.
> Take this man away.
> Take this man away!!!

The Stranger gets hold of himself and says without a hitch: 'In the name of all the ideals respected by humanity, we must restrain outselves.' The Old People calm down. The Stranger

draws up with still greater pride and says imperiously: 'I am
Professor Green from M.C.G.O. (Delivers another monologue from
Tumour Brainard). He points at the Somnambulist Prostitute
(Izia) and orders: 'Take her to the automobile and speed away in
fifth gear,' Roshulatyna screams: 'Help!!!' The Old Man With A Bike
(Tumour's Father) jumps up obediently and eargerly and asks in a
high-pitched voice 'In fifth gear?' then sweeps Izia out and drives her
away in his crippled bicycle-automobile. Green says calmly: I've done
my duty.' In reply, the Old Man With a Bike cries from afar to the
Old Man in the Loo (Tumour): 'You see, son, what you've come to?
Didn't I always tell you not to stretch the thread because it would
break?' Izia cries out: 'This is all a terrible dream, a nightmare.'

The Woman Behind the Window has been standing throughout
all this behind the third desk and, as always, looking on through her
window frame, now addresses everybody (In Balantyna Fermor's
lines from Act I of *Tumour Brainard*):

> You, children, go for a stroll. It's a glorious day
> today, Spring is definitely in the air.
> The trees are sprouting green all over.
> I've even seen two brimstone butterfiles which left
> their chrysalises encouraged by the warmth and circled
> in the scented air. The poor things, they don't know
> that there are no flowers yet and that they'll starve to death.

AN OUTING

The Old People obediently get up from their desks and meekly
stroll around the desks, two by two. Then they skip along and run
'until they are absolutely exhausted and dead-tired.' Gradually, they
move more and more slowly, everything calms down and for a moment
everybody stays motionless, until there is a sign from the conductor.

PART II

SCHEMING WITH EMPTINESS

Old Man Podophyllinic suddenly turns around and beckons to the Old
Man With a Bike, then whispers something in his ear with a grave,
mysterious countenance. Then Old Man Podophyllinic turns to the
Stranger as if to announce some very bad news and explain the
disastrous situation he is in. The Stranger (who is, in fact, indifferent to
other people's misfortunes) feigns interest, and then decisively signifies
that he'll have nothing to do with the matter. The Old Man With a Bike
appeals to the Podophyllinic; the latter violently orders him to do
something. The Old Man With a Bike makes a sudden decision and flees
the school room. All these developments have been followed closely by
the Old Man in the Loo who is evidently suspicious and thinks they

might be hatching some plot. Suddenly, he turns his suspicions against the Woman With a Mechanical Cradle who all this time has been quietly bestowing her automatic smiles on everybody present. The Old Man in the Loo, looking more and more suspicious, spits at her, spluttering saliva all around. Finally, he leaves the room in a dither, but the situation remains puzzling and unexplained. At this moment, the Woman Behind the Window gets up from her desk having apparently decided that the time to unmask the guilty one has come and calls out, pointing at the Old Man-Exhibitionist. 'It's you! It's him! It's been you all the time. It's absolutely revolting!' Worried, the Old Man-Exhibitionist decides to demonstrate his innocence and runs around the desks, his face emanating confidence and serenity. The Woman Behind the Window loses her self-assurance, draws back and mutters incoherently. The Old Man-Exhibitionist keeps running, looking more innocent all the time. The Woman Behind the Window tries to tell the others something but nobody listens and her face behind the glass is contorted with fear. The Stranger jumps up from his desk and runs alongside the triumphant Old Man Exhibitionist to inquire about something. The latter explains something in detail and the story must be important because the two go on running, gesticulating with great agitation. Then the Stranger remembers that he left his crippled friend behind at his desk. So he goes back to fetch his friend and now the three of them run together, gesticulating. However, the Cripple's lame leg gets in the way, so the other two push him out of the room, after which they move decisively towards the Woman With the Mechanical Cradle who continues smiling upon everyone around. They throw the Absent Old Man off the desk, sit on either side of the Woman and start cross-examining her. Meanwhile, the Absent Old Man picks himself up from the floor by the desk, and speaks his only lines in the whole spectacle, 'Just a moment, Mr. Executioner.' Then resignedly shrugging his shoulders, he leaves, tottering on his stiff legs. The Woman With a Mechanical Cradle suddenly shouts 'Fumtsekaka! Fumtsekaka' upon which the frightened Old People leap away, crying 'bzirkeke, bzirkeke . . . .' And then, they flee one after another. The school room grows empty. Only two persons remain in the second row of desks: the Somnambulist Prostitute who has been sitting throughout the scene in a trance, her eyes gazing fixedly into a vacuum, and Old Man Podophyllinic, now sitting quietly. Suddenly, the Somnambulist Prostitute turns to him with a sinister, sensuous smile. Frightened, like a boy, by this display of naked, rapacious eroticism, Old Man Podophyllinic reaches under his desk, snatches his school-bag and flees. The Somnambulist Prostitute remains at her desk, still wearing that strange smile. We can now see that one more survivor is left in the last row, the

Ordinary Old Man. Silence. Only the wooden balls rumble on.

Charwoman Death appears in the doorway. She moves with heavy footfalls to the Ordinary Old Man, brutally drags him out from behind the desk and takes him away. Only the Somnambulist Prostitute, still smiling mysteriously, is left. Perhaps she is to blame for the whole thing . . . .

THE FUNERAL

The conductor signals and the Old People enter the hall from the
back, moving like a funeral procession, or as in a demonstration. Each
holds a big white handerchief. They are in mourning for somebody,
or themselves. They begin prayers for the dead. Spoken in parts, they
sound like some eerie litany:

> Not so long ago
> Grass hasn't had time to grow
> Death cut her down
> She's been in the ground for a month . . .

The Repeater/Obituary Distributor runs in and hands everyone a
big black obituary with the name Josef Wgrzdagiel written in white. The
Old People form a compact group at prayer. Their faces are hidden
behind the obituaries. They read out a long list of the dead, the Roll
Call of the Dead. The names which are clearly those of rural folk
are taken from the reigster of one of the parishes near Cracow. The
unbearably long list drones on and on, for as long as the audience
can possibly stand. Finally, at a cue from the conductor, the
Waltz is heard.

The Dead Class, Part Two, 'The Funeral'. *Photo:* Wojciech
Szperl

The Dead Class, Part Two, 'A Simultaneous Orgy'. *Photo:*
Gallery 'Foksal' Archives

A SIMULTANEOUS ORGY

Having dropped the obituaries, the Old People throw themselves at one
another in a free-for-all. And again, as in all previous scenes, this develops
into a composition in which every single movement is premeditated, and
where the apparent disorder (watched by Kantor who walks around the
group) is in fact a set of simultaneous actions between particular
performers (characters); what might be a fight among a group of pupils
during a break gradually transforms itself into a paraphrase of a scene from
Act II of *Tumour Brainard.*

128

During that scene, Tumour meets with savage Malays on Timor island. To begin with, as the 'orgy' continues, two Old Men are undressed and two skinny figures practically in the buff appear among the black-clad characters, wearing only flesh-coloured briefs to which are attached enormous, sadly hanging penises made of the same material. They are Patakulo Senior and Patakulo Junior from *Tumour Brainard.* The Old Man in the Loo (Tumour) cries:

> I feel so terribly unsatiated,
> that my brain is changing into hot gruel
> Call Anak Agong Patakulo here!!!

The Old People lift Patakulo Senior up.
Tumour goes on:

> I am Tumour I, the rule of Timor,
> the son of the sky and a fiery mountain,
> and you are but the shadow of a shadow
> Compared to my White Power!!!

The Somnambulist Prostitute (Izia) laughs uncontrollably. Tumour shouts and kills Patakulo Senior. Then, he turns around and says:

> Boy, lemonade! I, Tumour, I,
> the ruler of Timor, am the only lord
> of this land! There is no other God!
> Bring her over here!

The Somnambulist Prostitute shouts: 'Tummy, you old idiot, you well-rested flounder.' Meanwhile, the Old People pick up Patakulo Senior's body, carry it to a corner and drop it there. The Woman With a Mechanical Cradle runs up with a riding crop and lashes the body. The Old Man (Tumour) says to Prostitute (Izia) in reply: 'I am helpless.'

AN EROTIC DIALOGUE

This is a considerably changed scene between Tumour, Izia, and Prince Tengah from Act II of *Tumour Brainard.* In addition to the Old Man in the Loo and the Somnambulist Prostitute, one more Old Man emerges from the crowd to 'play' the part of Prince Tengah (Patakulo Junior). He approaches Tumour and makes imploring gestures, pointing at Izia. His monologue is in a peculiar 'Dada-istic' language:

> V Z G Zh D A H A
> V Z G Zh A H A
> V Z G Zh A G E L
> V Z G Zh D A H A
> V Z G Zh D A G E L

Izia sways coquettishly with a come-hither look and keeps repeating a short poem—a clearly erotic, perverse paraphrase of a children's verse, also taken from *Tumour Brainard.*

Old Man-Tengah makes ever bolder advances to her. Furious, Old Man-Tumour cries, 'They've found a common language, the goddam aristocrats' and runs to Izia. Now Old Man-Tengah is angry and reproaches Tumour for his crimes with gestures and shouts. Tumour asks astonished: 'How is it that this blackamour knows about all that?' Izia keeps reciting her poem. Tumour cries: 'Oh, how common and vile all this is!' and throws himself at Izia. The two engage in a strongly erotic scene, while Old Man Tengah squirms in pain as he observes the Somnambulist Prostitute panting and heaving in the arms of the Old Man in the Loo (there is something both of voyeurism and gerontophilia in the scene). Izia, who keeps repeating the poem throughout, now moves to the Old Man Tengah, and Tumour is enraged as he watches them, but Izia backs away with the words 'This nigger has a very strange smell, like mouldy linen or dried mushrooms. It's awful.'

The Dead Class, Part Two, 'An Erotic Dialogue'. *Photo:* Wojciech Szperl

This simultaneous action within the triangle, with Izia's continuous recitation as the connecting element, now turns into a 'normal' dialogue between three characters. Old Man-Tumour says spitefully: 'You see, you silly European girl, our good old culture prevails after all.' Izia replies, 'This black idiot is absolutely revolting. A spring has come unscrewed within me.' Tengah, still ecstatic, asks: 'What are you saying, daughter of the moon?' Tumour: 'She is opening the treasure-house of the European culture wide open for you.' And soon afterwards he exclaims with amazement: 'I have come unscrewed, too, all over.' Izia turns away from Tengah with disgust: 'It's not sulphur you have on your breath but raw meat.' Tengah cries out: 'Be damned, you white worm, for whom I have betrayed all that is sacred!' He moves away in a wild leap and Izia comments: 'Well, I've finally got rid of that coloured beau.'

The Woman Behind the Window (Balantyna), so far silent and looking through her window pane, now says from behind it: 'A boat has put in at Bangaya Bay.' The Old Man Tumour turns around and says: 'Ah, yes. It's the Prince Arthur, a cruiser first class. Sacred blue, it's Green getting out of the boat . . . ' Izia cries out: 'Green's coming here. It's Green!!!' This has a stimulating effect on the group of oldsters who now come to life, after having remained relatively passive throughout the last scene.

A COLONIAL EXPEDITION

The Stranger-Green enters the room holding a black pirate's flag. He cries out: 'Hooray, let's take possession of this land.' A sign from the conductor and the same phrase of the *Waltz François* as before resounds from the loudspeakers. And again, and louder still. Like a real conductor Kantor brings it up to *fortissimo*. The whole crowd of the Old People turns abruptly to fall behind the Stranger as he marches forward. Carrying aloft first the naked Patakulo Senior and then Junior, they assemble for a group photo.

The Old Man With a Bike sneaks in along the left side, carrying an old-fashioned camera. A black bellows resembling an elephant's trunk comes out of the camera and sails above the group towards a few Old People in the background who form a Pieta with the body of Patakulo-Senior.

Throughout this scene, the Old Man in the Loo (Tumour), the Stranger (Green) and the Somnambulist Prostitute (Izia) conduct a disjointed dialogue composed of sentences lifted from Act II of *Tumour Brainard*. The Stranger pounces on the Somnambulist Prostitute shouting ' . . . Oh, Izia, how I love you . . . ' and drags her out of the school room. Izia cries: ' Oh, it was so nice, so unusual. What a pity, what a pity . . . ' Immediately afterwards, the Charwoman pulls the Old Man in the Loo (Tumour) away from the group of oldsters flapping about beneath the proboscis of the camera and drags him behind the curtain. The Woman Behind the Window repeats her lines about children

131

going for an outing and butterflies that came into this world not realising that nothing but death awaited them . . .

A TRY-OUT OF THE LAST RUN

The Woman With a Mechanical Cradle now moves to the foreground and sits on a pile of garbage. Her hair is dishevelled and her skirt hangs like a rag. The action freezes for a moment, and then the Woman Behind the Window raises her hand (holding the window frame with the other) and begins conducting. The Old People gallop around the desks. As they pass by the Woman With a Mechanical Cradle, they spit on her and throw garbage all over her. It looks as if they were stoning her. Finally they stop. The Woman sits covered by the garbage. Pause.

The Dead Class, Part Two 'A Try-Out of the Last Run'
Photo: Wojciech Szperl

PART III

The Woman With a Mechanical Cradle starts singing a lullaby in Yiddish,
to the accompaniment of the clattering balls in the cradle-coffin which
keeps rocking throughout the play.

> Az du vest zain raich zinele
> Vest du dich dermonen dos lidele
> rozhenkes mit mandlen *(repeated)*
> Dos vet zain dain beruf
> Mit dem vesta Yiddele handlen
> Shlof main zinele, shlof

Behind her, in the background, Charwoman Death begins the ritual of
washing corpses. The unintelligible singing-wailing continues over the
cradle in which the succession of births and deaths has been resumed.
Against this background, the Woman With a Mechanical Cradle and
the Old Man in the Loo engage in a dialogue, which Kantor has called
a 'dummy' dialogue. Each says one sentence but these sentences are
devoid of all meaning and allow for no real communication:

> somebody might say
> that it doesn't look like that
> but it's best not to say too much
> just in case
> one can never be sure
> because in fact
> there is nothing to keep secret

The Old Man With a Bike and the Ordinary Old Man show that they are
trying to eavesdrop on their conversation. The Stranger approaches the
Somnambulist Prostitute who is again 'walking the street' *(faire le
trottoir)* and they seem to be negotiating for her services. The 'dummy'
dialogue continues throughout all this. The Stranger moves up to the
Old Man in the Loo (Tumour) and tries to get scientific secrets out of
him:

> Tell me, Professor, just me alone,
> tell me how you arrived at the formula
> for the n-class of figures
> Tell me what *is* tumour-one.

The Old Man (Tumour) pays no attention to him, and his 'dummy'
dialogue with the Old Woman (Rozhulantyna) ends with a violent
quarrel: ' . . . I filed for divorce today . . . get out of my sight, you
goddamn bitch. I am the lord of the world!' The Old Woman
(Rozhulantyna): 'So that's how it is? So, all I've done for you is
nothing, is it? And I am to be kicked around as a reward for my
humiliation. And you dare insult what is most sacred in me? There,
you double clown!'

She takes out and mercilessly shows around what was in the cradle—
it looks like testicles, but in fact it's dried-up, dead wood—two wooden

133

balls. All action stops dead for a moment as everybody looks spellbound at this still-life image, this brazen mockery of death. Rozhulantyna hands the balls to the Old Man (Tumour) who draws back and takes them automatically, and then, frightened, puts them in his pocket. The cradle rumbles on but its sound is different now, hollow. The Stranger, who has been eavesdropping all the time, cries out: 'But Mrs. Brainard, you mustn't do things like that. It's barbaric.' The Old Man With a Bike (Tumour's Father), totally oblivious to what has happened, pesters everybody with silly questions. The Old Man (Tumour) tears the newspaper out of his hands and shouts 'Away with this rag, goddamit!' Then, ashamed, as if trying to apologise, he takes out the balls and gives them to him like a tip. The Old Man With a Bike takes them carefully, looks at them tenderly and says: 'Wouldn't even spare a child, the sons of bitches.' He walks stiffly to the cradle and delicately puts the balls in. The cradle keeps rumbling. The Old Man With a Bike turns around, puts his hand on the bicycle, pulls a handkerchief out, waves it, folds it again and puts it in his pocket. Then, he mounts his bicycle, rides away, turns around and comes back, repeating the whole procedure. From now on, he will keep waving good-bye and driving away . . . The Woman With the Mechanical Cradle cries: 'Your own dad, and he took a powder.' The Stranger replies: 'I am still here, I'll stay with him,' and the Old Man in the Loo starts cursing him (Brainard's monologue from Act III).

The balls in the cradle keep up their clatter. The Charwoman goes on washing the corpses. The Stranger tries to ingratiate himself with the Woman With a Mechanical Cradle.

The Old Man in the Loo walks up to the Woman Behind a Window and washes her window pane. The Deaf Old Man bursts in and shouts (in a paraphrase of lines from Act III of *Tumour Brainard*):

Listen! But pray
bear the news bravely
Tumour Brainard has fallen victim
to his own weakness . . .

Two Old Men get hold of him and begin cleaning his ears by pulling a tatty piece of string back and forth under his bowler. After a while the Deaf Old Man begins clearing his own ears. He breaks into a run and runs feverishly around the school room. The Old Man With a Bike rides into the room and back out again. The cradle rumbles on. The washing of corpses continues.

The Stranger cleverly draws the Old Man in the Loo and takes him to the naked bodies of Patakulo Senior and Junior. Like a sculptor, he begins forming them into a group. Having touched the two naked corpses, the Old Man in the Loo drops dead.

The Old Man With a Bike rides in and back out again. The cradle rumbles on. The Woman Behind the Window looks on. The Deaf Old Man cleans his ears, running around . . .

134

The Stranger crawls on the floor, carrying the black flag. He crawls up to the Woman With a Mechanical Cradle and begins courting her: 'Madam, is it your wish to become the Marchioness of the Fifth Maske-Tower?' The Woman With a Mechanical Cradle replies amid the clatter of the balls, contorting her face into a deliberately artificial 'actorish' grimace: 'But Mr. Alfred, this is so sudden.' The Woman Behind the Window looks on. The Deaf Old Man cleans his ears and runs around. The Old Man With a Bike rides in and back out again.

Charwoman Death disappears, unnoticed by the others. The Somnambulist Prostitute, the Repeater/Obituary Distributor and the Old Men from the first row of desks begin playing cards with the obituaries.

Charwoman Death enters and begins to play a chorus girl from a tawdry night club. She bumps and grinds, trying to dance. The cradle rumbles on. The Beadle tries singing the Austrian national anthem: 'Gott erhalte Unsern Kaiser . . . ' The Woman Behind a Window looks on. The Old Man With a Bike rides in and back out again. The Deaf Old Man cleans his ears with the string. This goes on and on and on . . .

Their movements become more and more automatic and repetitive—until someone in the audience begins applauding.

CHARACTERS IN *THE DEAD CLASS*
Tadeusz Kantor
Translated by Karol Jakubowicz

The characters in *The Dead Class* are neither individualised nor clear-cut and unambiguous. As if pasted or stitched together from ill-matched parts: remnants of their childhood, the vicissitudes of their (not always creditable) lives, their dreams and passions, they fall apart and become transformed with every minute, and through this continuous motion and theatre running riot, they progress inexorably to their final form which is irrevocably transfixed and is to encompass the *Entire Memory of the Dead Class.* Final preparations are hastily made for the *Grand Game With Emptiness.*

And since all this is happening in a theatre, the actors of *The Dead Class*—loyally sticking by the rules of theatrical ritual—take on some roles from a play. However, they seem to attach little importance to them; their acting appears mechanical, borne onwards by little more than the momentum of general habit; we even get the impression that they ostentatiously refuse to acknowledge the fact of role-playing and are simply repeating somebody else's lines and imitating movements, then moving on without regret or scruple. And the parts, as if poorly and carelessly learnt, collapse every few minutes, so that serious gaps appear; many fragments are missing and we are left with nothing but guesswork and intuition to fall back on.

Or perhaps no play is being performed after all, and if an attempt is being made to put an act together, it matters little compared to the 'Game' which is really being played in this *Theatre of Death.*

This creation of appearances, going through the motions of careless, shoddy, superficial acting, sentences that are never finished, gestures that expire in mid-air, the whole make-believe spectacle (as if some play were indeed being performed), all that 'futility', they, and they alone, make it possible for us to be allowed to experience the Great Emptiness and the most remote frontier—Death.

The scene in *The Dead Class Seance* entitled *Scheming With Emptiness* unequivocally contains the theatrical essence of that Great Game.

(Note: by trying to fill in the misssing fragments to gain full 'knowledge' of the play's plot, you would be displaying nothing but the unreasonable pedantry of a bibliophile.

That would be the simplest way to destroy the all-important sphere of *feeling.*

137

And that is why it is inadvisable to read *Tumor Brainard* by Witkiewicz, the play we used for the purpose described above.)

The School Room. In the last forgotten recess of our memory, somewhere in a cramped corner, are perched a few rows of shoddy wooden school *desks.*

Battered *books* are crumbling into dust . . .

In two *corners*, like geometric figures drawn in chalk on the blackboard there persist reminiscences of punishment undergone . . . The school *lavatory* where one got one's first taste of freedom . . .

Pupils, old men and women, some with one foot in the grave, some who are already absent . . . they put their hands up in class in the universally known gesture and remain like that . . . as if they were asking for something, something final . . .

They go out . . . the school room becomes empty . . .

And suddenly they all come back . . . the last game of illusion begins . . . a *grande entrée* of actors . . . All carry corpse-like infants with them . . . some hang lifelessly, others are clutched desperately, they are strapped on or dragged behind, as if they were qualms of conscience, a ball and chain; it's as if those creatures with the *warts* of their own *childhood,* so shamelessly displaying the secrets of their past, were pupae which had cast off their outer casing . . .

The Woman With A Mechanical Cradle. School jokes and antics, incidents that are so pitifully and painfully 'puerile' and 'wet behind the ears,' shamefully passed over in silence by adults, who view them as representing a simpler form of evolution—are in fact the 'primary' stuff of life. They are so disinterested and so devoid of practical purpose—though as jokes they may be very practical indeed—that they approach the sphere of art. They combine the air of nostalgia and longing with the clear ring of finality. Their 'mature' fulfilment in later life takes the form of nightmarish but accepted degeneracy.

The Woman With A Mechanical Cradle becomes the butt of a cruel joke on the part of the whole class: she is chased around, caught and forcibly put on a peculiar contraption figuring in the prop list as *The Family Machine.* It's functions are quite clear. Let us add, incidentally, that all the psychic and biological processes are outrageously 'materialized' in this theatre. In most cases, this is done with the use of various 'Machines' or more precisely childishly primitive contraptions of little technical worth but of great imaginative power.

The Family Machine is operated manually, causing the woman's legs to spread and draw up mechanically.

In order to dispel any lingering doubt that we are witnessing a birth ritual, *Charwoman-Death* brings on a *Mechanical Cradle* which in fact resembles a coffin more than anything else. It is only logical therefore that the *Mechanical Cradle* rocks (this time quite literally) two wooden balls, producing a dry, merciless clatter. The brutal *Charwoman's* own joke, this time . . . birth and death, two complementary patterns.

(All these events dovetail and overlap in a puzzling, enigmatic way with the missing parts of the play we mentioned earlier.)

It is little wonder that *The Woman With A Mechanical Cradle* (who keeps being subjected to outlandish 'ceremonies': she is almost ritually *spat upon* and garbage is thrown all over her) sings a *lullaby* which is really a desperate cry . . .

As of old, *The Old Man in the Loo* sits in the school lavatory, that extraordinary place where solitude bordered on freedom . . . Legs spread shamelessly apart, he is engrossed in endless accounts (perhaps he used to be a shopkeeper in a small town) . . . Wracked by pain and anger he keeps up an indefinite quarrel with his God . . . on that scandalous Mount Sinai.

The Old Man With A Bike never parts with his bicycle, a pitiful, shattered childhood toy . . . he is forever going on night rides on it, only their range has strangely shrunk to just the school room, around the desks . . . and it's not he who is on this bizarre vehicle, but a prostrate dead child. . .

The Somnabulist Prostitute was notorious for her scandalous behaviour while still at school . . . she pretended to be a mannequin in a shop window, a lascivious mannequin, often standing there in public stark naked . . . We do not know whether her dreams came true in later years or not . . . Now, in this *Dream of the Dead Class* she struts shamelessly around the desks, obscenely baring her breasts . . .

The Repeater-Obituary Distributor, a miserable lame pupil ignored by everyone . . . sadistically bullied by his mates . . . maybe they made him fag for them, carry their books, or satchels . . .

In his sleep, tied to his desk with a rope, he stubbornly recites a *grammar* lesson . . . showing off in this lesson, now of absolutely no use to anyone, in front of the totally and mercilessly indifferent class . . . and later he displays his notorious servility by taking round and distributing to his pals their own obituaries . . .

The Charwoman—a primitive woman who still quite literally performs her cleaning duties. Their futility in the disintegrating matter of *The Dead Class* underlines with a loud, almost circus-type effect the transient nature of all things. These lowly functions are transferred from objects to people, and the quite open washing of cadavers reveals the further duties of this *Charwoman-Death.* Her transformation in the final scene into a nightmarish brothel-keeper brings together diametrically different notions into some ruthless but human unity: death - shame - circus - rot - sex - tinsel - tawdriness - humiliation - disintegration - pathos - the absolute . . .

The charwoman reads out 'the latest news': 1914 . . . the outbreak of World War I . . . the assassination of the Austrian Crown Prince in Sarajevo . . . The Beadle sings the Austrian national anthem *"Gott erhalte Unsern Kaiser . . . '* (In that part of Poland, then occupied by Austria, the person of the gracious Hapsburg monarch was a symbol evoking both the sweet memories of our grandmothers' youth and ridicule for that impressive dummy).

The Beadle—a figure of the 'lowest rank' inextricably associated with

139

the school room, he is surrounded by all the nostalgia and melancholy air of bygone years, never to be relived again, and will remain sitting in his chair forever; when, suspiciously, he comes to life again, it's just another school joke, not to be taken seriously . . .

The Woman Behind the Window. The window is an unusual object which separates us from the world 'on the other side', from 'the unknown' . . . from death . . .

A face behind the window—wanting insistently to tell us something, determined to see something at any price.

With a sense of its own total helplessness, it follows everything that happens, comments more and more bitingly and fiercely, turns into a virago—and her lyrical invitations to a spring-time outing end with rampaging terror and death . . .

CONTEMPORARY POLISH OPERA
Tadeusz Kaczynski
Translated by Mariusz Tchorek

Although Polish music has been performed and appreciated
throughout the world, Polish opera is little known outside the
country, the one exception being Krzysztof Penderecki's *The Devils
of Loudun* which since 1969 has been staged in quite a number of
opera houses in Europe and America. But this is not to say that *The
Devils* is the only opera by a Pole to deserve more than just local
attention. Although it might be difficult to point to a work equalling
The Devils in every respect—music, drama and literature—the last ten
years have certainly seen several operas deserving of world attention.

Of most importance is *Tomorrow* by Tadeusz Baird, the main
representative (together with Lutoslawski and Penderecki) of the Polish
composers' school, and well-known outside Poland for his symphonies
and his chamber and vocal pieces. *Tomorrow* is a one-act musical drama
with libretto by Jerzy S. Sito based on Joseph Conrad's short story of
the same title. Although Baird often composed for theatre and his
symphonies designed for concert hall were subsequently adapted to the
stage to serve as background for ballets (e.g. by Maurice Bejart, director
of the Ballet of the XX century), *Tomorrow* (composed in 1965) is the
only genuine operatic piece by this eminent Polish composer.

The premiere of *Tomorrow* in Warsaw's Great Theatre in September
1966 was very well received. Baird's music was responsible for the success,
often functioning as a musical equivalent to the drama. The Warsaw
production of *Tomorrow* was seen in Prague during The Great Theatre's
visiting tour of Czechoslovakia in 1969 as well as in Wiesbaden and
Essen in 1972. The same year the work was produced—if only in concert
hall form—in Royaumont near Paris. *Tomorrow* was also recorded and
broadcast on Polish television to critical acclaim.

Romuald.Twardowski is another composer inspired by Joseph Conrad
(or, to be precise, by Jozef Teodor Konrad Korzeniowski, the real name
of that Pole who wrote in English): he adapted *Lord Jim* into a libretto
of his own. Even before this full-spectacle musical drama appeared, it
was awarded the Grand Prix at the Prince Rainier III Composers'
International Competition in Monaco. This success occurred in 1973
and then, in 1976, the work was produced in the Great Theatre in
Lodz where it was so well received that the Gdansk Baltic Opera
produced it a year later. Although the composer described it as a

'musical drama', the work is well established in the operatic tradition, with arias for the main characters, and a ballet scene.

Composing music for the stage is Romuald Twardowski's specialisation, and a very rare one it is in Poland. Apart from *Lord Jim* this forty-five year-old composer is responsible for three operas: *Cyrano de Bergerac* based on Rostand's play, *Tragedy or the Story of John and Herod* based on an old Polish Christmas Play and *The Fall of Father Suryn*, a radio opera, with a plot woven on a subject reminiscent of *The Devils of Loudun*. Twardowski has also composed music for two ballet pieces.

Witold Rudzinski is almost solely involved in opera composition: he is a composer of the older generation, a pupil of Nadia Boulanger. He is the author of five operas, including three full-spectacle ones. The most extensive is *The Countrymen* based on Wladyslaw Reymont's Nobel Prize winning novel. It is an abridged, but faithful musical and scenic adaptation, like its literary source, focusing on nature. With four parts corresponding to the four seasons, the composer not only spins out the narrative, but makes the music function in telling the story and illustrating natural phenomena. But the production of this musical epos at Warsaw's Great Theatre was not entirely successful. Polish critics preferred Rudzinski's earlier and smaller stage composition, *The Dismissal of Grecian Envoys* based on the play by Jan Kochanowski, the most eminent poet of the Polish Renaissance. It was for this opera that Rudzinski won first prize at the Composer's Competition in Monaco. Three years later the premiere took place in Cracow with Kazimierz Kord, the world-famous Polish conductor. It was subsequently staged in Warsaw and issued on a record. *The Dismissal of Grecian Envoys* owes its success to interesting vocal melodics and unconventional instrumentation. The austere shrillness of the music is particularly appropriate to the tragic fall of the mythical Troy. Witold Rudzinski is also the author of another, one-act opera linked as a dyptych with *The Dismissal of Grecian Envoys* though its subject matter is different. It is a lyrical biblical narrative dealing with the love of Solomon, King of Israel, for Sulamit.

One of the most interesting recent Polish operas is *The Twilight of Peryn* by Zbigniew Penherski, a full-spectacle work based on Kraszewski's novel *The Old Tale* dealing with prehistorical events in Poland, It does not attempt to revive the music of those ancient days, nor is it an avant-garde challenge to the opera tradition. However, it is outstandingly different in its unusual aesthetic premise that music is still the most important element in an operatic work. Unlike most present-day composers who give priority to the script or at most treat music as equal to the script. Penherski constructs his opera out of self-contained musical units which he 'illustrates' with appropriately selected scenes. According to the composer, the better the construction of those musical forms the greater the expressive force imparted to the dramatic scenes. *The Twilight of Peryn* is not just a cycle of scenes culminating in a dramatic whole: it is first of all a cycle of self-contained and independent musical forms.

142

Staged in Poznan in 1974, Penherski's opera was included a year later in the programme of the International Festival of Contemporary music—'Warsaw's Autumn.'

Bernadetta Matuszczak's debut in opera, with the libretto she herself adapted from Shakespeare's *Romeo and Juliet* was well received. Matuszczak approached the famous romance from a feminist point of view: she emphasised the experiences of the youthful heroine and went so far as to call her short opera *Juliet and Romeo*. The work is special in that the woman-composer wrote a minimal-size piece with a view to an expanded maximal opera, one to embrace sister arts such as poetry, dance, mime and visual arts. Although the traditional opera did combine some of each of those genres, they were primarily subordinate to music and dramatic action. Bernadetta Matuszczak applied music as one element functioning equally with voice, gesture, colour, light, and movement and silence and statics. Such an aesthetic concept was then developed by Adam Hanuszkiewicz, director of the premiere when he introduced three Juliets and three Romeos so that in addition to a pair of singers there were also a pair of reciting actors and a pair of dancers, all of them acting simultaneously. This inventive production designed by Marian Kolodziej and with the subtle music by Bernadetta Matuszczak was one of the most exciting and successful operas in Poland.

At the time of the premiere of this short opera by Bernadetta Matuszczak in September 1970, there was also the premiere of another short operatic work—*The Little Prince* by Zbigniew Bargielski, adapted from the popular book by Antoine de Saint Exupery. The piece, which the author described as a 'musical tale', was not well received by the critics or the public, because the music and the script did not correlate.

Much the same was true of *The Ring of the Great Lady* by Ryszard Bukowski to a libretto by Cyprian Norwid, one of the leading poets of Polish romanticism. It was a promising composition, but relied on the literary text to which the fine music was subordinated.

Any account of the most important operas recently produced in Poland must include two Silesian and two Cracow composers, Josef Swidra and Edward Boguslawski of Katowice and Juliusz Luciuk and Krzysztof Meyer of Cracow. Josef Swidra is the author of two operas, one of which—*Magnus*—takes up a local Silesian theme, while the other deals with Wit Stwosz, a medieval painter from Nuremberg who after settling in Cracow produced the main altar in the Church of the Virgin Mary, his magnificent and most famous attainment. Although the former piece was produced at two opera houses, in Katowice and Wroclaw, and the latter is likely to enjoy further premieres, neither of them were totally successful with the critics who found their musical expression eclectic and their style lacking in uniformity.

Another interesting composition is *Beelzebub Sonata* by Boguslawski based on Stanislaw Ignacy Witkiewicz's play of the same name. Self-effacing before Witkiewicz, just as his elder colleague

Bukowski was before Norwid, the writer made the music recede into the background. The first-night took place in November 1976 in Wroclaw under Robert Satanowski, a conductor of international repute.

Awaiting production are two interesting operas by Cracow composers: Juliusz Luciuk's *Demiurgos* based on Bruno Schulz, a writer often referred to as the Polish Kafka, and Krzysztof Meyer's *Cyberiada*. Luciuk's is a small-audience opera; Meyer's composition, initially conceived as a radio opera, was subsequently re-designed for the stage. In the meantime *Cyberiada* based on Stanislaw Lem's science fiction novel won the Grand Prix at the International Composers' Competition in Monaco.

A pupil of Krzysztof Penderecki, Krzysztof Meyer is by no means his imitator. The music he writes is 'pure' by comparison with his professor who keeps exploring foreign territories such as literature, theatre or religion. After the great success of the *Devils of Loudun* Penderecki received an honourable commission for an operatic work to celebrate the 200th anniversary of the United States. But the Polish composer failed to finish the work in time for the American centennial, in 1976. The premiere of *Paradise Lost* based on John Milton—the title and the theme of the second opera by Penderecki—is scheduled for 1978.

Contemporary Polish opera can not really be viewed as an integral body of work. Each work differs so much from the rest in its subject matter, style or form that it is a markedly distinct piece. If they have anything in common, it will be a lack of any interest in contemporary subjects. Opera composers tend to take their subjects from history or fantasy; they probably find present-day reality too concrete and robust to poetise with music.

In attempting a synthesis of Polish opera in the last twenty years, one can only arrange specific works according to a scale of values. This has been undertaken here by selecting the pieces of the greatest importance. If today's operatic compositions are visualised as a pyramid, one might say that the stones of which the pyramid is constructed are of many different kinds, while the apex is occupied by Penderecki's *Paradise Lost,* the latest, most mature work of the Polish composer whose fame is world-wide. Near the top, one should place *The Devils of Loudun* by the same composer and *Tomorrow* by Baird, followed below by the rest of the operas and musical dramas described here. There are not many because Polish composers seem to prefer other genres.

The quantitative, and to some extent qualitative, deficiency of Polish opera is by no means confined to the present period. Although the royal court in Warsaw was one of the first to develop interest in the new genre established at the beginning of the XVII century—King Wladyslaw IV opened an opera house in his castle accessible to the public—the taste for nearly two centuries was for Italian opera. The first opera with a Polish libretto was composed as late as the end of the XVII century, and the first opera composer of any stature was Stanislaw Moniuszko (1819-1872). Yet his works, impressive as they are, seldom appear outside Poland, and so remain of local significance only. Moniuszko did not generate outstanding successors, either. It wasn't until the twenties of this century that an operatic composition of high standard appeared: it was *King Roger* by Karol Szymanowski with Jaroslaw Iwaszkiewicz's libretto. But even this work failed to evoke a wide response and had only a few productions in Poland and elsewhere. Thanks to the successful production of *King Roger* by the English National Opera in London a few years ago it seems likely that at least one Polish opera will become established in the world repertory. Only time will tell. By and large the native opera tradition in Poland is humble. Small wonder, then, that contemporary Polish opera is represented by but a few works.

The Cuttlefish
or *The Hyrcanian Worldview*

by

Stanislaw Ignacy Witkiewicz

Motto: Don't give in even to yourself

Translated from the Polish
by
Daniel C. and Eleanor S. Gerould

CHARACTERS

PAUL ROCKOFFER *46 years old, but looks younger (his age becomes clear during the course of the action). Fair-haired. In deep mourning.*

THE STATUE ALICE D'OR *28 years old. A blonde. Dressed in a tight-fitting dress resembling alligator skin.*

THE KING OF HYRCANIA[1] *Hyrcan IV. Tall, thin. Vandyke beard, large moustache. A bit snub-nosed. Large eyebrows and longish hair. Purple cloak and helmet with a red plume. A sword in his hand. Under his cloak a golden garment. (What he has on under that will be revealed later on).*

ELLA *18 years old. Chestnut hair. Pretty.*

TWO OLD GENTLEMEN *In frock coats and top hats. They can be dressed in the style of the thirties.*[2]

TWO MATRONS *Dressed in violet. One of them is Ella's mother.*

GRUMPUS *The Footman. Grey livery coat with large silver buttons and grey top hat.*

JULIUS II[3] *Sixteenth century Pope. Dressed as in the portrait by Titian.*

---

[1] Hyrcania, on the Caspian Sea, was a province of the ancient Persian Empire. The Hyrcanian tiger, noted for its ferocity is mentioned by Pliny, Vergil and Shakespeare.

[2] *Sic. The Cuttlefish* was written in 1922!

[3] Giuliano della Rovera (1445–1513) was elected Pope in 1503. A patron of the arts, he commissioned Michelangelo to paint the ceiling of the Sistine Chapel.

*The stage represents a room with black walls with narrow emerald-green
designs. A little to the right on the wall in the centre of the stage
is a window covered with a red curtain. In places marked (X)
a light behind the curtain goes on with a bloody glow, in places
marked (+) it goes out. A little to the left a black rectangular
pedestal without ornamentation. ALICE D'OR lies on her stomach on
the pedestal, leaning on her arms. PAUL ROCKOFFER paces back and
forth, clutching his head in his hands. An armchair to the left of the
pedestal. Another one closer to the centre of the stage. Doors to the
right and to the left.*

ROCKOFFER.   Oh, God, God—in vain I call Your name, since I really
   don't believe in You. But I've got to call someone. I've wasted my
   life. Two wives, working like a madman— who knows why—after all,
   my ideas aren't officially recognised, and the remains of my paintings
   were destroyed yesterday, by order of the head of the Council for
   the Production of Handmade Crap. I'm all alone.
STATUE *(without moving her head in her hands).*   You have me.
ROCKOFFER.   So what? I'd rather I didn't. All you do is remind me
   that there's something else. But in yourself you're just a poor
   substitute for what's really important.
STATUE.   I remind you of the further road which opens before you
   in the wilderness. All the fortune-tellers have predicted that you'll
   devote yourself to Occult Knowledge in your old age.
ROCKOFFER *(with a contemptuous wave of his hand).* Oh! I'm
   absolutely incorrigible in maintaining a perpetual grudge against
   poor humanity, and I can't find a single drop of healing medicine.
   I'm like a useless, barren pang of conscience, from which not even
   the meagerest bud of hope for improvement can blossom.
STATUE.   You're a far cry from real tragedy!
ROCKOFFER.   That's because my passions aren't too strong. The
   life I've wasted escapes hopelessly into the grey distance of my
   past. Is there anything more horrible than the grey past which we
   still have to keep on digesting over and over again?
STATUE.   Think how many women you could still have, how many
   nameless mornings, softly gliding through the mysteries of
   noontime, then finally how many evenings you could spend in
   strange conversations with women marvelling at your downfall.
ROCKOFFER.   Don't talk to me about that. Don't rip open the
   innermost core of strangeness. All that is closed—forever closed,
   because of boredom: galloping, raging boredom.
STATUE *(with pity).*   How trite you are . . .

ROCKOFFER. Show me someone who isn't trite, and I'll let my throat be cut as a sacrifice on that person's altar.

STATUE. Me.

ROCKOFFER. A woman—or rather the personification of everything impossible about women. Life's unrealisable promises.

STATUE. At least be glad you exist at all. Just think—even prisoners serving life sentences are glad of the gift of life.

ROCKOFFER. What's that got to do with me? Should I be happy just because right now I'm not impaled on a lonely mound in the middle of the steppes or because I'm not a sewer cleaner? Don't you really know who I am?

STATUE. I know you're funny. You wouldn't be, if you could fall in love with me. Then you'd grasp your mission right here on *this* planet, you'd be a unique personality, itself and only itself—just that one, and no one else . . .

ROCKOFFER *(uneasily)*. So you recognise that there's an absolute, I repeat, an absolute hierarchy of Beings,[4] do you?

STATUE *(laughing)*. Yes and no—it depends.

ROCKOFFER. Tell me what your criteria are, I humbly beseech you.

STATUE. You've given yourself away. You're neither a philosopher nor an artist.

ROCKOFFER. Oh, so you've had your doubts about that anyway. No, I'm not.

STATUE *(laughing)*. Then you're just an ambitious nobody, aren't you? Despite everything, for them you're a genius at creating new metaphysical shocks.

ROCKOFFER. I'm pretending—just pretending because I'm bored. I know it's not even decent—it's not decent to pretend.

STATUE. Still, you've got something in you that goes way beyond anything my other lovers had. But unless you love me you won't get one step further.

ROCKOFFER. Stop talking about those eternal lovers of yours that you're always bragging about. I know you have influence in real life and that through you I could become who the hell knows what. But somebody real, not just somebody in my own eyes . . .

STATUE. You're exaggerating: greatness is relative.

ROCKOFFER. Now I'm going to tell you something: you're trite, worse—you're thoughtful; still a hundred times worse—you're basically good.

STATUE *(upset)*. You're wrong . . . I'm not good at all. *(Suddenly in another tone)*. But I love you! *(She stretches out toward him.)*

ROCKOFFER *(staring at her)*. What? *(Pause.)* That's true, and that's

---

4 The "hierarchy of Beings" probably comes from the work of the German philosopher and biologist Ernest Haeckel (1834–1919), who popularised Darwinism and traced the chain of being from one-celled creatures to man.

why it doesn't matter to me. The light of the Sole Mystery has been extinguished for me . . . (X) *(A knock at the right; the STATUE assumes her former pose.)* and its unfathomableness . . .

STATUE *(impatiently)*. Quiet—the Pope's coming.

ROCKOFFER *(in another tone)*. I beg you, introduce me to the Pope. He's the only ghost I still feel like talking to . . . *(Enter the POPE.)*

JULIUS II. Greetings, daughter, and you, my unknown son . . . *(PAUL kneels. The POPE gives him his slipper to kiss.)* Only let's not talk about Heaven. Alighieri was 100 per cent right. Even a child knows that, but I still have to say that the human imagination cannot conceive such happiness. That's why it was hell that our son Dante portrayed with so much talent.[5] I'll even go so far as to say that Doré's illustrations[6] express quite well the inadequacy of human concepts and the human imagination to portray this kind of, as it were . . .

STATUE. Boredom . . .

JULIUS II. Quiet, daughter. You don't know what you're talking about. *(Emphatically.)* This kind of happiness. *(Jokingly.)* Well, my son: get up and come over here and tell me who you are . . .

STATUE. Holy Father, he's the great artist and philosopher, Paul Rockoffer.

JULIUS II *(raising both hands up in horror)*. So it's you, is it? You, wretched infidel, who dared reach out for the fruit of the Highest Mysteries?

ROCKOFFER *(proudly, getting up)*. It is I!

JULIUS II *(with humility, his hands on his stomach)*. I'm not talking about you as an artist. You're great. Oh, I was a fierce patron of the arts. (+) Now that's all over, all over! Yes, I've learned to appreciate decadence in art. They don't understand it, and yet that's the only way they live themselves. I'm talking about the people of your time. *(Indignantly.)* What a terrible thing—all your paintings burned. My son, eternal reward awaits you in Heaven.

STATUE. In heaven? Ha, ha, ha.

JULIUS II *(good-naturedly)*. Don't laugh, daughter. Heaven has its good sides too. Nobody suffers there, and that counts for something.

ROCKOFFER. I'm a philosopher, Holy Father, but I've continued to be a good Catholic, too. I can't stand that lie any more.

JULIUS II. Yes—you're a Catholic, maître Paul, but not a Christian. There's a great difference, a very great difference. And what lies can't you stand any more, my son?

ROCKOFFER. That I'm pretending as an artist, that is, that I've been pretending up to now. All my art is a hoax, a deliberate carefully planned hoax.

---

[5] Dante Alighieri (1265–1321), in *The Divine Comedy*.

[6] Gustave Doré (1832?–1883), French illustrator and painter.

JULIUS II. I'm disregarding the fact that there can be no question of
Truth once we start discussing Beauty in the abstract. But that's
what's so awful, that your art and the art of people like you is the
sole Truth. You've discovered the last possible consolation, but
I've got to take it away from you. *(Solemnly.)* Your art is the sole
Truth on earth. I didn't know you personally, but I do know your
paintings very well, in marvellous divine reproductions.
(Gloomily.) That's the sole Truth.
STATUE. And what about the dogmas of faith?
JULIUS II *(hurriedly).* They're Truth too, but in another dimension.
In earthly terms they're Truth for our poor understanding. Only
there *(He points to the ceiling with his finger.)* their mystery
blazes forth in all its fullness before the dazzled intellect of the
liberated.
ROCKOFFER *(impatiently).* Holy Father, theology isn't my
speciality, and I'd prefer not to talk about philosophy. With Your
Holiness's kind permission, let's talk about Art. I know I lie, and
that's good enough for me. No one will make me believe that my
Art is genuine, not even you, a guest from a genuine Heaven.
JULIUS II *(with his finger pointing toward the ceiling).* Up there,
where I come from, they know about that better than you do,
you miserable speck of dust. But after all an artist's worth comes
from either rebellion or success. What would Michelangelo have
been if it weren't for me or other patrons of the arts (may God
punish them for it). A few madmen eager for new poisons raise
up the man who concocts them to the apex of humanity, and
then a crowd of non-entities adore him, gaping at the agony and
ecstasy of the ones who've been poisoned. Isn't the fact that the
Council for the Production of Handmade Crap burned your works
a proof of your greatness?
STATUE. You're beaten, Paul baby. Bow down before His
Holiness's connoisseurship. *(*ROCKOFFER *kneels.)*
ROCKOFFER. Something terrible's happened. I don't know any
more whether I'm lying or not. And I was the one who knew
everything about myself. Holy Father, you've taken away my
last hope. I'd finally found one thing I was absolutely sure of, and
you, you cruel old man, you've destroyed even that.
JULIUS II *(to the* STATUE, *pointing at* ROCKOFFER). That's
what comes from pursuing the absolute in life. *(To* ROCKOFFER.)
My son, in life as in philosophy, relativity is the only wisdom. I
was a believer in the absolute myself. My God, what respectable
person hasn't been. But those times are over. Now, what all of
you fail to realize is that not every biped who's read Marx or Sorel[7]
is highest in the earthly hierarchy of Beings, nor do you realise that
I, for example, and the rest of you are two different kinds of Beings,

---

7 Georges Sorel (1847–1922), French Sociologist and theorist of revolution.

and not just varieties of the human species. Only Art, despite decadence, has remained on a high plane.

ROCKOFFER *(getting up, in despair)*. She tells me the same thing. I'm surrounded by treachery on all sides. I don't have any enemies. I look for them night and day in all the back alleys and only find some sickening jellyish mess, but no opponents worthy of me. Can Your Holiness understand that?

JULIUS II *(puts his hand on* ROCKOFFER's *head)*. Who could understand you better, my son? Do you think that history has given me full satisfaction in that respect? Who do you take me for? Can you suppose that I, Julius Della Rovere, was content having as my chief foe that mediocrity Louis XII? *(With deep emotion.)* Oh! Like God without Satan and Satan without God is he who has not acquired an enemy worthy of him.

STATUE. It's dangerous to base one's greatness on the negative value of one's friends. It's worse than admitting the relativity of Truth.

JULIUS II *(drawing near her and stroking her under the chin)*. Oh, you, you cute little dialectician! Who educated you so well, my nice little woman?

STATUE *(sadly)*. Unhappy love, Holy Father, and not only that, but for somebody I despise. Nothing can teach us women dialectics so well as the combination I just mentioned.

JULIUS II *(to* ROCKOFFER). Poor maître Paul, how you must have suffered with that *précieuse*. In my day that type of woman was a little different. They were real titanesses. I myself, my God, even I . . .

ELLA *runs in from the left. Dressed in a sky-blue dress. A man's straw hat with sky-blue ribbons. She has grey gloves and a whole pile of different coloured packages in her arms.* GRUMPUS *follows after her in a grey servant's coat and a grey top-hat, carrying twice as many packages as she is. Both of them pay absolutely no attention to* ALICE D'OR.

ROCKOFFER. Help! I forgot, I have a fiancée.

ELLA *(throwing the packages on top of* GRUMPUS *and running up to* ROCKOFFER). My dearest! But you're happy you have one, now that you've remembered she exists. My one and only: look at me. *(She cuddles up to him.* GRUMPUS, *laden down, stays where he is.* JULIUS II *goes over to the left and stands leaning on the base of the* STATUE.)

ROCKOFFER *(embraces her gently with his right arm and looks straight ahead madly)*. Wait, I have the impression that I've fallen from the fourth floor. I don't understand myself very well. You know, Mr. Della Rovere has just proved that my Art is Truth. I've lost the prop for my carefully planned hoax.

ELLA *(chattering away)*. I'll do everything for you. Just rely on me. I've fixed up our little apartment divinely. The small sofas have

already been covered—you know, the golden material with the tiny
rose stripes. And the sideboard is just the most beautiful thing.
All the furniture for the dining room is really pretty, but there's
something strange about the sideboard. There's some sort of dreadful
mystery in those faces made out of iron-grey wood. They were done
by Zamoyski[8] himself. You can keep all your drugs in there. I won't
bother you, I'll let you do everything you want, only in moderation.
(ROCKOFFER *smiles vacantly.*) Aren't you happy? (ELLA
suddenly grows sad.) Mother furnished my boudoir for me herself.
Everything's covered in pink silk with sky-blue flowers.

ROCKOFFER *(embraces her with sudden tenderness).* But of course—
I am happy. My poor little thing . . . *(He kisses her on the head.)*

JULIUS II *(to the* STATUE). Look daughter, how this little bird's
chattering lulls our good docile snake to sleep.

ELLA *(looking around.)* Who's that old man?

ROCKOFFER. Don't you know? It's Pope Julius II: he's come
straight from Heaven to bless us.

ELLA *(turning to* Julius II). Holy Father . . .*(Kneels and kisses his
slipper.* GRUMPUS *puts the packages on the ground, kneels down
too and kisses the* POPE's *other slipper.)* Oh, how happy I am!

JULIUS II *(to the* STATUE). Well, what can you do with such
innocence and goodness? *(To all those present.)* I bless you,
my children. I wish you a swift and unexpected death, my little
daughter. You'll be the most beautiful of all the angels whose
garlands twine about the throne of the Almighty.

ROCKOFFER *(falling on his knees).* Oh, how beautiful this is! I
feel that from now on I could start painting like Fra Angelico.
All decadence has vanished without a trace. Thank you, Holy
Father.

JULIUS II *(to the* STATUE). See how it's possible to be a sower
of good in this world without even meaning to be. Look at the
blissful faces on those two children. Maître Paul has grown at least
ten years younger.

STATUE. Not for long, Your Holiness. You don't realise how
quickly time passes for us. Time is relative. You know Einstein's
theory, Holy Father. Transfering the concept of psychological
time to physics produced a wonderful flowering of knowledge
about the world, an indestructible creation of absolute Truth.

ELLA *gets up and goes over to* PAUL, *who also gets up. They kiss
in ecstasy.* GRUMPUS *gets up likewise and looks at them, deeply
moved.*

JULIUS II. My, my, my! In Heaven, where we live, no one believes
in physics, my child. It's only a simplified system for all of you to
understand mathematical phenomena since your brains stopped

8   Jan Zamoyski (1910–   ), a Polish artist and friend of Witkiewicz.

154

short at the frontier beyond which the creation of metaphysics is possible. Every step in the hierarchy of Beings has its own boundary. Human philosophy has got itself all bottled up. The co-efficient of all knowledge is infinite only within each boundary. But what about what's happening on the planets of Aldebaran! Ho ho! They know their 'Einstein' there too, but they've known how to place him in his proper sphere.

STATUE *(anxiously)*. And so the world really has no bounds?

JULIUS II. Of course not, my child.

STATUE. Then even you, Holy Father, won't live eternally? And what about Heaven?

JULIUS II. Heaven is only a symbol. You people must accept the theory of diverse bodies united in a single individual. But the number of these bodies is limited. Eventually we'll all die for good. The sole mystery is God. *(He points to the ceiling* (X)).

STATUE. Ah! *(She falls down on the pedestal.* JULIUS II *sits on the chair on the left side).*

ELLA *(drawing away from* ROCKOFFER). What's that? I heard a voice inside me saying something about eternal death (+)

ROCKOFFER *(pointing to the prone* ALICE d'OR). That statue said it. It just passed out. It's a symbol of the past which I sacrificed for you.

ELLA *(astounded)*. But there's nobody there!

ROCKOFFER. Didn't you hear how His Holiness was philosophising with it?

ELLA. Paul, stop joking. The Holy Father was talking to himself. Don't stare so blankly: I'm afraid. Tell me the truth.

ROCKOFFER. You wouldn't understand anyhow, my child. Let's not talk about it.

JULIUS II. Yes, daughter, maître Paul is right. A good wife shouldn't know too much about her husband. Within certain limits, a husband should be a mystery.

ELLA. I have to know everything. You're torturing me, Paul. Our little apartment, which made me so happy, is beginning to terrify me in this vision of the future you and the Pope have created together. A kind of shadow has fallen on my heart. I want my mother.

ROCKOFFER *(embracing her)*. Quiet, little girl. I've begun to believe in my future. I'm returning to Art and I'll be happy. We'll both be happy. I'll start painting again calmly, without any orgies with form, and I'll end my life as a good Catholic.

JULIUS II *(bursts out laughing)*. Ha, Ha, Ha!

ELLA. End your life? I'm just beginning it with you.

ROCKOFFER. I'm old—you must understand that once and for all.

ELLA. You're forty-six—I know. But why does your face say something different? Can the soul be so different from the face?

ROCKOFFER *(impatiently)*. Oh, quit bothering me about my soul. It's an essence so complicated that I've never been able to see myself as a whole. It was only an illusion. Stop thinking about me and accept me as I am.

ELLA. Paul, tell me who you really are. I want to know you.

ROCKOFFER. I'm unknowable even to myself. Look at the paintings I've already done and you'll see who I used to be. But if you look at what I'm going to do now, you'll see what I want to be. The rest is a delusion.

ELLA. And is that what love is?

ROCKOFFER. Love? Shall I tell you what love is? In the morning I'll wake you with a kiss. After a morning bath, we'll drink coffee. Then I'll go paint, and you'll read books, which I'll suggest for you. Then dinner. After dinner, we'll go for a walk. Then work again. Tea, supper, a little serious discussion, and finally you'll fall asleep, not too fatigued by sensual pleasures, to conserve strength for the next day.

ELLA. And so, on and on, without end?

ROCKOFFER. You mean: to the very end. Such is life for those devoid of absolute desires. We are limited, and Infinity surrounds us. It's too trite even to talk about.

ELLA. But I want to live! With that hope in mind I've fixed up our dear little apartment, I've looked after everything. I've got to really live.

ROCKOFFER. Tell me, please, what is life 'really'?

ELLA. Now I don't know anything any more and that terrifies me.

ROCKOFFER. Don't force me to make speeches. I could tell you things, beautiful and horrible, deep and infinitely remote, but it would be just one more lie.

STATUE *(waking up* (X)*)*. A little drama is beginning. Our little Paul has decided to become sincere.

ELLA. I'm hearing that evil voice of a strange being inside me again. *(Looking around.)* That's funny—I feel that there's somebody here, but I don't see anyone except you and the Pope (+).

STATUE. I am the lady Pope for fallen titans. I teach them the grey wisdom of daily existence.

ELLA *(in fear)*. Paul—stop hypnotising me. I'm afraid.

ROCKOFFER. Don't say anything more. I'm beginning to be afraid myself. I don't even know myself how I know that person.

ELLA. What person? Oh, my God, my God—I'll die of fright. I'm afraid of you. Holy Father—save me. You've come from Heaven.

JULIUS II *(getting up, speaking with cruelty)*. How do you know that Heaven isn't a symbol for the most awful renunciation?— renouncing one's real personality. I'm a shadow, just as she is. *(He points to the* STATUE.*)*

ELLA. But there isn't anyone there, is there? Take pity on me, Holy Father. All this affects me like a bad dream.

JULIUS II. Dream on, my child. Maybe this moment of terror is the most beautiful in your whole life. Oh, how I envy all of you. (ELLA *covers her face with her hands.*)

ROCKOFFER. A strange force is entering me again. Ella—I can't conquer decadence with you.

ELLA *(without uncovering her face).* Now I understand you at last. I've either got to die for you or stop loving you. *(Uncovers her face.)* I love you now that I see how you're descending into the abyss. This is my real life.

STATUE. That little virgin's making progress like crazy. Now I'll never get you back again, Paul love.

ELLA. That voice again. But I'm not afraid of anything now. It's already happened. My fate's already sealed somewhere. And the sooner the better, Paul. Now I won't go back to mother. I'll stay with you now.

JULIUS II. Don't be in such a hurry, daughter. You've already entered on the right path. But it doesn't mean you've got to be in quite such a hurry.

ROCKOFFER. Holy Father, the speed of my transformations terrifies me too. In a moment I may become a statesman, an inventor, who the hell knows what. Whole new layers have shifted in my head like an avalanche.

JULIUS II. Wait—I hear footsteps in the hallway downstairs. I have a rendezvous with King Hyrcan today.

ROCKOFFER. What? Hyrcan IV? Is he still alive? You know, he was a classmate of mine at school. He was always dreaming about an artificial kingdom in the old style.

JULIUS II. And he created it. I guess you don't ever read the newspapers. *(He listens.)* That's him—I recognise his powerful, commanding footsteps. *(Suspense.)*

ELLA. But is he real or is he something like Your Highness?

JULIUS II *(outraged).* Something like! You're taking too many liberties, my daughter.

ELLA. I'm not afraid of anything now.

JULIUS II. You've already died—you have nothing to fear.

ELLA. Nonsense. I'm alive and I'll create a completely normal life for Paul. He'll fall slowly, creating wonderful things. I'm not at all as innocent and stupid as all of you think. I've got a little venom in me too . . . (X)

From the right enter HYRCAN IV *in a purple coat which comes down to the ground. He has a helmet on his head with a red plume. A huge sword in his hand.*

HYRCAN IV. Good evening. How are you, Rockoffer? You weren't expecting me today. I've heard you're getting married—it'll never work. *(Kneels quickly in front of the* POPE *and kisses his slipper; getting up.)* I'm glad to see His Holiness is in good health. Heaven agrees with him very well. *(Approaches the* STATUE.) How are you doing, Alice—Alice d'Or, isn't it? Remember our orgies in that marvellous dive—what was it called? *(He squeezes the* STATUE's *hand.)*

STATUE. Perdition-Gardens.

ELLA *turns around at the sound of her voice.*

HYRCAN IV. Exactly.

ELLA *(pointing at the* STATUE), She was the one who was here! It was her voice I kept hearing as though it was in me. It's not nice to eavesdrop on our conversation that way!

STATUE. It's not my fault that you didn't see me, Ella . . .

ELLA. Please don't call me by my first name. I'm asking you to leave this house. I'm staying here with Paul now. *(To* ROCKOFFER.) Who is that woman?

ROCKOFFER. My former mistress. I'm letting her live in this room. I was a little afraid in this huge house and that's why . . .

ELLA. You don't have to justify yourself. From now on I'm going to be here and I'm asking you to get rid of that lady immediately.

JULIUS II. Not so fast, my daughter. You may over-reach yourself.

ELLA. I don't want her here and that's all there is to it. Paul, did you hear me? *(She sits down in the armchair to the left.)*

ROCKOFFER. Certainly, my dear. That's no problem. *(Goes toward the* STATUE.) My Alice, we must part. Get down off that pedestal and clear out. This is the end. You'll get money from my bank. *(He pulls out a cheque book and begins to write (+))*

HYRCAN IV *(to* ROCKOFFER). If I may be permitted to ask—who's that broad? *(He indicates* ELLA.) Is she your new mistress, or is she the fiancée I've been hearing about?

ROCKOFFER *(he stops writing and remains indecisive).* My fiancée.

HYRCAN IV *(to* ELLA). Oh—in that case perhaps you'll allow me to introduce myself: I'm Hyrcan IV, king of the artificial kingdom of Hyrcania. You'll be so kind as not to order my friend about, or you'll find I make short work of things.

STATUE. You talk marvellously, Hyrcan.

HYRCAN IV. I don't need your advice either, Alice. I'll settle things with you too at the proper time. The situation—apart from my kingdom, which is the only really unusual thing—is the tritest in the world: a friend decided to free his friend from women—the ordinary bags, masculettes, and battle-axes who've fettered him.

ROCKOFFER. To prove what? Isn't your kingdom only a badly disguised form of insanity, my friend?

HYRCAN IV. You'll find out soon enough. You're already suffering from a prison psychosis living in freedom. Over-intellectualised sex combined with fluctuation between decadence and classicism in art. First of all, to hell with art! There's no such thing as art.

158

JULIUS II.   Excuse me, sire. I won't allow maître Paul to be made an ordinary pawn in the hands of Your Royal Highness. He's got to go to pieces in a creative way.

ELLA.   I've been saying the same thing . . .

HYRCAN IV *(speaks to the* POPE *without paying any attention to what she has said).*   He doesn't have to go to pieces at all. That's just the way perverse young girls jabber when they sniff for carrion or the way deprived patrons of the arts think. Paul won't go to pieces: he'll make himself into someone new and different. None of you have any idea what conditions are like in my country. It's the sole oasis left in the whole world.

JULIUS II.   The world is by no means limited to our planet . . .

HYRCAN IV.   Holy Father, I don't have time to plumb the depths of Your Holiness's posthumous knowledge. I am a real man, or rather a real superman. I create a reality which is the incarnation of Hyrcanian desires.

STATUE.   There's no such thing as Hyrcanian desires . . .

JULIUS II *(politely to the* STATUE).   That's just what I wanted to say. *(To* HYRCAN.) That word doesn't even exist, it's just an empty sound without meaning.

HYRCAN IV.   Once I give it a definition, this empty sound will become a concept, and from then on it will exist in the world of ideas for all eternity.

JULIUS II *(laughing).*   But only ahead in time, not behind, sire.

HYRCAN IV.   That's just the point. No behinds for me. I reverse events, and life too only goes ahead, and not behind.

ROCKOFFER.   You know, Hyrcan, you're beginning to interest me.

HYRCAN IV.   Experience it—it's wonderful. Once you experience it, you'll be so thrilled and have such a sense of power, you'll go out of your mind. *(To the* POPE.) You see— I call Hyrcanian desire the desire for putting the absolute into effect in life. Only by believing in the absolute and in its realisation can we create something in life.

JULIUS II.   And what good will that be to anyone? What will come of it?

HYRCAN IV.   That's senile scepticism or rather senile doddering. Oh, that's right—I forgot that Your Holiness is practically 600 years old. What'll come of it is that we'll experience our life on the heights of what's possible on this damned small globe of ours, and not waste away in a continual compromise with the ever-growing strength of social sticking-togetherness and regimentation. Some consider me an anarchist. I spit on their rancid opinions. I'm creating supermen. Two, or three—that's enough. The rest is a pulpy mass—cheese for worms. 'Our society is as rotten as a cheese.' Who said our society is as rotten as a cheese?

JULIUS II.   Never mind about that, sire. I came here for a serious discussion on saving art from a total decline and fall. The fight against so-called *pur-blaguism*.[9] It's finally got to be proved that Pure Blague is impossible. Even God, although he's all-powerful, wouldn't really be able to blague anything perfectly and completely.

HYRCAN IV. Humbug. As I was coming here, I gave some thought to the problem of Art. Art has come to an end and nothing will ever revive it. There isn't any sense to our discussion.

JULIUS II. But, sire, as I see it, Your Royal Highness is a follower of Nietzsche, at least in social questions. Nietzsche himself recognised Art as the most important stimulus for personal power.

HYRCAN IV *(threateningly)*. What? Me a follower of Nietzsche? Please don't insult me. He was the life philosophy for a bunch of dunderheads willing to drug themselves with absolutely anything. I don't accept any drugs and therefore I don't accept art either. My ideas arose completely independently. I didn't read any of that trash until after I'd created my country. That's enough. Our conversation is over.

JULIUS II. All right. But just one more thing: such a formulation of the question, with your goal already in mind, isn't that Pure Pragmatism? You can believe in the absolute in life or not, but to believe in it as a preconceived theory for experiencing on the heights, as Your Royal Highness put it, this wretched life of ours on our small globe—likewise your expression, my son—is a self-contradiction and a devaluation of Hyrcanian—yes, I repeat Hyrcanian desires themselves! Ha, ha!

HYRCAN IV. That's pure dialectics. Maybe in Heaven it's worth something. I'm a creator of re-al-i-ty. Understand, Holy Father. And now that's enough—don't get me upset.

JULIUS II. Sire, I beg you, just one more question.

HYRCAN IV. Well?

JULIUS II. How's religion doing over there in your country?

HYRCAN IV. Everyone believes whatever he wants. Religion has come to an end too.

JULIUS II. Ho, ho! That's rich. And he wants to create old-time power without religion. Really, sire, that strikes me as a stupid farce. Look at the most savage tribes, at the aboriginal Arunta or whoever they are. Even they have religion. Without religion there are no countries in the old sense of the word. There can only be an anthill.

HYRCAN IV. No, no—not an organised anthill, only a great herd of straggling cattle, over which I and my friends hold power.

JULIUS II. But what do *you* believe in, my son?

9 Pure humbug, or pure hoax, was itself a hoax by Witkiewicz. In the early twenties he announced a new theory of art called "Purblaguism" and anonymously published a small pamphlet which purported to contain works by various authors in the new pur-blague style.

HYRCAN IV. In myself and that's good enough for me. But if I ever need to, I'll believe in anything at all, in any old fetish, in a crocodile, in the Unity of Being, in you, Holy Father, in my own navel, what difference does it make! Is that clear?

JULIUS II. You sir, are a combination of a very clever but ordinary bandit and the worst kind of pragmatist. You're not a king at all, at least not for me. From now on we won't have anything more to do with each other.

He goes to the left and sinks exhausted in his armchair. HYRCAN stands looking angry, leaning on his sword.

STATUE. Well, they demolished you, my petty chieftain. The Holy Father is really a first-class dialectician.

ROCKOFFER. You know, Hyrcan, actually His Holiness is partly right in all this. Besides, I must point out that the tone of our group deteriorated as soon as you came in. The conversation became downright crude.

JULIUS II. You're quite right, my son; to talk to slobs you've got to talk like a slob.

ROCKOFFER *(to HYRCAN)*. I don't entirely agree with you in the matter of fundamental principles either.

ELLA. Oh, Paul, then all's not lost yet.

HYRCAN IV *(waking up form his meditation)*. Yes—I'm a slob, but I'm what I am and there's no one else like me. Listen to me. I'm talking to all of you as an equal with equals for the last time. Paul—make up your mind. Alexander the Great was a slob too. And anyhow, we have a ruler here with us. You can read about Mr. Della Rovere and his doings in any outline of history.

JULIUS II *(getting up)*. Shut up! Shut up!

ROCKOFFER *(quietly to HYRCAN)*. Leave him alone. *(Aloud.)* I won't allow anyone to insult the Holy Father in my house, not even the King of Hyrcania.

JULIUS II. Thank you, my son. *(Sitting down.)* A pragmatist on the throne! No—this is absolutely unheard of. It's actually funny. Ha-ha-ha!

HYRCAN IV. Well, Paul, go ahead. Maybe your objections will be somewhat more to the point. Believe me, I only want your happiness. If you don't leave with me now for Hyrcania on the eleven o'clock express, you're through. I won't come back here again. I'll break off diplomatic relations and start a series of wars. Digging up and buring down anthills and moronhills. A lovely business.

ROCKOFFER. You've already done one thing for me. All the little problems I used to be concerned with seem completely insignificant to me now.

ELLA *(sits in the armchair to the left; suddenly wakes up from her stupified condition)*. And the problem of love, too?

ROCKOFFER. Wait a minute, Ella, I'm in a different dimension right now. *(To* HYRCAN.*)* But I must confess I don't see greatness on your side either.

HYRCAN IV. What do you mean?

ROCKOFFER. His Holiness used a word that I can't get out of my head—but you won't be offended, will you, Hyrcan?

HYRCAN IV. At you—never. Go ahead. What word?

ROCKOFFER. Bandit. You're actually a petty robber baron, not an important ruler. You're only great given the extremely low level of civilization in your country. Nowadays, Nietzsche's superman can't be anything more than a small-time thug. And those who would have been rulers in the past are the artists of our own times. Breeding the superman is the biggest joke I've ever heard of.

HYRCAN IV. You're talking like a moron. You don't understand the first thing about my concept of Hyrcanian desires. You're living your life as an absolutist—that's a fact. You're too much either for yourself or for so-called society. You're a perfect specimen of 'moral-insanity,' but you've got the strength of at least four normal people, according to the standards of our times.

ROCKOFFER. Yes, that's a fact. That's why I've decided to end it all right now by committing suicide.

ELLA *(getting up).* Paul, what's happening to you? Am I dreaming?

STATUE. He's right. I never dared tell him that, but it's the only, really obvious, trite solution.

HYRCAN IV. Shut up, you sluts! One's worse than the other. *(To* ROCKOFFER.*)* You fool, did I come here from my Hyrcania to see the downfall of my only friend? I've already got two strong types. I've absolutely got to have a third. You're the only one who can do it.

ROCKOFFER. But what's a regular work day like in this Hyrcania of yours? What do you really occupy yourselves with there?

HYRCAN IV. Power—we get drunk on power in all its forms from morning till night. And then we feast in an absolutely devastating glorious fashion, discussing everything and viewing everything from the unattainable heights of our reign.

ROCKOFFER. A reign over a heap of idiots incapable of organising themselves. An ordinary military dictatorship. Under favourable conditions a really radical state socialism can do the same thing.

HYRCAN IV. But what was humanity in the past but a heap of beings, a formless pulpy mass without any organisation? In order to hold on to their power, the pseudo-titans evolved by socialism have to lie. We don't. Our life is Truth.

ROCKOFFER. So it's a question of Truth. Is Truth also an integral part of the Hyrcanian worldview?

HYRCAN IV. Of course. But if all humanity wears a mask, the problem of Truth will disappear all by itself. I and my two friends, Count de Plignac and Rupprecht von Blasen, are creating just such a mask. Society masked and we alone who know everything.

ROCKOFFER. But isn't there something of a comedy in it all? You know what's chiefly discouraged me? Your costume.

HYRCAN IV. But that's nothing. I thought you were more impressed by scenery and that's why I dressed up this way. I can take this fancy stuff off. *(He goes on talking as he takes his clothes off. Under his coat he reveals a golden garment. He throws it off and stands in a well-tailored, normal cutaway. He takes off his helmet as well. He puts the clothes in the middle of the stage. He continues to hold his sword in his hand.)* But you knew what greatness consists of? Attaining isolation. To create such an island of brutalised, bestial spirits amidst the sea of regimentation engulfing everything, now that takes a little more strength than Mr. Della Rovere had in the XVI century. Not to speak of the Borgias—they were just common clowns.

GRUMPUS. Most gracious lord—I'll go to Hyrcania too. If you're going to serve, you might as well serve real masters.

HYRCAN IV *(to ROCKOFFER)*. See? That dolt's recognised my true worth, but you won't even try to understand me.

ROCKOFFER. Wait; my daimon has split in two. It's an unheard of event in the history of mankind. I hear two secret voices telling me two parallel truths which will never meet. The contradiction between them is of an infinite order.

HYRCAN IV. I keep a certain philosopher in my court, one Chwistek[10] by name. On the basis of his concept of 'the plurality of realities' he's establishing the systematic relativisation of all Truth. He'll explain the rest to you. He's a great sage. I'm telling you, Rockoffer, come with me.

ROCKOFFER. My conscience as a former artist is growing to the dimensions of an all-encompassing tumour. A new monster feeds on itself. Monsters, till now tormented in cages, have conquered unknown areas of my disintegrating brain.

ELLA *(getting up)*. He's simply gone mad. Most gracious lord, ask whatever you will, but don't take him away from me. Now that he's a madman, he'll create wonderful things as long as he's with me.

ROCKOFFER. You're mistaken, little girl. I'm clear-headed as never before. Long ago I recognised my madness—for me it was much less interesting than my extremely cold, clear consciousness.

ELLA *sits down, stunned.*

---

[10] Leon Chwistek (1884–1944), Polish logician, aesthetician, mathematician, essayist, painter, and close friend of Witkiewicz. In *The Plurality of Realities* (1921) he postulated four different kinds of reality which gave rise to four different kinds of art.

STATUE. That's the Truth. Once, when I was with him, he overcame a fit of madness. It was metaphysical madness, of course, but my life was also hanging by a thread. He's a psychic athlete, and a physical one too—sometimes.

HYRCAN IV. Alice, believe me, for him you were only a sort of vinegar in which he preserved himself until my arrival. I'm grateful to you for that. You can come with me to Hyrcania.

STATUE *(climbing down from the pedestal)*. All right—you can make me into the priestess of whatever cult you want. I'm ready for anything.

JULIUS II. So you've also become a pragmatist, my daughter. I didn't expect that.

STATUE. But Holy Father, in the depths of your soul aren't you really a pragmatist, too?

JULIUS II *(getting up)*. Perhaps, perhaps. Who's to say? My worldview is subject to constant transformations.

HYRCAN IV. To have my concept recognised I'm even willing to let art disappear from my realm for good. I appoint you patron of the dying arts, Holy Father, on condition that you won't tempt Paul Rockoffer. He can be an absolutist only in life, not in art.

JULIUS II. All right, all right. I give in. In any case, you've opened up new perspectives for me. Just between you and me, you have no idea how madly, hopelessly bored I've been in Heaven. Starting today I'm extending my leave for at least three hundred years. (HYRCAN *and* ROCKOFFER *whisper*).

STATUE. Julius Della Rovere, you can count on me: with my dialectics, I'll make twenty of those three hundred years a delight for you. In the evening, after a tiring day's work, you'll tell me all about it and have a really serious talk with a woman who's both wise and moderately perverse.

JULIUS II. Thanks, daughter. I'm going to Hyrcania.

ELLA *(getting up)*. I can't take any more! This is some ghastly nightmare, all these discussions of yours. I'm not at all good and noble, and I feel as though I've been asphyxiated by some hideous poison gas. And besides, all this is boring. You're tearing my heart apart just as a game, a stupid, boring game. I want to go to Hyrcania, too. When Paul feels unhappy, at least he'll have me and I'll save him. Sire, will Your Royal Highness take me with him?

HYRCAN IV. Out of the question. Paul must forget his former life. You'll start tempting him right away to make artistic excuses for why he fell or who the hell knows what. All creative impulses must be stifled in embryo.

ELLA. And how's it all finally going to end? What then?

HYRCAN IV. Then, as usual, death takes over, but along with it the feeling that life has been experienced on the heights, and not in the filthy cesspool of society, where there's art instead of morphine.

ROCKOFFER. So you're opposed to drugs? I can't get along without them.

HYRCAN IV. I still approve of alkaloids, but I have the greatest contempt for all psychic drugs. Aside from the fact that you won't create anything, you can do whatever you want.

ELLA *approaches* PAUL *and they whisper.*

JULIUS II. Your Hyrcania, Sire, strikes me as a kind of sanitorium for people sick of society. The way you describe it, of course. Actually it's the lowest kind of whorehouse for the playboys in life . . .

HYRCAN IV. But they're absolutists every one of them—if they don't manage to get through the wall, at least they leave the bloody marks of a smashed skull on it. That's where my greatness lies.

JULIUS II. But after all, you could have been a pickpocket, Sire, like the Duke in *Manon Lescaut.*

HYRCAN IV. I could have been, but I'm not. I'm the king of the last real kingdom on earth. Greatness lies only in what succeeds. If I'd been completely unsuccessful, I'd have only been ridiculous from the very start.

JULIUS II. You still can fall. And then what?

HYRCAN IV. I'll fall from a certain height. After all, there's never been a tyrant who didn't fall.

JULIUS II. That's just where the pettiness lies: in the idea of a certain height.

HYRCAN IV. I can't fall through Infinity. Even in the world of physics we have finite speed, since there's nothing beyond the speed of light. Practically speaking, it's infinite.

JULIUS II *(ironically).* Practically speaking! Pragmatism's at the bottom of everything. But it doesn't matter. For the time being, I prefer that to Heaven.

HYRCAN IV. Rockoffer, did you hear that? No one has ever received a greater compliment. The Holy Father is with us.

ELLA *(clinging to* PAUL*).* Answer me, at least make up your mind.

ROCKOFFER. I'm going. It's always worth abandoning the forseeable for the unknown. Besides, it's the basis for the New Art, the art of vile surprises.

HYRCAN IV. Thanks, but don't even compare Hyrcanianess and art. Hyrcania must be experienced.

ROCKOFFER. The dadaists said the same thing about dadaism, until they were all hanged. No—that's enough. I'm yours. Everything's so disgusting that there isn't any stupidity great enough not to be worth sacrificing everything in our lives for it. Let me die, but not in all this petty shabbiness. I had intended to die in Borneo or Sumatra. But I prefer the mystery of becoming to the mystery of staying the same. I'm coming.

ELLA. Paul, I beg you. I won't bother you. Take me with you.

ROCKOFFER.   No, child. Let's not even talk about it. I know your spiritual traps. As a woman, you don't exist for me at all.

ELLA.   Paul, Paul—how cruelly you're tearing me apart inside! I'll die. Think of our poor, lonely little apartment, and my unhappy mother.

ROCKOFFER.   I'm terribly sorry for you. Now I really love you for the first time . . .

ELLA.   Paul! Wake up from this hallucination. If you can't stay, at least let me go to my death and destruction!

HYRCAN IV *(pushing her away from* ROCKOFFER).   Lay off him. She's a cuttlefish, not a woman. Did you hear me? This is the last time I'm telling you this.

ELLA *(flaring up).*   Then kill me—I won't leave him myself.

From the right enter two matrons and two old men elegantly dressed in black.

MOTHER.   Ellie, let me introduce you to two of your uncles you don't know. They're the ones who are financing your marriage with Paul. Mr. Ropner and Mr. Stolz—my daughter—my daughter's fiancé, the well-known painter Mr. Paul Rockoffer.

The two old men greet ELLA.

ROCKOFFER.   First of all, I'm no longer her fiancé, and secondly, in introductions a person's first name and occupation should never be mentioned, particularly since I've changed my occupation. You'll have to pardon me, Maria, but unknown perspectives are opening up before me. I'll be something along the line of a cabinet minister in Hyrcania. Hyrcanian desires gratified at last! It would take too much time to try to explain it all at once now. I hardly understand it myself.

MOTHER.   I can see that. You must be drunk, Paul. Ella, what does this mean?

ELLA.   Mama, it's all come to nothing. He's not drunk, and he hasn't gone mad. It's the most obvious, cold cruel truth. The King of Hyrcania is taking him with him. He's stopped being an artist. *(The* MOTHER *is dumbfounded.)*

HYRCAN IV.   Yes, Ma'am, and we'll settle things amicably. I don't like big scenes in the grand manner when I'm not on my own home ground. I'll pay you whatever damages you ask.

MOTHER.   I'm not concerned about money, but about my daughter's heart.

HYRCAN IV.   Don't be trite, please. And besides, I'm not just any lord or master, I'm a king.

MOTHER.   I've read about that Hyrcania of yours in the newspapers. It's the theatre critics who write about it. Not one decent politician even wants to hear it mentioned. It's an ordinary theatrical hoax, that Hyrcania of yours. A depraved and degenerate band of madmen and drunkards took it into their heads to simulate a regime in the old style! You ought to be ashamed, Mister! Hyrcania! It's simply a disgrace, 'bezobrazia' à la manière russe.[11]

HYRCAN IV *(throwing his sword on the pile of clothes).* The old lady's gone crazy. Be quiet. Rockoffer's agreed and I'm not going to let any mummified battle-axes get him in their clutches. Let's go.

PAUL *remains undecided.*

ELLA. Mama, I won't live through this. I want to go too.

MOTHER. What? So you're against me too? Aren't you ashamed in front of your uncles you've just met? If you keep behaving this way, we won't get a single cent. Ella, come to your senses.

ELLA *(clutching her head).* I don't want to live! I can't Only I don't have the courage to die. *(To the king.)* Hyrcan, most poisonous of civilized reptiles, crowned slob, kill me. I want pain and death—I've already suffered too much today.

MOTHER. Ella, what a way to talk! Who taught you such dreadful expressions?

ELLA. I don't even know myself. I'm playing a role—I know that—but I'm suffering terribly. *(To the king.)* I beg you—kill me.

HYRCAN IV. You want me to? That won't cost me anything. In Hyrcania everything is possible. The absolute in life—can you understand that, you vile dishwashers of plates others licked long ago?

ROCKOFFER. Wait—maybe it can all still be settled by a compromise. I can't stand scenes and rows. Ella will go quietly back to her mother, and I'll at least leave with a clear conscience.

ELLA. No, no, no—I want to die.

MOTHER. Do you want to poison the last days of my old age? And what about our little apartment, and our nice evenings together, just the three of us, and later surrounded by children: yours and Paul's, my darling grandchildren.

ELLA. Mama, don't torture me. I'll poison your life worse if I stay with you than if I die right now at the hands of the king.

MOTHER *(in despair).* What difference does it make who kills you. You die only once, but my old age will be poisoned to the very end.

ELLA. No—I must die right away. Every minute of life is unbearable anguish.

HYRCAN IV. Do you mean that seriously, Miss Ella? (X)

ELLA. Yes. I was never so serious.

HYRCAN IV. All right, then. *(He picks up his sword, which is lying on the pile of royal robes, and strikes* ELLA *on the head with it.* ELLA *falls without a groan.)*

---

[11] 'Bezobrazia,' which is Russian for 'disgrace,' is a common expression of indignation and outrage.

MOTHER. Oh!!! *(She falls on* ELLA's *corpse and remains there until almost the end of the play.* HYRCAN *stands leaning on his sword. The old men whisper vehemently among themselves.* MATRON II *remains calm (+).)*

ROCKOFFER. I'm just beginning to understand what the Hyrcanianess of Hyrcanian desires actually is. Now at last I know what it means to put absolutism into practice in real life. *(He clasps* HYRCAN's *hands in his,)*

JULIUS II. I've committed many atrocities, but this pragmatic crime has moved me deeply. I bless you, poor mother, and you, spirit of a maiden pure and lofty beyond all earthly conception. *(He blesses the group on* HYRCAN's *left.)* Well, sire, she lived her life as an absolutist, too—you've got to admit that.

HYRCAN IV. Her death has moved me too. I've come to recognise a new kind of beauty. I didn't know that there could be anything quite so unexpected outside of Hyrcania.

ONE OF THE OLD MEN *(drawing near).* Well, all right, gentlemen, but what now? How are we going to settle all this? We understand, or rather we can guess what it's all about. Actually it's a trite story, but how can it all be explained and justified?

JULIUS II. Well, gentlemen. I'm a tolerant person, but I can't stand your company any longer. You understand—I was the Pope. Kiss me quickly on the slipper and clear out, while you're still in one piece. I can't stand dull, commonplace thinking masquerading as phony good nature. *(The old men kiss his slipper and, crumpling their hats in their hands, go out to the right with astonished faces. Meanwhile, the others continue talking.)*

HYRCAN IV. Paul—go with this flunkey right now and get ready for the trip. The Hyrcania-express leaves in an hour. I'm here incognito and don't have my special train with me.

ROCKOFFER. All right—Grumpus, leave these ladies here and come along.

He and GRUMPUS *pass to the right.* MATRON II *comes up to* HYRCAN. ROCKOFFER *and* GRUMPUS *stop on the threshold.*

MATRON II. Hyrcan—don't you recognise me? I'm your mother.

HYRCAN IV. I recognised you instantly, mama, but you're the one hidden shame in my life. I'd prefer not to apply the Hyrcanian worldview to my own mother. My mother, mother to a king—an ordinary whore! How ghastly!

JULIUS II. And so even you have sacred treasures hidden in the depths of your pragmatic-criminal heart? I didn't expect that.

HYRCAN IV. Holy Father—don't meddle in what's none of your business. *(To* MATRON II.) Mama, I advise you, get out of here and don't cross my path ever again. You know, I inherited a bloody and violent disposition from my father.

MATRON II. But couldn't I be a priestess of love in your

country? In olden times the daughters of Syrian princes deliberately offered up their virginity to an unknown stranger for a couple of copper pieces.

HYRCAN IV.   That was in olden times and that made it beautiful. You didn't get started that way. You were the mistress of our idiotic aristocrats and obese Semitic bankers. I don't even know whose son I am—me, a king. What a nasty mess.

MATRON II.   Why should you care? All the more credit to you that starting from nothing you've raised yourself up to the height of a throne. A ridiculous one, but still a throne.

HYRCAN IV.   Still, I'd prefer to know my genealogy and not get lost in guess work.

MATRON II.   You're funny. What difference does it make whether you're Aryan or Semitic or Mongolian? Prince Tseng, ambassador of the Celestial Empire, was one of my lovers, too. Nowadays . . .

HYRCAN IV.   Shut up—don't get me in a rage!

JULIUS II.   Common pragmatic snobism. So even in Hyrcania there are irrelevant issues. Yes—Napoleon was right: recherche de paternité interdite.

STATUE.   Ha, ha, ha! Hyrcan and the mother problem, that's a good one!

HYRCAN IV.   I'm leaving. I don't want to have a new row. If I weren't here incognito, you'd see it would all end quite differently.

He goes to the door and leaves at the same time as ROCKOFFER *and* GRUMPUS.

MATRON II *(running towards the door).*   Hyrcan, Hyrcan! My son!

She runs out.

JULIUS II *(to the* STATUE).   That's a fine kettle of fish! And what do you say to that, my daughter!

STATUE.   I knew we wouldn't get off without a few discordant notes.

Behind the scenes, a shot is heard, and then a dreadful roar from HYRCAN IV.

JULIUS II.   What's that now? Some fiendish surprise. My stay in Heaven has made my once nerves-of-steel too sensitive. I've grown unaccustomed to shots.

ELLA*'s mother didn't even bat an eyelash.*

STATUE.   Quiet. With Paul, anything is possible. Let's wait: this is a really strange moment. I feel an extraordinary, non-Euclidean tension throughout all space. The whole world has shrunk to the dimensions of an orange.

JULIUS II.   Quiet—they're coming.

ROCKOFFER *runs in with a revolver in his hand, followed by*
MATRON II.

ROCKOFFER. I've killed him. I've avenged the death of poor Ella.

JULIUS II. Who? Hyrcan?

ROCKOFFER *(embracing* MATRON II). Yes. And you know what
alienated me from him most? That scene with his mother. I don't
remember my mother, but I feel sure I wouldn't have treated
her that way. If you want absolutism in life, there's absolutism in
life for you. He drove me to it himself, the dog.

JULIUS II. Well, fine—that's very nice of you, my son. But what's
going to come of it?

ROCKOFFER *(to* MATRON II). Just a minute. First of all, I ask
you, in memory of your son and my friend, to consider me as
your second son. He was unworthy of you. A matron—a whore—
where could I find a better mother?

MATRON II *(kissing him on the head)*. Thank you, Paul—my son,
my true, dear son!

ROCKOFFER. That's enough. Let's go.

JULIUS II. But where? What'll we do without that thug Hyrcan?
Worse still—what'll we do without Hyrcania? Now that our
Hyrcanian desires have reached their peak and, so to speak,
run absolutely wild?

ROCKOFFER. Oh—I see Your Holiness has really lost all his wits.
Is there anyone who deserves to be King of Hyrcania more than
I do? Is there any absolutist who's carrying out his ideas in real
life more than I am? Give me the whole world and I'll smother
it with kisses. Now we'll create something diabolical. I feel
the strength of a hundred Hyrcans in me. I, Paul Hyrcan V.
I won't be a joker the way he was. Out with this junk. *(He
kicks the royal robes and sword on the floor.)* I'll create a really
cosy little nook in the Infinity of the world. Art, philosophy,
love, science, society—one huge mishmash. And not like grovelling
worms, but like whales spouting with sheer delight, we'll swim
in it all up to our ears. The world is not a rotten cheese. Existence
is always beautiful if you can only grasp the uniqueness of
everything in the universe. Down with the relativity of truth!
Chwistek's the first one I'll knock off! We'll forge on in the
raging gale, in the very guts of absolute Nothingness. We'll go on
burning like new stars in the bottomless void. Long live finiteness
and limitations. God isn't tragic; he doesn't become—he is. Only
we are tragic, we, limited Beings. *(In a different tone.)* I'm saying
this as a good Catholic and I hope I won't offend Your Holiness's
feelings by doing it. *(In his former tone.)* Together, we'll create
pure nonsense in life, not in Art. *(Again in a different tone.)*
Hm—it's revolting! They're all different names for the same gigantic,
disgusting weakness. Completely new—everything new. *(Clutches*

his breast.) I'm getting tired. Poor Ella! Why couldn't she have lived till now. *(He falls into deep thought.)*

STATUE.   Didn't I say that with good old Paul you can expect anything?

JULIUS II.   But you won't leave me for him, my daughter?

STATUE.   Never. Paul is too intense for me—and too young. *(She kisses JULIUS II's hand.)*

JULIUS II.   I'm only afraid that the actual results may not live up to such a promise. I'm afraid of humbug.

STATUE.   I am, too—a little. But it's always worth trying.

ROCKOFFER *(waking up from his meditation).*   And you, Holy Father, will you go with us? In Heaven, will they grant you an extension of your leave?

JULIUS II.   To tell the truth—in Heaven they think I really belong in Hell. But you see, as a Pope they can't decently do . . . that to me . . . you know? That's why I can get a leave to any planet I want without any difficulties whatever.

ROCKOFFER.   That's great. Without you, infernal old man, I wouldn't be able to take any more. You appealed to me because your inner transformations were sincere. But poor Ella—if it were only possible to bring her back from the dead! What wouldn't I give for that right now! He was the one who made me do it: that damned Hyrcan. (ELLA *springs up suddenly, pushing her* MOTHER *aside.)*

ELLA.   I'm alive! I was only knocked out. I'm going with you! I'll be queen of Hyrcania!

ROCKOFFER *(embracing her).*   What happiness, what endless happiness! My most dearly beloved, forgive me. *(He kisses her.)* Without you, even Hyrcania would be only a ghastly dream.

MOTHER *(getting up in tears).*   You're a good man, Paul. I knew you wouldn't abandon poor Ella.

PAUL *goes over to her and kisses her hand.*

ROCKOFFER.   Adopted mother and mother-in-law, I'll take both of you with us to Hyrcania. I know how to value the advice of older women who've experienced a great deal. Even the uncles—those two old idiots, we'll take them with us too. Let's go—whatever he's done, Hyrcan opened a new way for us. May his memory be sacred to us.

JULIUS II.   What generosity, what generosity! This is one of the most beautiful days of my life beyond the grave. In any case, God is an inscrutable mystery (X). Come, my daughter.

ROCKOFFER.   Matrons, let's get a move on—the Hyrcania-express leaves in ten minutes—we've got to hurry.

The MATRONS *leave, passing by* GRUMPUS.

GRUMPUS.   His Royal Highness just breathed his last in my arms.
ROCKOFFER *(offering his arm to* ELLA*)*.   Well, may he rest in
  peace. Now I am king of Hyrcania. And even if I have to stand on
  my head and turn my own and other people's guts upside down,
  I'll carry out my mission on this planet. Understand?
GRUMPUS.   Yes, Your Royal Highness.

ROCKOFFER *goes out with* ELLA. JULIUS II *goes out after them
with the* STATUE. (+)

JULIUS II *(as he leaves)*.   Even the worst fraud that scoundrel
  perpetrates on society has the strange charm of a finished work
  of art. I wonder if I'll be able to create a new artistic centre in
  this infernal Hyrcania.
STATUE.   In artistic matters, you're the almighty power, Holy
  Father . . .

They go out, followed by GRUMPUS. *The packages and the clothing
of the king remain in the middle of the stage.*

APRIL 1922

Ninety-Three

by

Stanislawa Przybyszewska

Adapted by Jerzy Krasowski
and
Translated by Edward Rothert

Characters in order of appearance:

DE LA MEUGE

MAUD

DENIS

FATHER MICHOT

JOSSE

ACT ONE

Scene One

DE LA MEUGE. But, Maud, what's wrong?

MAUD. *(sobs)*

DE LA MEUGE. Oh, of course. That poor girl . . .

MAUD. What poor girl?

DE LA MEUGE. The one I presume you're crying over. Our
Judith . . . Charlotte Corday.

MAUD. How dare you call her a poor girl! If I were to shed any tears
on her account, it would only be out of envy. God! How I wish I
could love something or someone to the point of complete
self-sacrifice . . . to the point of murder.

DE LA MEUGE. But, in that case, what were you crying about?

MAUD *(slyly)*. You really want me to tell you?

DE LA MEUGE. Very much.

MAUD. Over him. The victim.

DE LA MEUGE *(sighing)*. Oh. You mean you were merely
experimenting on me?

MAUD. Does it still surprise you that, surrounded by puppets, I yearn
for a man so passionately that I go to pieces over Marat dead,
while alive . . .

DE LA MEUGE. No, it's not that. Death and blood excite you.

MAUD. Have you noticed, Papa, how we have lost all sense of our
relationship? A year ago I would never have presumed to address
you familiarly. What has become of my *piété filiale*? All trace of
respect for my father has vanished.

DE LA MEUGE. I suffered a defeat and that is enough to forfeit
all respect. Human nature contains a streak of contempt and
abhorrence for losers. And quite right too. Every defeat leaves a
stigma like leprosy. What's more, we are living in squalor, and
nothing, not even the most infamous knavery, so humiliates . . .
so irredeemably debases a man as that. Poverty rules out even
elementary human dignity. It is impossible for a poor man, no
matter how much of a hero he may be.

MAUD. You are mistaken about poverty inviting contempt. Marat
wore the same shirt all year, yet Paris adored him . . . Fr. Michot
and Josse are even poorer than we are, but are still respected.

DE LA MEUGE. No doubt, my dear, but you have never seen them
buttoning up their shirts right to the neck to conceal their patched
underwear. Nor have you slept in the same room with them . . .
Incidentally, do I snore? (MAUD *shakes her head vigorously*.) Thank
God. But they perhaps do. You should be grateful to me, my love,
for sparing you the more 'human' sights and scenes.

175

Ninety-Three by Stanislawa Przybyszewska, directed by
Jerzy Krasowski, at the Panstwowy Theatre, Cracow, 1977.
Photo: Zbighiew Lagocki

MAUD *(stubbornly).* No, it's not that. In some way you seem to have
let me down. Look, in all the time that we have been living in a
single room, continually in each other's company, has it . . . have you
ever noticed that I am a woman?

DE LA MEUGE. Have I, by God! Every word that passes from your
lips tells me that you are *only* a woman.

MAUD *(pale with anger).* You know perfectly well what I meant.
Have you ever desired me?

DE LA MEUGE. That is not the sort of question one asks.

MAUD. You old coward!

DE LA MEUGE. Very well, I shall tell you, though the answer is
insulting. No, my dear, I have never desired you.

MAUD. Thank you.

DE LA MEUGE. My poor, dear child, why not tell me what's the
matter with you? Is it simply that our circumstances have become
more than you can bear? In London we shall all breathe more
easily. I still have a part of my fortune intact there.

MAUD. The trouble is that leaving Paris would be a wrench for me.

DE LA MEUGE. It will not be for long, I promise you. This grisly
farce cannot last forever.

MAUD. But that is precisely what appeals to me. It is not a farce,
but the most beautiful tragedy that life has ever precipitated
upon our ugly world.

DE LA MEUGE. Our peril here grows from day to day. I am
absolutely positive that the Terror of August and September
will return shortly, which means that we shall have to hide in
holes and corners and live like stray animals until we are run
to earth by the Committee and packed off to the guillotine. I was,
after all, a party to the plots before the coup and at the Chateau on
August 10th itself. What's more, I was standing in a window
overlooking the courtyard next to the very man who opened fire
on the Marseillais just as they were beginning to fraternise with the
Swiss. That shot was responsible for all of the carnage that followed.
It only needs one of those Marseillais to recognise me—and I must
confess I would sooner be accused of forgery or theft than that.

MAUD. Why?

DE LA MEUGE. It is too hideous a crime.

MAUD. So it was not you who fired?

DE LA MEUGE. Surely you know me better than that, Maud?

MAUD. I didn't mean to offend you.

DE LA MEUGE. Never mind. Now, to come back to our
predicament . . . consider one further point: were our correspondence
with my brother—on Prince Condé's staff no less—to come to light,
my fate would be sealed . . . even in the present circumstances. You
and Denis would be imprisoned for the duration of the war. You will
appreciate, therefore, that the situation seems desperate. As a man in
the best of health I do not in any way hanker after a martyr's death.

In any case I cannot bear to see you dressed like that, ruining your hands with kitchenwork. Denis worries me . . . a sickly boy and losing what self-composure he ever had. To put it bluntly, I fear for him.

MAUD. Quite unnecessarily. *He* is safe enough.

DE LA MEUGE. Finally, I also find this wretched poverty an ordeal, even though I am less sensitive than you. So, Maud, think it over carefully. If you insist on staying behind, you are letting yourself in for hardships which you cannot begin to imagine—and probably for death as well.

MAUD. Is life really so precious that it is not worth sacrificing for a whim?

DE LA MEUGE. *Our* life, yes, unquestionably so. Only your whim will prove a complete will-o'-the wisp.

MAUD. How on earth could I lay down your life?

DE LA MEUGE. Do you imagine that I would leave you here on your own?

MAUD. Why not?

DE LA MEUGE. What a question! Though, come to think of it, I'm not sure. Pride, I suppose.

MAUD. Not because you love me too much?

DE LA MEUGE. To be frank, no.

MAUD. I'm beginning to find you engaging. But perhaps the two of us might stage ourselves a small, private drama of our own . . . strictly *entre nous.* I shall stay on here. *(Lowering her voice.)* You know, Father, the guillotine fascinates me. It is a death for heroes, swift and bloody.

DE LA MEUGE. The point, Maud, is that I do not in the least share your aspirations. I shall stay on *very* reluctantly.

MAUD. Can it be that the Duc de la Meuge quails at the very thought of the guillotine?

DE LA MEUGE. Of course—like anyone in his right mind. You are excused by youth.

Scene Two

DENIS. Father . . . Maud. I have . . . I have arranged . . . passports.

DE LA MEUGE & MAUD *(simultaneously).* What?

DENIS. Yes, genuine, perfectly legal passports. Not for crossing frontiers, you understand, but they will take you to the Department of Calvados.

DE LA MEUGE. But . . . How on earth?

DENIS. Through Josse. I risked my life. But let me begin at the beginning. We were talking about Marat's death. Now, Josse maintains that Marat, for all his thorough-going radicalism, was an astute man of sound judgement, which prevented him from throwing reason wholly to the winds in the pursuit of his ruthless ends and demands. Apparently, by terrorizing all the demagogues, he prevented them from pushing his radical programme to absurd lengths. Josse is sure that Marat would have sized you up correctly. But his successors lack both his sense and scruples . . . I then considered the wisdom of confiding our secrets.

DE LA MEUGE. What secrets?

DENIS. That you were among the royal family's entourage on the night of August 10th. But he believed me—I could see his look of relief—when I added that you went and returned unarmed. The moment was right. I took the plunge and told him point-blank that you were hoping to slip across to London. He pounced like a tiger. On my word of honour I vouched for your political neutrality. I am sure, after all, that you have no intention of plotting and scheming abroad.

DE LA MEUGE. No, Denis. You are quite right. *(Smiling.)* I would never have thought you capable of judging me so acutely.

MAUD. Perception of the heart . . . Well?

DENIS. In the end I managed to persuade him that, since you do not propose to engage in any counter-revolutionary activities, it makes no difference whether you live here or in London. He gave it some long, hard thought, but eventually saw my point. We then went straight out to arrange the papers and Josse vouched for the names and particulars. So all you have to do now is to call on the section committee and have the passports endorsed and issued.

MAUD. Well, well, Denis, how touching! To risk one's life—what could be easier? But the lives of others, and loved ones at that— that would daunt most people. Because you must surely have known that Josse was virtually duty-bound to report your indiscretions instantly.

DENIS. I suppose so . . . but Josse is basically honourable and I was sure anything so despicable would be beyond him.

MAUD *(scornfully)*. Despicable? Why, he would be furnishing proof of his genuine maturity and his willingness to offer up not only his shabby life, but also his conscience.

DE LA MEUGE. You are becoming tiresome, Maud. You have no right to make superhuman demands.

MAUD. Come, come, Papa, spare us the pathos.

A knocking at the door.

Scene Three

FR. MICHOT. Josse sent me. I understand you have passports with
the dates open. I beg both of you to make use of them at the
earliest opportunity, preferably tomorrow. The last three days
have been immensely critical. The silence at Marat's funeral was
ominous. The populace of Paris has grown into a dangerous force
since it ceased to be a rabble.

DENIS. We might still be in time today, Father.

FR. MICHOT. No, tomorrow. To collect papers in the evening is
ill-advised. It suggests haste and suspicions are too easily aroused
these days . . . Why do you look so doubtful?

DENIS. The two of you must leave tomorrow.

MAUD. The two of us?

DENIS. I . . . I have other plans.

FR. MICHOT. What?

DENIS. I belong, though only in heart and spirit, to a heroic
and doomed party. To share its triumphs is denied me; but
I can share in its battles, its tribulations, its defeat. Don't try
to stop me. My one purpose in life would be in vain if I were to
betray my first and only faith.

FR. MICHOT. So you are a Girondist, are you? But you're mistaken .
That isn't a faith.

DENIS. Not a faith?

FR. MICHOT. A man of faith, Denis, does not accept that his cause
is doomed, even if it suffers ten defeats running. Nor does a man
of faith enter the fray in search of death. On the contrary: he
calculates the odds and takes the greatest pains to avoid it.

DENIS. I am not cut out for life . . . I do not love it. I long for only
one thing: some great exploit which would consume this whole life
with the speed of a forest fire and be a blessing to the victim
himself. If only by destroying him.

FR. MICHOT *(with grim intensity)*. Idiotic, iniquitous nonsense.

DENIS *(quietly, haughtily)*. I won't stand for remarks like that.

FR. MICHOT. What makes you think that you're not cut out for
life? That it means nothing to you? What, after all, do you know
about it. Make him see sense, Mademoiselle.

MAUD. But I applaud my brother's decision wholeheartedly. To
my mind, he could make no more noble use of his life.

FR. MICHOT. M. de la Meuge?

DE LA MEUGE. My apologies, Father, for my daughter's words.
You have my sincerest thanks. Needless to say, I agree with you
entirely. But I doubt that anything can temper their youthful
fanaticism. So we had better yield with good grace.

FR. MICHOT. But it's their lives that are at stake!

DE LA MEUGE. You see, Father . . .

They begin to whisper.

DENIS. So the revolution has also affected you, Maud?

MAUD. Oh, far more deeply than you. I like you, Denis.

DENIS. Now you are making fun of me. But what do you plan to do?

MAUD. Stay on here as the lion's jaws close and revel in the spectacle of . . . of, well for one thing, your heroic death.

DENIS. We shall both die, Maud, the only martyr's to a faith without a God.

MAUD. Certainly we shall die.

DENIS. One sacrifice deserves another?

MAUD *(furiously)*. Oh no! Not in my case. I, my dear, am laying down my life from pleasure. I, at least, am not a coward, either physically or morally.

DENIS *(after a pause)*. But what of Father, Maud?

MAUD *(with exaggerated venom)*. He will marry again in London. If someone will still have him, that is . . . He was relieved when Mother died in Coblenz last autumn. An emigré wife is a terrible embarrassment . . .

DENIS. But, Maud, Father is not a coward. The very fact that he did not join the emigrés . . . Why do you hate him so?

MAUD. You see, Denis, I wonder if he is not a coward after all. On August 10th he came back from the Tuileries without even a scratch.

DENIS. But, Maud, he went unarmed.

MAUD. Exactly. But why? What am I to make of that? I'm sure that he would be good at getting himself butchered gracefully.

DENNIS *(calmly)*. You are play-acting, Maud. There are limits to the amount of leg-pulling I can take. But tell me this: why did you insist on moving in with him? He was perfectly willing to share a room with Josse and leave this one to us.

MAUD *(morosely)*. I was making the best of a bad bargain. If one must live in one room with a man—and my own flesh and blood at that—a father is a fractionally less repugnant prospect than a brother. The properieties would have been better served really by sharing with Josse.

DENIS. You are being evasive, Maud. You had other reasons.

MAUD. If I'm being evasive, it must mean that I do not care to confide in you. And what is this, anyway? A cross-examination?

DENIS. I feel sorry for Father.

MAUD. Pity?

DENIS. For heaven's sake, Maud, what are you on about? No, not pity. I simply feel sorry for him. Tell me, won't you feel a little bit sorry when they chop off my head?

MAUD. You're being a bore. As for whether I shall feel sorry, I very much doubt it. But if you succeed in not looking ridiculous on the scaffold, I promise the odd tear.

DENIS. I shall be most obliged. But remember that you have promised.

181

I like you, Maud.

MAUD. I can't stand people who harp. I would prefer to know what, exactly, you plan to do in order to share the sad fate of the Gironde.

DENIS. I shall help them to set France ablaze.

MAUD. But you don't know the first thing about political organisation. You'll simply get in the way. Oh, Denis—

DENIS. Stop needling me, Maud.

MAUD. You've no idea how comic you are. You are so totally under the influence of Josse. I mean, it's only through him that the gravity and beauty of revolution ever even dawned on you.

DENIS. I suppose you're right.

MAUD. Of course I am. But you're so anxious to preserve some semblance of having a mind of your own that you picked precisely the side which he opposes.

DENIS. There you're wrong . . . I admire Josse, but by and large I find the Jacobins loathsome. They are cold, cruel, boorish and unfeeling. They lack all sense of beauty. Their criteria are unrelievedly utilitarian.

DE LA MEUGE. Excuse me, children, but I have a request to make of Denis. Would you come along with me to see Josse? I have to consult him on a certain matter which also concerns you.

MAUD. But does not concern me? I'm intrigued.

DE LA MEUGE. Oh, it does, if you so wish. Fr. Michot will fill you in.

Scene Four

MAUD. There's no need to be afraid of me, Father. I'm not a witch.

FR. MICHOT. That stands to·reason. Witches are sorely afflicted women who deserve nothing but compassion, hapless creatures whose bodies have matured, but whose spiritual development has been arrested at the level of a child. Physically, they feel the instinctive desires of their sex, but are unable to gratify them in the normal way.

MAUD. What's that little speech supposed to mean?

FR. MICHOT. To demonstrate that no one could take *you* for a witch.

MAUD. Have you no problems of your own?

FR. MICHOT. Naturally. Trifles, mostly. Not long ago, for example, I ran out of money.

MAUD. Don't make fun of me.

FR. MICHOT. I see you haven't yet learned how serious financial difficulties can be. The exquisite sufferings of the soul are child's play by comparison.

MAUD. But those, no doubt, are outside your experience?

FR. MICHOT. Of course not. I'm only human.

182

MAUD. But no pokes around in *your* wounds with their dirty great . . . hands.

FR.MICHOT. True, but that's because they are scratches. Problems of greater consequence are decided not by my whims, but by the word of my confessor or the ruling of the bishop.

MAUD *(astonished)*. What? You mean to say you don't resolve your own doubts?

FR.MICHOT. My dear child, do you think I am infallible? But shouldn't you be more interested in the matters your father and brother have gone to discuss?

MAUD. No. On the other hand, I am passionately interested in your soul and the conflicts your bishop settles. What dilemma has been on the agenda recently?

FR.MICHOT. A mere point of doctrine. It would bore you.

MAUD. Now you really have me bursting with curiosity.

FR.MICHOT. Very well. As you know, I come from the working class and I've never risen above that station in life. I remember vividly the environment I grew up in. I remember winter nights when the streets were full of people tramping up and down, trying to avoid falling asleep at home and freezing to death. We had no wood, but all around us smoke from palace chimneys filled the sky. And laughing women, wrapped in furs, riding carriages made of the finest timber sent the frozen passers-by flying. I remember long months of hunger. And walls . . . and pickets guarding the warehouses of the rich corn merchants. I remember the remedies used by the government to relieve disasters. Six such remedies twelve foot high, were erected next to each other in the square. By the end of the week many more than six bodies had hung from them. So for me the Revolution was the dawn of divine mercy. And I was more or less forced to accept its actions lock, stock and barrel. At least understand. That would have made me a Jacobin. But the Revolution was bound to declare war on the Church, and the Church to denounce the Revolution. On both sides there was the same implacable necessity. I found myself the servant of two hostile powers. A choice had to be made. But this time conscience, instead of coming to my aid, categorically forbade me to choose. It plumped with equal conviction for both sides. I entreated the Holy Father, needlessly really, since I knew in advance what the answer would be. Any participation whatsoever in revolutionary activities, any public demonstration of support was anathema.

MAUD. What choice did you make? In the end?

FR.MICHOT. None at all. Barred from any kind of work, I try to justify my existence somehow by doing everything in my power to help individuals . . . provided, of course, that it does not endanger the security of the revolutionary republic. For example, I would be happy to assist in your departure, since I know that your father will not break his word. Otherwise I would try to stop you.

MAUD. All right, all right, but that's not the point . . . At a time when even cowards like my brother are rushing to take up arms on one side or the other, you sit on the fence with your hands folded, neither fish, nor fowl . . . *lukewarm* . . . Sit down, for God's sake—I'm confused enough as it is. A compromise . . . but what kind? One that has turned you into a nothing, a cipher. Don't you feel?

FR.MICHOT. Yes, but that's a trifle . . .

MAUD. Trifle? For the Revolution you could be a second Marat, for the Church the kind of gladiator it lacks. Instead you're a cipher. You can't summon the courage to cut the reassuring cord of obedience. You let yourself be led like a puppy. You are despicable.

FR.MICHOT. I don't have wings—I can't take off and fly. That's why I love man—and here on earth above all. It is a mistake. Moreover it is a love so foolish, so obtuse, so . . . desparate that it equals my love of God—the Lord does not come first in my heart. And in a priest that is a terrible sin. Christ made clear his contempt for a servant like me.

MAUD. You love man. But not enough, it appears, to sacrifice eternal salvation for him. For you, therefore, there is only one way out . . . death. Not suicide. Simply sport your cassock in public and go about your duties, and in no time at all you will have achieved your purpose.

FR.MICHOT. To invite death is also suicide. I don't crave death. I hold life sacrosanct—in me as in every creature. No, for me there is no way out. Couldn't I help you?

MAUD. No, *now* you can no longer be of any use to me. *(She breaks into a throaty, insultingly demonic chuckle.)*

FR.MICHOT *(softly, in an ordinary voice which nevertheless commands unwilling obedience).* Stop it.

MAUD. What?

FR.MICHOT. That cackle is disgusting I wanted to warn you.

MAUD. It is too late, Father. Oh, an hour ago I would have been thrilled if you'd dared to order me about. But now . . .

FR.MICHOT. I have failed you.

MAUD. Dreadfully. *(With a stifled cry.)* For pity's sake can't you see that I need a hero? The city is throbbing to the rhythm of an epic, but the only people I ever meet are miserable worms . . . Vermin . . .

FR.MICHOT. You long for a hero? You'll find one in the crowd. Yet they are all, almost without exception, average people. Anyone ignorant of the richness of human nature would never suspect they had heroism in them. In any case heroism is a flame which leaps forth suddenly from a log which burns just the same, whether expensive or common. Fire cannot be a lasting condition of wood. Yet you expect a man to be a hero while putting on his shoes, eating his lunch, going about his daily business. No, your search for this ideal hero is in vain: you wouldn't recognise him, if you saw him.

You are at cross-purposes with life and people. Just next door, you
have a man worthy of admiration and love, but you are blind . . .

MAUD. Who . . . who is he?

FR.MICHOT. You know who.

MAUD. Well now, Father . . . Perhaps you would be good enough to
tell Josse that I wish to speak with him in private.

FR.MICHOT. Very well. *(He leaves quickly)*

Scene Five

MAUD *(alone, getting to her feet, gradually stiffening as though
going into a trance).* Admiration . . . and . . . love . . . Admiration
. . . Oh, my God! *(All at once she snaps out of it and assumes a
natural bearing.)*

JOSSE. Here I am. At your service.

MAUD. No . . . Not yet . . . Let me go . . . Let me go . . . Let me go . . .

JOSSE. Oh no, my dear. There are limits. Your little game's gone sour
on you, right? And it's so nice pulling a puppet on the string. Ah well,
are you all right now? Your first kiss, it appears. Well, I'll make
myself scarce so you can cry your heart out. Bye. *(He turns towards
the door.)*

MAUD *(halting him with a smile so natural as to be strange).* Don't
go . . . silly. *(Bursting out laughing.)* What makes you think that I'm
going to cry?

JOSSE. Because that's the habit of girls new to the game. You are
evidently one.

MAUD. There is absolutely *no* cause for tears. You are a brute, but
never mind. I must have a serious talk with you. Sit down.

JOSSE. Excellent. In that case I also have a few questions to put to
you . . .

MAUD. I'll answer them . . . today. You start.

JOSSE. I must admit that you have me completely baffled. You took
great pains to make sure that I didn't slip through your fingers, that I
would always be there at your beck and call. But you never betrayed
the least sign of liking for me. Furthermore, you were fond of
experimenting with me, in the manner of every girl who knows she
is . . . loved. But now I think I have an inkling of what is inside you.
You need a man whom you would have to obey. I suspect that I could
fulfil this need. In other words, will you agree to become my
mistress? All your spiritual torments, your tiresome nerves, can be
accounted for by your virginity. For a mature woman it is a painful
handicap. Free yourself of it at last, and you will be like new. For
that matter, you can become my wife, if that matters to you, though
I doubt if it will do either of us much good. Well, now, make your
mind.

MAUD. Josse, I . . . I don't know. No, no, Josse, it isn't the normal hesitation of a virgin. It's something else.

JOSSE. Come on, don't let your capriciousness make a fool of you.

MAUD. Don't be angry with me, Josse. Let me think it over.

JOSSE. Of course. But—

MAUD. Who knows? Perhaps at last I will be able not only to love, but also to admire . . .

JOSSE. Listen to me, Maud. If you agree to our liaison, it would be the answer to at least two problems. I know that you want to stay in Paris and watch the course of the Revolution. Well, as the mistress of a prominent Jacobin official, you would have both security and freedom of movement. There is no danger of our party coming to grief: It alone draws honest breath, the breath of the people. My personal position is equally secure. The Republic has allowed me to work for myself: I have been appointed prosecutor-general of the Commune. At the same time, once you had the safest protection imaginable your father would be able to leave . . . You must know how fervently he desires to get away from a country where he is regarded as an enemy and where he may at any moment perish for a cause which is indifferent to him . . .

MAUD *(trembling, with a pathetic, almost childish moan).* But I don't want him to leave me . . . I don't want my father to go . . . *(Close to tears.)* I mean, he won't abandon me . . .

JOSSE. Talk sense, Maud. How can you be abandoned when you're under my care? And I am sure I can make that dear ass, Denis, see reason . . . So you love your father as desperately as that? Maud, it's . . . unnatural.

MAUD. I don't love him . . . not a bit. I merely can't live without him

JOSSE. Ah, I see. How clear and simple it is. Only I'm not that stupid. Now I'm completely in the dark.

MAUD. So am I . . . Perhaps it's the result of my upbringing. As a child I grew up with strangers. My parents were so absorbed by their social life that they had neither the time nor the inclination to care for me. Nevertheless of the two I saw my mother more often. And I have always thought that by the time I was ten I had seen right through her. You can't even guess, Josse, what a desolate feeling it is for a woman when she has become convinced of her spiritual superiority to her parents.

JOSSE. Perhaps you're right. Incidentally, I loved my mother dearly, without expecting either understanding or help from her.

MAUD. You are a man, a strong one. But I . . . it sometimes seems to

me that I was created solely to become an object for which some
big, powerful man would put forth all his energies and abilities . . .

JOSSE. That's a disastrous mistake, Maud. Any great man who lived
and worked only for some individual would simply be wasting his
life and work. No individual has the right to claim another person's
energies and abilities; only the masses can demand them exclusively.

MAUD. After my disillusionment with my mother, I came to hate
her. You will understand how fiercely I fastened on to the image
of my father. He was unapproachable. I rarely saw him, and always
in the plumes of a man of the world. But, on the other hand, God,
how handsome he was! Infernally handsome . . . He wouldn't allow
his hand to be kissed. And familiarity, like a kiss on the cheek,
upset him. I doubt that I would have had the nerve to touch him.
But I did manage to steal a pair of his gloves which had the
imprint of his knuckles and even a whiff of scent. At night I would
get out of bed and kneel to bury my face in those gloves. They're
still there, in my drawer. You know what? Burn them for me, or
throw them away.

JOSSE. Those are things you have to do for yourself.

MAUD. Surely it comes to the same thing.

JOSSE. If it had been love . . . but even then you loved only yourself.

MAUD. The shadow of my father grew in me into inordinate
dimensions. The Revolution threw us together, but far too closely.
My shining hero was cut down to size. Seen at close quarters my
dream god was revealed as an ordinary, average man. Ah! And yet . . .
yet I was unable to get his measure. He never lets his mask slip.
He sleeps in it. Never once have I had the chance of glimpsing him
at a truly critical moment, in some sudden danger. But even if I
have to wait ten years, I must discover once and for all if he is
worth anything. I must.

JOSSE. He is difficult to see through. But, Maud, you must free
yourself of this mania. You're no longer a child . . .

MAUD. I asked you here, Josse, to learn something from you that is
very important to me. What is it that Father wanted that made him
call on you with Denis?

JOSSE. Your life. He admitted frankly that he would much prefer
to leave, but that you wanted to stay and why. But since your
situation would be growing more dangerous every day, your father
asked me to help him find a post in one of the offices of the
Republic. So he could acquire political standing as an able and
trustworthy official and you would be completely free and safe.
But he said he would change his mind unless Denis abandoned
his crazy plans . . . or if I had any doubts as to his honour. I said I
trusted him But that it was a risky business. Your father would
have scores of enemies, who would pounce on him en masse. Your
father is a shrewd man, but quixotic, taking such a dangerous step
merely to gratify a girlish whim. My plan is sounder.

187

MAUD *(slowly, with clenched teeth)*. Ah, so that was what he wanted . . .
Do you really imagine that he is concerned with my safety and not
his own?

JOSSE. I'm positive of it. It's not just you he's worried about, but
also his son, whom he is anxious to save from his own folly. And
if he personally prefers to live quietly and work rather than die
senselessly, that only does him credit . . .

MAUD. Really? So it is honourable if a man who has been defeated
saves his own skin when he sees his cause crushed?

JOSSE. When will you get into your head, Maud, that your father
is not a Royalist? With his intelligence he knew from the start
that the monarchy was dead.

MAUD. He took part in the intrigues of the court. But circumspectly,
soberly, careful to take no risks.

JOSSE. Are you quite sure he took part?

MAUD Listen, Josse. I think I will accept your offer. But for that
very reason I must be absolutely honest with myself. Tell me why
exactly you have honoured the Duc de la Meuge with such trust?

JOSSE. I know him . . . a little . . . Michot is convinced that he is
a man to be believed—and Michot is an unerring judge of
character.

MAUD Well, this time he's mistaken. De la Meuge is a very, very
wily conspirator and spy. That is why he stayed in Paris instead
of emigrating, why he now talked me into foiling our departure. Why
I pretended that I wanted to watch the course of the Revolution on
the spot. That idiot Denis hasn't the faintest idea of any of this.
The Duke lies low, but he misses little, and every week all sorts
of interesting facts about revolutionary capital make their way
secretly to the Prince Conde.

JOSSE. What was *your* part in this assignment?

MAUD. None. He let me into the secret only after Denis had wangled
the passports, never suspecting how unhelpful he was being to his
father. You can imagine what I went through then . . .

JOSSE. I couldn't care less about that. You're lying. You knew and
colluded with him all along.

MAUD. If you want, I'm prepared to swear.

JOSSE. That won't be necessary. In any case I shall be watching
you. And now, evidence please.

MAUD. Evidence! *(She leaps to her feet and starts towards the
wardrobe, but freezes in her tracks sensing a few seconds in
advance a knock on the door which is then heard.)*

Scene Six

DE LA MEUGE *(entering the room without waiting for a reply).* Maud,
   list . . . Excuse me, I didn't know . . . What are you doing here?
MAUD *(walking over to him and placing a hand caressingly on his
   shoulder).* It's I, papa, who apologise. But I'm in the middle of talk
   talking to Citoyen Josse. About matters of principle.
DE LA MEUGE. So you've actually succeeded in changing my Maud's
   mind? With your eloquence, the Republic possesses a priceless
   treasure, Monsieur Josse . . . *(He releases himself affectionately from
   his daughter's embrace.)* For the moment I shall return to Fr. Michot.
   I will not intrude any longer. *(Exits.)*

Scene Seven

JOSSE *(takes the letters, places them on the table, and, still standing,
   leafs through them in a businesslike, concentrated manner).* No dates.
   And nothing incriminating in this correspondence either. Nothing!
MAUD. You have to know the key. Let's take just one example. You
   are, of course, aware that my mother died a few months before the
   outbreak of the Revolution, in other words before July 14th. But these
   letters keep referring to 'Your wife'. Mother's name was Florence
   yet some of these letters are full of references to a certain Pauline.
   For instance . . . *(Taking a letter.)* 'Pauline bade me to thank you
   for your news. She had been waiting for it on tenterhooks. She will
   follow your advice.' That grateful, dutiful Pauline is the conference
   in Pilnitz. And the 'wife' is the army of Prince Conde.
JOSSE. How do you know?
MAUD. He told me . . . everything . . . Josse . . . What provoked the
   massacre of the Swiss on August 10th? The Marseillais burst into
   the courtyard of the Louvre. Whereupon . . . a shot was fired . . .
   from the floor where there was still a handful of . . . courtiers.
   It was . . . my father. He was standing at a window.
JOSSE *(collecting the letters and tucking them inside his tunic).* Get
   this clear: I warn you, if you tip him off, if you warn him, you will
   be put in the dock as an accomplice.
MAUD. Joosse . . . Joosse! Where are you going?
JOSEE. The section headquarters.

189

Scene Eight

DE LA MEUGE *(entering almost cheerful)* I decided not to bother
    Fr. Michot . . . Maud . . . Maud . . . my dearest child . . . What is
    the matter?

MAUD   You have powerful arms, even if they are now trembling
    slightly . . . No, you are not one to be paralysed by fear. Would
    you still have the strength to carry me?

DE LA MEUGE *(making to lift her).*   Naturally, but where?

MAUD *(releasing herself with an almost amorous gentleness).*
    Thank you, darling, but I am perfectly all right. So you were
    not with Fr. Michot?

DE LA MEUGE.   No, I was pacing the corridor. As a result I saw
    Josse come out. He was looking very pensive. When he reached
    the staircase he stopped and for a while just stood there. Then
    he looked around as though he had forgotten something—his hat,
    no doubt—and turned back.

MAUD   So you did not bump into each other?

DE LA MEUGE.   No . . . You seem to be close to fainting, Maud.
    And no wonder, in this heat . . .

MAUD.   It is not the heat, Papa.

DE LA MEUGE.   I know, darling.

MAUD.   What . . . do you know?

DE LA MEUGE *(now smiling broadly).* That it is not the heat. Come,
    child, there is nothing to fear. Am I one of those legendary
    fathers in German ballads who make scenes instead of offering
    consolation? Maud, calm down, please. Getting into a state
    will do you no good.

MAUD.   What on earth are you talking about, Papa?

DE LA MEUGE.   About what you tried to hide from me. Be your
    age, Maud. There is no cause for hysterics. How you choose to
    arrange your life . . . afterwards is entirely up to you. *(She makes
    no answer, apparently dazed.)* You must see that there is absolutely
    no reason for despair.

MAUD.   Father . . . How much time can have elapsed since you
    left?

DE LA MEUGE.   Fifteen minutes, perhaps.

MAUD.   Fifteen minutes . . .

DE LA MEUGE *steps across to the wardrobe to fetch a clean
handerkerchief and wipes her brow. Maud notices and terror jerks
her to life. DE LA MEUGE leaves the drawer open, turns and moves
towards her. He addresses her as though she were hypnotised.*

DE LA MEUGE.   Maud!

MAUD.   You are about to be arrested.

DE LA MEUGE.   For what?

MAUD.   Look in that drawer.

Ninety-Three by Stanislawa Przybyszewska, directed by
Jerzy Krasowski for Wroclaw TV, 1969.
Photo: Zbigniew Lachowicz

DE LA MEUGE *(dumbfounded, but imperturbable, does as she has bid. He has guessed that only the letters could be the corpus delicti.).* I see . . . *(He speaks ruminatively, without emotion. Finding the one remaining letter, he takes it out, puzzled.)* And this one? *(Holding it, he turns towards her gently.)* Who did this, Maud?

MAUD. Josse . . .

DE LA MEUGE. In that case, why did he leave this one letter?

MAUD. I do not know . . .

DE LA MEUGE. Because it compromises you. Poor lad . . . *(He hands her the letter, which she takes dully, then places his hand on her shoulder and speaks firmly.)* Maud, do you hear me?

MAUD. Yes.

DE LA MEUGE. You must burn this letter the moment you are alone. Apart from that, Maud . . . look after Josse. Out of love for you he has suppressed evidence and in his eyes that is a crime which will haunt him . . . He must have thought himself insulted . . . decided that I had violated his trust . . . in some truly dreadful way. That being so, he obviously felt that he was duty-bound to denounce me . . . Ah well, it cannot be helped . . . But, Maud, one thing I beg of you. Don't tell him I'm innocent. Promise me Maud! You have no idea what conscience can do to a man!

MAUD. Save yourself, Father. Go!

DE LA MEUGE *(turning towards her with an amused smile).* While you deputise for me before the Revolutionary Tribunal and on the guillo–? Now look, Maud. In the first place, there is no knowing that they will convict me. The misunderstanding may be cleared up. And even if they do . . . a natural death is infinitely more cruel, and you yourself know how little store we set by our lives, valueless as they are, we who are incapable of faith . . . But you, my dear . . . you deserve to live. You have found the ardent love of a man above the ordinary run. That is to be prized. If you are only strong enough to surrender yourself to this force unquestioningly, life will acquire a beauty, a power, a glow that you cannot yet even conceive. Courage, Maud!

MAUD. But, Father don't you understand that it was I who betrayed you? Stop clutching at straws, stop deceiving yourself, old man. One wretched *word* can ruin you. It was I, yes I, who betrayed you. Who knew of those letters apart from me? But that's not all! I hinted that they were coded messages. So you'll be accused of a crime which is so abhorrent to a delic . . .

DE LA MEUGE. Stop! So you're not pregnant?

MAUD. Me? Pregnant!

DE LA MEUGE. Good. Give me back that letter.

MAUD. What on earth for?

DE LA MEUGE. I need it. Don't make me recover it by force!
(He leans across and she removes her hand hesitantly, her eyes fixed on him fearfully. He scoops up the letter as though pulling

it out of a fire and tucks it away). Now hurry up and collect whatever you need. Or am I to pack for you? The gendarmes will be here any minute and we must be ready to leave, they won't be kept waiting.

MAUD. But I want to live!

DE LA MEUGE. Really? I thought you wanted to die with me.

MAUD. No, you swine! Get that straight! Why do you think I removed that particular letter? Why? In order to destroy *you* and only you! And now you, you bastard, are try . . .

DE LA MEUGE. When did I ever get in your way?

MAUD. All the time. I was chained to you—you were the only thing that mattered to me in the whole world. And you carried on as if you hadn't the slightest idea! I was just one of two children to be loved within reason. And the worst thing was that I didn't know if you were worth my love. Now do you understand? Hand over that letter. It is my turn to live!

DE LA MEUGE. Too late.

MAUD. Getting your own back, you bastard?

DE LA MEUGE. No, Maud, it's not revenge. Simply human duty. You cannot be allowed to live, Maud. Whether it's my fault or nature's I don't know, but you have grown into a monster with no control over yourself. You say that I stood in your way. In fact you were dependent on me because you were incapable of fending for yourself. As you would discover quickly enough— even in the agony of death—if you were to survive me now. You would latch on to Josse with desperation. But a lover is not the same as a father. Sooner or later he would either have to discard you without mercy or go under. No outsider could take on an incubus like you. Abandoned for the second time, the third, the seventh, you would sink to the very bottom. You would become a helpless starving, animal. That, thank God, I can still prevent. And that, Maud, is why I am taking you with me. Pull yourself together, child. Right now you look awful.

DE LA MEUGE *has finished packing. He looks to see if he has forgotten anything. Then he leans against the wardrobe and contemplates the almost empty drawer. Suddenly a gleam of curiosity flashes from his dulled eyes and he pulls out a pair of very elegant men's gloves. He looks at them incredulously, wrinkles his brow, struggling to keep out the tempting thought that perhaps it was all a dream . . . Slowly, almost distractedly, he pulls on one of the gloves. It fits to the last crease.*

Scene Nine

DE LA MEUGE. Come on in, Denis.

DENIS *(entering with a shopping bag from which a long French roll protrudes, he stops in his tracks by the charged atmosphere of tragedy).* Father . . . What's happened?

DE LA MEUGE. Pull yourself together, Denis. All right? You see, my son, we have to part . . . you will lose me and your sister. You will be on your own. I am to be accused of being an emigré agent. A mistake, but no matter. This . . . patriot . . . has reported me and supported the accusation with convincing evidence. Maud and I are doomed. Don't waste time thinking you can rescue us, but listen carefully . . . The patriot in question is our friend Josse, *(Denis utters an animal howl.)* Shame on you, Denis! Now, what you must understand is that he has committed no crime whatsoever: for him it was simply his inescapable duty—and I can assure you that discharging it did not come easily to him.

DENIS. But, in that case who . . . who?

DE LA MEUGE. Is guilty? Chance, my boy . . . So I hope you will see that Josse truly had no choice . . . as a patriot . . .

DENIS. The devil take his patriotism! Oh God, my God!

DE LA MEUGE. Be quiet, Denis and listen. It is Josse I am thinking of. I want you to remain under the influence and care of a truly honourable man, and Josse is blameless. So you are to treat him not only with the same respect and, if you possibly can, the same friendship as before, but above all never—never!—allow him to learn that it was a mistake, that I was innocent. Is that clear, Denis? If he discovered too late that he had committed so terrible a mistake, he might be inclined to think of himself as a murderer. I wish to spare him that no matter what. Can I rely on you?

DENIS. You can, Father. I will not refuse to shake his hand, even though mine were to wither at the touch . . . Father . . . Father . . . Fa—ather! Papa!

DE LA MEUGE. Quiet, Denis, qui—et. Death is not so terrible. You I entrust with a more difficult task: you must live.

DENIS. No . . . No . . . No, Papa! Take me with you! Dear Papa, take me with you! Father . . . Fa—ather, have mer—cy! Father, I . . . I . . . shall go mad . . . I shall lose my mind! Oh, take me with you, Papa, take me with you!

At her brother's first outburst, MAUD *half comes to, opens her eyes, and now, lying on her back and staring at the ceiling, she is listening intently.*

DE LA MEUGE. No, my boy, we shall not be so foolish . . . neither you nor I.

DENIS. Oh, Father!

DE LA MEUGE. It's no use, my son . . . I order you to live. Because

my own life has been as empty as an abandoned tomb. For forty
years I have struggled on with a heart like a piece of wood, while
other people blazed with passion. I was amazed. I couldn't believe
it was possible to live so vehemently, so vibrantly. No ideal had
the power to set me alight; my soul had shrivelled. But love of
one's children . . . that is something which no heart can resist.
You became the sum and substance of my life . . . much too
late. I failed in your upbringing. I could have fostered in you
those mighty forces whose seeds are planted in every human
being . . . but I didn't have the time to try. I was too involved
in my work. Today I will breathe my last. But it doesn't matter.
I can no longer be of any service, though I am still comparatively
young. Maud will accompany me . . . That can't be helped. But
that is precisely why you must stay. Do you understand?
DENIS. No . . . not yet, Father.
DE LA MEUGE. For you to die, my dear son, would be to damn
me. To make my life a meaningless mockery. I would be worth
less than the humblest domestic animal, which is at least
of *some* use! Redeem me, my son. Repay my immense debt.
Give meaning to my life, the meaning that at least I fathered a
human being.
DENIS. Now I understand.
DE LA MEUGE. But don't ever think you are to live for my memory!
God forbid! A father should live for his children, but the reverse
is monstrous. Be what you please . . . Jacobin or priest, duke or
baker . . . but whatever be it totally. Stop mooning and dreaming,
pull yourself together, don't shrink from life. And now farewell,
dear son. I hear them coming for us.

MAUD *has so far been lying open-eyed. At the words 'And now farewell'
she raises her head, struggling with a terror as primitive as life itself.
She fights it down.*

DE LA MEUGE. Remember: there is nothing you can do to help us
and you would probably only endanger yourself. All my hopes,
my last wishes, would then be lost. Do not, Denis, do me that
disfavour.

Scene Ten

Knocks on the door are heard at last. MAUD *shudders and her
expression turns to terror.*

DE LA MEUGE *(lightly, almost jauntily).* Come on in, gentlemen.

JOSSE *appears in the doorway, looking pale. Puzzled,* DE LA MEUGE
*cranes his neck, seeking out the rest of the arresting party, but makes
out only the silent presence of* FR. MICHOT *in the dark corridor.*

DE LA MEUGE. Please, Father, come in. (MICHOT *steps inside without a word.*) I suppose you have come to give us time to get ready. I'm most grateful, gentlemen, but fortunately we are both packed. If you wish, we can leave at once.

JOSSE (*completely stunned*). Leave? Where to?

DE LA MEUGE. Where no one goes of his own free will . . . Come on, Maud, snap out of it.

JOSSE. Ah, so I take it you know. That makes it easier for me . . . But, please, that won't be necessary. (*He takes out the letters and places them on the table.*)

DE LA MEUGE. I . . . I don't understand.

JOSSE. Michot categorically insists that you are innocent, and I have never known him to be wrong. Since my mind is now full of such serious doubts, I cannot hand you over to the authorities.

MAUD. Oh! It is you! Go away . . .

DENIS (*hugging her*). But, Maud dear, nothing has happened. The whole matter has been cleared up . . . Maud, what has come over you.

MAUD (*frantically pulling herself free and crossing her arms over her breast*). I cannot stand the sight of you . . .

FR. MICHOT. You'd better not upset her any more . . . Let us leave.

DENIS. But, Father, what has got into her?

MAUD. Papa . . . Oh God! (*She goes out.*)

DE LA MEUGE. Have I shocked you, my son? (*He puts an arm around DENIS, and the contact steadies him.*) Don't regard me as a monster, Denis. You're obviously not aware that one has to treat nervous attacks with a certain brutality.

FR. MICHOT. I asked her to go to my room. She can rest there. (*His eyes switch to DENIS, who understands that he ought to leave.*)

DENIS. If you will excuse me, Papa . . . (*DE LA MEUGE gestures with his hand and DENIS goes out.*)

FR. MICHOT. When all is said and done, she may still go mad. Even if she doesn't, she will certainly go to the wall. Unless you save her . . .

DE LA MEUGE. How could I still help her?

FR. MICHOT. By not rejecting her. The main thing is to see that she does not feel rejected from all human relationships. But I take it that you won't carry out so simple a gesture?

DE LA MEUGE. No, you can't take it. After all, madness might be her salvation?

FR. MICHOT. How can you presume to condemn a young woman to that?

DE LA MEUGE. A woman . . . But she is a mons—. No, I doubt that her nature can want life.

FR. MICHOT. Any more than yours. I have, as you know been a

196

confessor. And no one knows better than us the mire in the depths of men's hearts. No, Maud is not a monster.

DE LA MEUGE *(with a rueful smile)*. I would like to believe you.

FR. MICHOT. No, If you approach her as a hopeless case, the poor girl will feel condemned beyond reprieve. She will cease to feel human.

DE LA MEUGE. Well, we shall see. I will do everything in my power. Thank you. Oh, I almost forgot. I still have to have a word with Josse.

FR. MICHOT *(calling)*. Josse! Come here a moment!

DE LA MEUGE. Do I need to make it clear that all along I was aware of the necessity of your conduct . . . and that it aroused nothing but my respect. I feel no rancour. I appreciate the significance of the fact that you returned those letters. For that reason I want you to keep them. I insist. They are the only earnest of loyalty that I can give you. And I have no right to demand your trust. I'm well aware that you are now bound to refuse me assistance. You can no longer vouch for me.

JOSSE. You're right. I can't vouch for you . . . But . . . What on earth will you do now?

DE LA MEUGE *(with a broader smile)*. I don't know. First, I must come to accept the joy of knowing that I shall be allowed to live. Then— *(He stops short.)*—Do not despise me my happiness. I would have managed somehow had things gone otherwise.

JOSSE *(with for the first time a hint of a grin)*. You forget that I had the chance to see that for myself.

DE LA MEUGE *(ignoring the compliment)*. Anyway don't take it to heart, since I don't take it to heart myself. *(He goes out.)*

Scene Eleven

JOSSE. If you have really prevented me from making a mistake, Michot . . . But you haven't saved him. You have merely postponed his death, his inevitable death.

FR. MICHOT *(matter-of-factly)*. True . . . unless you help him.

JOSSE. But, Michot, I can't help him! Proof, proof, I lack proof! Look, Michot, are you honestly certain—certain!—of his innocence? Would you be prepared to swear to that under oath?

FR. MICHOT. Yes, even that.

JOSSE. In that case, Michot . . . would that be enough?

FR. MICHOT. No, what I believe is not proof. It would be wrong for you to do anything to defend him unless you were absolutely clear in your own mind.

JOSSE. Why, then, did you try to save him?

FR. MICHOT.   But, Josse . . . Strive for that truth and then you will be able to care for him as if he were your own father!

JOSSE.   But where am I to find that truth?

DENIS.   Not so loud, gentlemen. I can't help overhearing you.

FR. MICHOT.   There stands your truth—come forward of its own accord.

JOSSE.   Of course! Oh, what a fool I've been . . . The only trouble is that it somehow seems to smack . . . of spying.

FR. MICHOT.   Could you join us for a moment, Denis?

DENIS.   At your service.

JOSSE.   What you must think of me I can't imagine . . . Perhaps you are struggling to forgive me for an act you can't understand. This is, I promise you, the last time I shall ever impose on you. But you must answer a few more questions. What was your mother's name?

DENIS.   Pauline. But—

JOSSE.   Wait. For the moment *I* am asking the questions. She died a few months before the storming of the Bastille?

DENIS.   Who ever told you that? No, she died much later . . . in the autumn of ninety-two.

JOSSE.   Where?

DENIS.   Never mind.

JOSSE.   Where?

DENIS.   I refuse to answer.

FR. MICHOT.   Abroad. In Koblenz.

JOSSE.   As you can see, I know the facts. In any case, it isn't necessarily a crime to die in Koblenz. It's something else that interests me. Still she did die there?

DENIS.   Yes.

JOSSE.   Did you know that your father was corresponding with a certain emigré officer?

DENIS.   Of course I did. I added a postscript to each letter.

JOSSE.   So you knew this . . . officer?

DENIS.   He is my uncle.

JOSSE.   Ah, I see. *(Returning to the attack.)* What forced you to take part in such an incriminating correspondence? And what was its nature?

DENIS.   Before I can answer that question, I must have my father's permission. I'm sure he'll give it, but he has forbidden me to discuss—.

JOSSE.   What? What did he forbid you to discuss?

DENIS.   Look, I said I would tell you, except that . . .

JOSSE *(seizing his arm spinning him round and flinging him into a chair).* Now! Tell me now! What did he forbid you to discuss? Out with it, you fool.

FR. MICHOT *(almost shouting).*   Tell him, Denis! You can tell him.

DENIS.   That . . . Josse was wrong . . . that Father was not guilty . . .

FR. MICHOT *(leaning forward and hooting with laughter)*.   Oh . . .
you ass . . . you priceless ass! Be off with you, Denis, before *I*
wring your neck. Your brittle little bones would snap like a
chicken's. *(Composing himself.)* Oh, God almighty!

DENIS.   What are you laughing at?

JOSSE.   At you, you idiot! And from sheer glee at the lunacy of
it all.

FR. MICHOT.   And at Satan whom God has contrived to make a
complete fool. Which is a rare satisfaction.

DENIS.   Actually, all things considered I'm not all that curious . . .
now that everything seems to have sorted itself out. What was it
that you were asking me about? Ah, I remember. Well, the subject
of our correspondence was my mother. When she decided, against
Father's advice, to leave, he entrusted her to his brother's care
and asked to be kept informed. I presume you've read those letters
and are familiar with their contents.

JOSSE *(sighing, resting his elbow on a crossed knee and his head on
his hand)*.   I only skimmed through them. But, now I know the
whole story. *(After some seconds of gratifying silence.)* Tell me,
Girondist and respected foe, have you made up your mind about
your plans?

DENIS.   I've abandoned that assinine idea I had.

JOSSE.   You know Denis, I may yet find myself relishing the
thought of having been a hair's breadth from despatching your
father to kingdom come. And you know what saved him? And you?
My hat. Yes, but for my hat, my good old hat, your father would now
be roasting in hell. The simple fact of the matter is that I didn't want
to go to the section committee bareheaded, so I came back to collect
it. And that was when I fell into Michot's clutches.

DENIS.   I say, gentlemen, are we not completely forgetting my sister,
who has probably had the hardest time of this ordeal? What . . .
something has happened to her and you're keeping it from me . . . I
can see it in your expressions.

FR. MICHOT *(with a forced smile)*.   No, Denis. If we have not
mentioned her, it is only out of . . . embarrassment. But don't
worry about your sister.

DENIS *(heaving a sigh)*.   Thank God . . . I was a little frightened. But
I shall take your word for it, Father . . . My head has started to
ache, so if you will excuse me . . . Goodbye, Father.

Scene Twelve

JOSSE. I feel like kneeling before you, Father. But no, no, I shall not.

FR. MICHOT. A fine father I am! Does it not strike you that we may have outstayed our welcome?

JOSSE. I'm in no hurry to go. I feel so elated. But I think you find my exhilaration a little puzzling.

FR. MICHOT. You think right.

JOSSE. Because of Maud? Is that it?

FR. MICHOT. You are perceptive!

JOSSE. The thing is, Michot, right now Maud means as much to me as last night's dreams. There are more important things than Maud. Like honesty. Her father's honesty has come to loom so large in my mind that she fades into insignificance. My spirit is weak, Michot. Disgracefully weak. That faith in man, that faith which inspires us seems to teeter at the slightest touch. And when I sense it, I feel as though I were suffocating. Physically, you understand. As though I were in a vacuum. Think of all the disillusionments we have suffered! Add them up, Michot . . . Add up all the people in whom we have entrusted our salvation. We have trusted all and sundry! We've carried one blackguard after another, on our shoulders, while they deliberately marched us to our doom . . . This time it would probably have been the last straw. He was, I grant you, only a private citizen, but I *had* to trust him. I was so overpowered by that absolute purity in his gaze that I felt that to suspect such a man would be utter stupidity. If eyes like *that* masked squalid treachery, then . . . But now it's as though I had experienced a miracle. Consider his behaviour when confronted by the severest test of all. There I was, the instrument of his death, and he, instead of swearing his son to vengeance, ordered him to be silent . . . to assure me, a murderer, of an untroubled conscience. That, Michot, is too strong a wine for me.

FR. MICHOT. A wavering of faith, Josse, is not necessarily a sight of weakness.

JOSSE. The memory of a man who emerged untarnished from an ordeal by fire will serve me as a shield. Because he is neither a hero nor a saint. No, he is just like thousands of other men, utterly ordinary. He has his flaws, as I do, as everybody does . . . And yet, Michot, he is a victor.

FR. MICHOT. Beware, Josse! You have not plumbed the deepest recess of the human soul. Because there is no such thing. Today, de la Meuge behaved magnificently; tomorrow, he may falter. So what if he hasn't yet disgraced himself? Believe me, Josse, every man is splendid and abject by turns and between these two poles of life lies commonplace human nature.

JOSSE. Do you really think that Maud has a chance of becoming human?

200

FR. MICHOT.   What nonsense! She is that already. And I am confident that she can also get well and develop into a normal woman. All she needs is a father's hand . . . a wise, restrained, but dominating love . . . and in due course a husband and children. *(Bluntly.)* Why must you part? Marry her.

JOSSE.   You are experimenting on me, Michot.

FR. MICHOT.   You know very well that I'm not in the habit of doing such things. It seems the best answer, that's all.

JOSSE.   Have a heart! Am I to put her in a cage and sap my own energies? Today, when the Republic needs us, when it must have an *exclusive* claim on our existence?

FR. MICHOT.   What has that got to do with it? A revolutionary does not cease to be a human being. As for you Josse, you are already on the brink of pride. Because it was granted to you to devote your existence to a great cause, you are already inclined to regard yourself as more than an average man, to think you are outside the laws of nature. The sordid mundanity of marriage is beneath you, is it? And the demands of the flesh . . . how destructive you must feel them to be! But marriage renders that preying monster harmless. If you break with Maud, you will only exacerbate its cravings.

JOSSE.   I think, Michot, that for once you are mistaken. I feel in my very marrow that I am wedded to the Revolution. I shall never marry. Nature, Michot? I thumb my nose at it!

FR. MICHOT *(warningly)*.   Don't you dare talk like that, Josse! You are not a saint.

JOSSE.   Surely every vow taken by a monk is an affront to nature! Yet it has not been counted a sin. If I am defeated, I know that before I draw my last breath, perhaps in the very instant of death, the scales will suddenly fall from my eyes. I shall see my life, my frenzied activity, its glowing joy, my own self, as one monstrous lie. I shall realise that, instead of serving man, I harmed him. Compared to that, what does Maud's and my lust amount to? Now, Michot, let's go and eat. I am damnably hungry.

Hamlet 70

a television drama in two acts

by

Bohdan Drozdowski

Translated from the Polish
by
Mariusz Tchorek and Catherine Mulvaney

Characters:

GUERILLA

AMBASSADOR

ACT 1

Film shown from news reels: riots, shooting in the capitals of Latin America, neon-lit cities, screaming police sirens, political campaigns, rapid flashes of political figures in various situations, such as on platforms waving their hands over batteries of microphones etc. Against this background run the title and credits. Sirens off, shooting. Cut. The inside of a room on a high floor of a skyscraper from which the city's multitude of lights can be seen.

A man, his head covered by a sack and his arms tied, enters the room followed by a GUERILLA. The door behind them slams loudly shut: someone walks away. The echoes reverberate in the empty stairway. In the room we see a clock on the wall, a palm in a pot, radio, cupboard with glasses, soda siphon, refrigerator. The GUERILLA opens the fridge and we see bottles of drink and a little food. He looks at the clock, then inspects his wristwatch: the times correlate.

AMBASSADOR.   Remove this sacking, please.
GUERILLA.   Certainly.
    Now know the wager. Here the odds are laid
    as well befit Your Lordship's higher station.

The GUERILLA takes the sack from the AMBASSADOR's head who looks around the room, moves his handcuffed arms and observes his guard intently.

AMBASSADOR.   Who's th' equipped that stayed me in th' escort?
GUERILLA.   One Fortinbras.
AMBASSADOR.   'Twas not a gentle sport.
    How come this pit of darkness? What's afoot?
GUERILLA.   Mehr Licht?
AMBASSADOR.   You mock me, sir.
GUERILLA.   No, by this hand.
AMBASSADOR.   Mehr Licht.
    You play the villain's game exceeding measure.
GUERILLA.   Excellency, your threat is ill addressed:
    I've naught to lose, alas infinite little—
    that merchandise in price reduced called Life.
AMBASSADOR.   I see, you play at ransom, do you not?
GUERILLA.   Aye, maybe.
AMBASSADOR.   How much?
GUERILLA.   Only fifty.

The AMBASSADOR starts as the price seems far too low.

205

AMBASSADOR. Thousands?
GUERILLA. Nay, persons. You, sir, are taken hostage.
AMBASSADOR. What, sir?
GUERILLA *(passing chair).*
　　Your Grace be seated. I know the action
　　has caused your envoy's shield a certain damage.
　　I also know of no blade cutting sharper
　　in strife and combat 'gainst the world's mean outrage
　　than outrage. There is no other way.
AMBASSADOR *(sitting down).*
　　Young fellow, you amaze me.
GUERILLA. Thank you.
AMBASSADOR. You put your life in peril, you make
　　your flesh into but chaff, and speak
　　of mine?
GUERILLA. Speak not of that at present.
　　The choice befell you in no random process,
　　but with reason. Your Grace's name
　　is wide esteemed, cherished the whole world over.
　　So innocent as only it could be
　　for a good man in a world full of goodness.
　　You, sir, are come from Europe, which means to us
　　Love's oasis, all harmony and grace . . .
　　You frown, most noble Lord? You know this Land
　　did see your brother Spaniards cutting hands,
　　tongues, noses, breasts; the odds were made
　　with single belch of falchion slash
　　a girl from crotch right up to virgin throat.
　　From yon sweet Europe you are, noble Lord,
　　which offered religion, words withal.
　　You are from such a country capable
　　of making killing business, industry—torture.
　　Yet you alone—God only knows how—
　　those monstrous quagmires skirted dry o'foot,
　　as only Christ could on the holy lake.
　　You are most rare, in you take refuge
　　the tortured and the sentenced. Am I clear?
AMBASSADOR. Your enemy was I never.
GUERILLA. Indeed, as though
　　I held in you a foe, while sooth
　　I hope to give you my heart for a Friend.
AMBASSADOR. I am thirsty.

The GUERILLA *opens the fridge, takes out a bottle of dry wine,*
pours some into a glass and passes it to the AMBASSADOR.

GUERILLA. Here, please take this wine.
AMBASSADOR. Just water.

GUERILLA. It seems the heat does you no good, sir.
AMBASSADOR. I wish to be unfettered. I'm trustworthy.

The GUERILLA *unfastens a link of the handcuffs from one of the* AMBASSADOR'*s wrists and secures it to the arm of the chair.*

GUERILLA. You are semi-free.
AMBASSADOR.   Let's survey our positions.
  You and fellow comrades in broad day
  the city's heart usurp, with armed force
  charged towards the outer power's envoy.
  It comes to shooting, men fall slain all round,
  government is furious, police defeated.
  The world is stirred to horror, what's the purpose?
  Yes, indeed, a noble purpose looms
  over this carnage: freeing the imprisoned.
  Who are those worthy lads?
GUERILLA.   Sir, girls as well.
AMBASSADOR. Aye, girls as well, who are they?
GUERILLA.   They are nought.
  Hence I have the honour of your company.
  Your Grace gives them value where none was before.
  and thus non-entity comes before the world.
AMBASSADOR. Profound indeed; mark you, I remember the Minister.
GUERILLA. You think of him? That's promising for us.
AMBASSADOR. He's loathe to yield to any degree of pressure;
  indeed he'd rather have your comrades shot.
  His temper will not suffer blackmail.
GUERILLA *(sounding hurt).*   Blackmail?
AMBASSADOR. My government might offer you some help,
  . . . the Red Cross . . . certain agents . . . ways are many.
  You're better to run the way of the world's conscience
  than make it run against you. Do you hear?
GUERILLA *(bursts out laughing).*   Ha!
  In your profession words only have meaning
  when looked at from behind—on the reverse.
  You've come from the vitals of this snake:
  come, bite your own tail now, leave me in peace.
AMBASSADOR. A stranger in this country, I'm not empowered—
  by definition neutral—to judge a thing,
  otherwise I'd be *persona non grata.*
GUERILLA. Not so very gratifying, perish the thought.
AMBASSADOR. Come take a ticket and a bag of money—
  it's not too late to pull out of this trap.
  I know its insides, friend, how noble souls
  are but forgiveness for our wrong-doings.
  We use their torment and we use the shadow
  they cast from the gallows where they hang
  to hide the mediocrity we are.

207

GUERILLA. We are?

AMBASSADOR *(jerking his handcuffed arm).*
This globe is directed, my dear fellow,
by gears ill-suited to such noble hands.
The lubrication of this globe, brave fellow,
depends upon mechanics who think themselves
so serious they offer their grimy paws
for others to kiss—as though it were the people
and their good they toiled and laboured for.
Recall Hamlet, "To be or not to be",
for "not to be" put Cowardice, for cowardice—Treason.
Now what is Treason? Be sure it's nought but claptrap.
Who can say he knows what "faithful" means?
Faithful is treason, treason—faithfulness, boy;
friendship, enmity—but chartered carriers.
Fear, fear alone bestows on humanity
the vehicle through which it takes its birth.
Let us pray, friend, to the god of fear,
for he is our refuge and only he.

GUERILLA. I thought, therefore I was, I fear, so I am?

AMBASSADOR. Such thought alone to different ends is geared,
especially so since men taken *en masse*
think no such thoughts which might engender danger—
that weapon being used by a tiny minority,
a classlet rather, if you'll pardon the expression.
I think it's not your style.

GUERILLA. Do you indeed?
Then you believe the government will free them?

AMBASSADOR. I believe that you'll free me.

GUERILLA. It's true,
You are my tool, with me lies your fate.
So pray to me, Your Lordship, how about it?

AMBASSADOR. Ultimately, it is a law of nature:
to kill to live. I'm sure it's not your course.
Not that I place myself above you, no,
not even beyond your heads, you striplings brave . . .
Yet should it come to killing me, then woe!
Naught but a volley will light them to the grave—
must terror nothing else but terror grow?

GUERILLA. What would you say to a drop of gin?

AMBASSADOR. Untie me
from this chair, my arm's completely numb.

The GUERILLA *undoes the handcuffs and throws them to one side.*

Unless I watch the fits of twitching ads
what else is there to do in such a cell?
Let's drink the health of your ongoing thought:
thus far you've been ruled by instinct alone.

208

The GUERILLA *passes him a tot of gin. They touch glasses.*

GUERILLA. There are moments, excellency, when it seems
    that Life conceals the bar 'twixt plus and minus.
    Life's magnet ceases, its sparkle's snuffed out.
    A man halts at the crossroads with no beacon,
    the sun has long-past set, he cannot judge
    directions in the starless sky above,
    no passer-by is seen, nor one to guide.
    The traveller is lost. Yes, at such moments
    you gauge yourself and toss the thought of death.
    And what else? Love? Love you have known indeed.
    What else? Defeat? Yes, by the flesh you own.
    And then? On Nature's pure beauty dwell you?
    Shall I love Autumn's mists, or Spring's charms?
    I am a soldier, shall I throw off my arms?
    Why are you laughing?
AMBASSADOR *(smiling with amusement)*
                            Shall we have some food?
    This shot of gin has put my head astir.

The GUERILLA *takes some food from the fridge.*

GUERILLA. Will you please empty out all your pockets?
    I'm sorry, really, those are my instructions.

The AMBASSADOR *obediently takes odds and ends out of a few
pockets, however he is hesitant about one of them and seeing this, the*
GUERILLA *comes over, looks, and finds inside it a bundle of
papers. He starts to read one of them.*

    Looks interesting. You wrote this?
AMABASSADOR. *(trying to make light of it)*
                            Just a list.

The GUERILLA *goes over to the window and reads in the light of the
flickering neon.*

GUERILLA.   12th January: kidnapped Buonfina
    released after father paid unknown sum.
    28th: Tennenbaum, Abraham,
    kidnapped, soon freed 'gainst ransom.
    27th February: Hernandez,
    Appollo, assassinated in the street.
    No comments either from the Left or the Right.

The AMBASSADOR *turns his back to the* GUERILLA *and observes
the second hand of the wall clock.*

    27th: Minister Fuentes
    Mohr—a nice list—held by the Left,
    freed for J Cavillo, Marxist.

8th March: Biguria, lawyer,
released for enormous ransom.
Jose Bernabe Linares—murdered,
Marxists claim responsibility.
March 23rd: city, shooting.
Police clash with Marxists. Corpses
in "Zone Eleven". Comprehensive list!

The GUERILLA *sinks into thought, mechanically screwing up the other pieces of paper. The senseless work of the neon lights goes on outside the window.*

AMBASSADOR.   So you see, we are not all quite blind.
GUERILLA. *(mechanically reading to the end)*
   "Sean Holly, Second Secretary, released
   in exchange for four jailed Leftists.
   The US put pressure on the authorities."
AMBASSADOR.   Now you can see I have some antecedants.
GUERILLA.   Your rundown makes optimistic reading.
AMBASSADOR.   Government's patience is not without its limits.
   Govenor must show power, especially in
   moments of weakness. Then the power strikes:
   and striking its allies is the quickest blow.
   Unless they take the time to walk in line.
   I say, it strikes the allies first of all—
   this is the way to crush adversary:
   trap him in one net with his enemy.
   This brings him quickly to his knees,
   arrests his actions, frustrates his assaults,
   squashes his slogans and turns upside down
   all thoughts of resistance: should you seize
   power one day, remember this iron rule:
   first finish the combatants on your side.
   You'll hardly build a system on the shoulders
   of some such giants who for some idea
   were eager to pay with their own lives.
   Fit to fight an enemy, once they've finished fighting
   they must be impeached. That they are wrong
   shows right at the surface. Those who stay behind
   err not, they'll be the ones passing the sentence.
   One day you'll be called to the prosecutor . . .
   You who play at wager will find you trump
   not with your own fate. You'll see
   yourself before the pitiless faces of your brothers
   and lose your life, 'cause the world you now harrass
   will regain its values, whilst you remain
   a pimple of past days.
GUERILLA.   Trying to crush?
AMBASSADOR.   Trying to make you question,

GUERILLA.   Let's draw up the balance.
  I have got you here, for you they let them free,
  and in the end they'll seek to erase me
  for my trespass of whoever's law.
  I accept the prize.
AMBASSADOR.   Congratulations.

The GUERILLA *passes the* AMBASSADOR *some food.*

GUERILLA.   Have something to eat, c'mon, you are hungry.
AMBASSADOR *(eating).*
  Your chances seem to be precarious.
  Nothing is that was not, and all will be the same.
  Turn on the radio. What's on the news?

The GUERILLA *turns on the radio, brash music is heard.*
He tunes in to different stations quickly.

GUERILLA.   Music everywhere, canned trash, that's all.
AMBASSADOR.   What is your name?
GUERILLA.   Hamlet, you said, my Lord.
AMBASSADOR.   Nice, Alfonso, that's a good nickname.

The GUERILLA *searches through the Ambassador's wallet, examining*
photographs etc.

GUERILLA.   Your little boy? He's cute, a lovely face.
AMBASSADOR.   Yes, that's him, Eduardo, he's our darling.
GUERILLA.   What if you drop a few lines to your son?
AMBASSADOR.   Agreed, Bernardo, give me a piece of paper.
GUERILLA *(handing over paper and an envelope).*
  You can write anything you like.
AMBASSADOR.   Shall I write how sorry I feel for you, Enrico?
GUERILLA.   Go ahead, the contents count for little,
  your handwriting's needed, that's all.
AMBASSADOR.   Water, Horatio.

The GUERILLA *passes some water.*

GUERILLA.   They will surely see your soul before . . .
AMBASSADOR.   Stop it, damnation! What's wrong with you!
GUERILLA.   Please begin to write. We'll send it now.
  This minute they're smashing my brothers' bones to pulp.
  Inserting electrodes
  into our girls' vaginas.
  Write, write anything, but do it now!
AMBASSADOR *(murmuring).*
  Dear ones, I am in good hands, I love you.
  Will come back soon when the authorities
  free those desperados—that bunch
  of madcaps, who can be rearrested

once outside the prison gate. They
firmly believe that their sacrifice . . .
GUERILLA.   Write this! In this country
honour is mockery, law—for words too funny!
I am the victim of this tension, darling!
Should I fall by their hands, they will weep
over my corpse with you and share your tears.
They do not wish to kill, nor are they guilty,
but will not bargain down their conscience pure.
Aren't you writing, dad?

The AMBASSADOR *has stopped writing and is listening.*

AMBASSADOR.   I'm with you, Umberto.

The GUERILLA *points to the paper in his hand.*

GUERILLA.   The confrontation we've been brought to
is revolution, which simply escapes
all our governance, so said Rockefeller,
bloodshed is at stake.
AMBASSADOR.   Pretty good logic.
GUERILLA.   D'you want some whisky? Let's get drunk together.

The AMBASSADOR *writes in silence, comes to an end, seals the
envelope and hands it to the* GUERILLA.

AMBASSADOR.   Send it out, they'll answer in the press.
GUERILLA.   Father, I heard that in the last war
three hundred used t'be shot for one. True?
AMBASSADOR.   'Twas so, Rodrigo, only I didn't shoot.
GUERILLA.   You've studied the sort of reactions
a woman, in the ninth month, has
when faced with a gun? What did you find?
AMBASSADOR.   No more!
GUERILLA.   Exactly at this time, a girl
up there will see the squad.
AMBASSADOR.   Playing on my tender feelings, Petrucio!
GUERILLA.   Hamlet, good sir, please, call me Hamlet.
This was my name even as a student.
AMBASSADOR.   All right, Hamlet. Who was your father?
GUERILLA.   All men.
AMBASSADOR.   Look at this.

The GUERILLA *slips the letter through the gap, under the door,
the letter disappears.*

GUERILLA.   Mother slept with all
who gave her food. Syphilis devoured her.
AMBASSADOR.   Then you are a son of your class, Hamlet.
You feel no shame.

GUERILLA.   Me? Why should I?
   Shall we play chess?
AMBASSADOR.   Good idea, odds being?
GUERILLA.   Time.
AMBASSADOR.   You would fain lose it, but I would gain.

The GUERILLA *takes two pawns in his hands and conceals them behind his back.*

GUERILLA.   Which one?
AMBASSADOR.   Well, right, I'm from the Right, and so . . .

The GUERILLA *opens his right hand to reveal a black pawn.*

GUERILLA.   Black.
AMBASSADOR.   Typical Right.
GUERILLA.   You believe in spectres?
AMBASSADOR.   Yes.
GUERILLA.   Not me.
AMBASSADOR.   Fancy, a Hamlet who doesn't!
GUERILLA.   Okay, I do, if it pleases your Lordship.
   My move. *(Makes a move on the chessboard.)*
AMBASSADOR *(moves)*.   Queen's gambit.
GUERILLA.   Silence on the air.
AMBASSADOR.   Yet some broadcasters must know everything.
GUERILLA.   The hungry, the beguiled, exist no more.
   Only the mob is there. Law and order
   cannot suffer the riff-raff in action.
   With smashing down shop windows crash ideals.
   Nothing immobilises a man more
   than ridding him of honour.
AMBASSADOR.   How awful.
GUERILLA.   You deem yourself a worm upon a hook,
   a fly in a spiderweb. *(Makes a move.)* Your move.
AMBASSADOR *(making a move)*.
   The radio says nothing, cheers us up—
   jig-a-jig, rumba, samba, habanera.
GUERILLA.   Dictatorship's terror waxes lyrical.
   How can you be so smart—it baffles me.
AMBASSADOR.   The 20th century: open secrets reign.
GUERILLA.   Men must be able to up against the wall.
AMBASSADOR.   Against the wall? That one you mean
   the squad will put you all before?
   I'll give you all my learning—acquired
   in playing political games. They are
   all subject to the same rules the world over.
GUERILLA.   Keep your ears and mind open.
AMBASSADOR.   I do.
GUERILLA.   You must know then that in Reform Alley

walking barefoot is not allowed. The rules.
You must have known Rogelia Martinez—
a beauty—whom students carried in their arms
when she was announced Queen. Yes, you met her.
The TV showed you giving your parent kiss.

AMBASSADOR. Poor dear.

GUERILLA.   You may have seen her body
when it was found in a trench quartered,
like a piglet.

AMBASSADOR. I saw it, friend.

GUERILLA. You know the reason? Because her boyfriend
used to read Lenin. This is your move.

AMBASSADOR *(approaching the window)*.
It's not the best time for chess, let's stop.

GUERILLA. Bentham, you know, held death as most efficient
against reprisals.

AMBASSADOR. What do you want to say?

GUERILLA. To say, long live philosophers, dad.

AMBASSADOR. Except he does add, in his next discourse
that such a measure is extravagance.

A piece of paper is slipped under the door, the GUERILLA *picks it
up and reads.*

GUERILLA. "Arana puts a deaf ear to the swap.
Already tanks surround the jail. Tomorrow
at the time appointed—firing-squad".
The last hope would be that Arana softens.

AMBASSADOR. Unless . . .

GUERILLA.   Tomorrow you get out.
In martyr's glory. The best periodicals
will offer you big money. Just routine.
Notes From the Hideout. It will be a sellout.
Your face'll be run a hundred thousand times
and every coolie, any poor fishmonger
packing fresh cod in yesterday's gazette
will see your Lordship's face, all wreathed in smiles.
A minor envoy, hitherto obscure,
banished to this place, at the world's edge
is elevated to the rank of hero.
Not bad, is it?

AMBASSADOR. Not bad, yet will be true.

GUERILLA. Your son, when he sees all this news of you,
will grow so proud at having such a dad.

AMBASSADOR. In brief, you say you render me a service?
Shall we divide the profits? That would be funny.

GUERILLA. They pray for your release in all the churches.
  Parliaments echo with thunderous speech,
  pealing with anger. You are at the focus
  of the world's conscience. Finally a conscience!
  You have a right to be proud of yourself.
AMBASSADOR. I'll not accept a penny for my memoirs.
GUERILLA. That would be unwise after getting out.
  Take all that you can get, write everything.
  I hope you are honest enough not to
  lie more than need be 'bout those bravados.
AMBASSADOR. You play with the death of the innocent.
  Me? In this affair I'm chaff and husk.
  You'd better save your friends, and yes, the face
  of all your troupe, for if the volley's fired
  you'll soon see how hatred becomes the people.

The GUERILLA *goes to the door and knocks, there is no
reply. He lifts up the receiver—silence.*

GUERILLA. We are alone.
AMBASSADOR. Roberto, you know you have an enlightened mind.
  Rather than war, why don't you make degrees?
  Do some thinking first, become "someone",
  then begin your service for your people.
GUERILLA. Gramsći said, 'It's not for me to judge
  why intellectuals aren't capable
  of having real love bonds with their people.'
  I prefer to have that bond than your degrees.
AMBASSADOR. Then never comb your hair, and belch at dinner.
  This will draw you closer to that band.
GUERILLA. Jokes aside.
AMBASSADOR.   There is no third way out.
GUERILLA. There is: to fight.
AMBASSADOR.   Utopian solution.
  And you hate shooting, that is obvious.
  Your mind is too tender to pull the trigger.
  It's better to deprive the poor of their needs
  than incite them, then fail to meet the goal.
GUERILLA. Epicurean bias! Cheap Mandevillism!
AMBASSADOR. Promise then! You'll earn their hatred,
  for you'll just promise to keep your promises.
  Stuff their stomachs and give them the vote
  and lo, thick overgrown with fatty callops
  of civilisation they'll sink into gimmickry,
  torn from your creed like the oyster's shell:
  when the oyster has died the form alone remains.
  Yet, you are not of formalist stock, are you?
GUERILLA. How perfect your hatred is, father.

215

AMBASSADOR. My diet's unspiced, that's all.
GUERILLA. A true son of the soldier's tribe. Yet they
   call your unprocessed bread a luxury.
   They must fill themselves up for a start
   before embarking on anything profound.
AMBASSADOR. You are a man of faith: Faithful Umberto.
GUERILLA. How many more names have you in store for me?
AMBASSADOR. You are a million men, it's hard to reach you.
GUERILLA *(over the chessboard, making a move)*.
   Let's play the game. Check.
AMBASSADOR.   I'm not playing.
GUERILLA. Am I not a good enough match, Your Grace?
AMBASSADOR. A match?
GUERILLA.   Indeed how could I dare? O fie!
   Yet as this barrel peeps into your eye
   —this index finger trigger-happy is—
   my lofty target I'd be loathe to miss.
   Your knees will soon feel weaker .
AMBASSADOR   You reckon . . .
GUERILLA. Aha! Not that I reckon on you,
   Your Grace's fate does.
AMBASSADOR. Poor souls! Led in the dark!
GUERILLA *(reciting from memory)*.
   Our free nation's safest security
   is the broad mass of the toiling poor.
   The poor supply the surest breeding
   for servants, valets, guards and soldiers.
   To allow a community peace and quiet
   the rabble must stay ignorant.
   Learning feeds desires and demands.
   You know Mandeville, don't you, baron?
   He phrased it well, he forestalled you.
AMBASSADOR. Such stuff's not for the present, I'm afraid.
GUERILLA. You are afraid? This frankness is so telling.
   Come, drink, my Lord, we've day and night to spare.
   Let's keep "I am afraid" for bigger shot . . .
   A drinking aristocrat with a sansculotte!
   To your life, sir!
AMBASSADOR. To your life, your life.
   I see you're weak, you wish to dull the senses.

Shooting in the street.

   Sounds very near.
GUERILLA.   Hunting with battue.
   Pass me the whisky, excellency.
AMBASSADOR. You look frightened, my prince?
GUERILLA.   Just a trifle.

Someone lies, I stand. It's not a rifle
I need, but a whisky.

The AMBASSADOR *slowly pours out some whisky and passes
it to the* GUERILLA.

AMBASSADOR. To your health, prince.
GUERILLA. Surely by now your letter has arrived.
AMBASSADOR. I have a father complex.
GUERILLA. Mine's a pariah's.
Do me a favour, don't call me son.

The AMBASSADOR *moves a piece on the chessboard.*

AMBASSADOR. Retreat with the king. You suffer from delusions.
Legends are fashioned thus and there is many
a youthful grave. You sadden me, my boy.
GUERILLA *(making a move).*
Check, excellency, checkmate at that.
AMBASSADOR *(astounded).* Checkmate!
GUERILLA. Illogical? Reversible?
AMBASSADOR. With this move, I offer obeisance.
GUERILLA. I thought I was the loser when all of a sudden
I saw your flank unshielded, then it was
I struck.

They eye each other up and down.

You try to read my thoughts, old chap?
AMBASSADOR. Systems are crushing. Ethics and aesthetics,
immunities go to hell and reach rock bottom.
While here we put each other to the test.
In such a flood of trouble, insane helter skelter,
amidst these kidnaps, outrage, homicide,
Shakespeare would perish. To us his tragedies
are like a wanton boy's tomfoolery—
with words, sighs, mimics, abstract logic . . .
GUERILLA. Rest, rest, perturbed spirit!
AMBASSADOR. You said, my prince?
GUERILLA. Hamlet said it.
AMBASSADOR *(sotto voce).* And has us in mind?
GUERILLA. Words I heard.
AMBASSADOR. The age of words is dead.
GUERILLA. "Aye sir, to be honest as this world goes
is to be one man picked out of the thousand!"
AMBASSADOR. "That's very true, my lord . . . "

The GUERILLA *laughs.*

That's very true.

The GUERILLA *stabs at the* AMBASSADOR *with an imaginary poniard.*

GUERILLA. Rat! Rat!

AMBASSADOR. That's far better. Again you used a poniard:
this is far nobler than knuckle-duster steel.

GUERILLA. Suppose I ever wrote about it all,
it would be a farce.

AMBASSADOR.   Tragedy clichéd.

GUERILLA.   How?

AMBASSADOR. You playing the hangman.

GUERILLA.   You, the oppressed.

AMBASSADOR. You turn sentimental.

GUERILLA.   Pit, pitch darkness.

AMBASSADOR. To realise the light? That's good for fools.
You, man, sowing light make empty gimmicks.

GUERILLA. Darkness is your kingdom, lit by wood dust.

AMBASSADOR. Light you want? So lepers can see each other?
What if you sleep?

GUERILLA.   "What frightened with false fire?"

AMBASSADOR. "Give me some light away". Once I played the King.

GUERILLA. I followed Hamlet.

AMBASSADOR.   You use the past tense?
Manneken you are and Piss, not more.

GUERILLA *(putting a cigarette into his mouth, his hands show
trembling).*
"Give me some light away!"

AMBASSADOR *(lighting the* GUERILLA*'s cigarette with a lighter).*
                          Fool, fool.

GUERILLA. My bladder's full.

AMBASSADOR.   Then leak into the vase.
Feel free, feel radical, if the door is shut.
And parry the blows!

GUERILLA *(looking at the door).* No one's out there.
You are to me confined.

AMBASSADOR.   And you to me.
The noise down there made all your friends disperse.
What to do?

GUERILLA. What? . . . "Ay, good, my lord!"
"What do you call the play?"

AMBASSADOR. "The mousetrap. Merry, how?"
Prince . . . *(shooting is heard in the street, and
sirens.)*   The orchestra makes us cheerful.
(Handing him a drink).
Drink, unhappy prince!

GUERILLA.   I will, my lord.

AMBASSADOR. You raise my spirits. Go on playing, son.

GUERILLA. The whisky is warm, goes straight to the head.

Hamlet 70 by Bohdan Drozdowski directed by Jerzy
Krasowski, at the Panstwowy Theatre, Cracow, 1978 with
Krzysztof Jedrysek (the Guerilla) and Andrzej Bakerznak
(the Ambassador). *Photo:* Wojciech Plewinski

The AMBASSADOR *takes a siphon and sprays soda water on the*
GUERILLA's *face.*

GUERILLA.   May heaven reward you, king. My king of spades.
AMBASSADOR.   Spades mean death.
GUERILLA.   In the realm of symbols.
   If you complained . . .
AMBASSADOR.   O yes, and why should I?
   There are fifty of them, I am one.
   It's worth it to stay here in this mousetrap.
GUERILLA *(mockingly)*.   A model situation, isn't it? A victory
   of great spirit over the privacy of flesh.
   Beautiful indeed.
AMBASSADOR.   Your breath smells impure.

GUERILLA. My breath impure, conscience impure.
  I'm all from dirt, dad, and the dump
  I come from such infertile land
  that even cactus doesn't grow.
AMBASSADOR. It's dark, turn on the light, if you know how.

The GUERILLA *turns on the light.*

GUERILLA. Lie down, dad, it's night, goodnight.
AMBASSADOR *(lying down on the sofa).* Goodnight, prince.
GUERILLA.   Tomorrow we'll be woken
  by the jubilant free, or the whine of the broken,
  whose eyes have been blindfold with iron bars—
  who are soul-tied in cellars fit for dogs.
  (He ponders, looking into the twitching neon lights.)
  While here I set to thinking. O my God,
  am I come to a planet so thickly wrapped
  with blood, with filthy, manacled conscience mapped,
  to seek therein support from their philosophers
  and look for lofty lines in slushy verse?
  That they my conscience's burning fire quench?
  Coming from dust, in dust I roll. One day
  I turn in Horace's dust: one speck of it
  will irritate the eye of their conscience.
  To die? This question—mortal's blasphemous breath.
  To die means to avoid death, O unbold.
  To die means to cut off a bond with Death
  before he comes to wrap us in a fold
  of his silent gown fashioned for eternity.
  To die, to be a coward? To live in absurdity?
  To sleep? Cheeks on fluffy cushions lay
  and pray to their Guardian Angel for Rainbow Dreams?
  Wake, recommence this cross, their only means
  not having better options for the journey of Life?
  For what high stakes does this battle rage?
  What dawn do I compel to rend my night?
  You move a stone and die in an avalanche grave,
  or stay and watch the hailstorm, ever nearer,
  near the crops soon to face destruction.
  And wait for thunder in a hero's posture
  ever ready to die: to yield ne'er fain.
  Whence this conviction that the silent thousands
  would raise a finger at my call? What if
  my voice turns rancid into a tongue mouthed?
  A crew of joiners is always there
  eager to erect a scaffold their eyes' height.
  O God, what heaviness to you am I?

Unable to grasp your world with my thought.
Show me the third way, You must be that one,
for in my soul all routes I have searched down
and found the exit not. This puts my mind
to shame, the very worst torment. O Sire,
you did bestow me with a mind so tender
I plainly see the cogs and wheels of your clock.
I want but little, I wish to be useful,
have no desires, although I desire . . .
I live because I am lived by your will,
and hate myself for being too cowardly weak
out of the trap of Destiny to break.
And every single speck with thought I mark—
yet nothing shines but mould into my dark.
How do I save my mind from this madness?
Clinging as I am to puny conquests!
My fate is not your fault, I am all firmness.
Nothing you saved with your Martyr's death,
as I save none with my struggling deeds.
(Loud, but unwittingly loud.)
O Lord, indifference from you I need:
that I can just see, and feel, and hear,
and that nothing is able to unsaddle me
from spirit's heavenly poise.
Are you listening Lord? Do you heed?
AMBASSADOR.   Boy of boys!
Go to sleep, that's all I can say,
goodnight, prince.

ACT II

Some time passes, the AMBASSADOR *is half asleep,
the* GUERILLA *cannot sleep. The flash of the neon lights goes on
intruding the room, otherwise all is still. The* GUERILLA *stands up
and goes over to the fridge where he takes something out and drinks.
He goes to the radio, turns on: no power. He picks up the telephone
receiver: no signal. Complete isolation. He goes to the door and
listens: silence. He knocks gently at the door hoping that someone is
on guard behind it. No answer. He looks at the sleeping ambassador,
anger boils in him. Why should he be able to sleep? On the spur of
the moment the* GUERILLA *kicks the chair, which lands in the corner
with a broken leg. The* AMBASSADOR *opens his eyes but
doesn't react, he closes his eyes again and turns away. This is an*

221

obvious provocation, which the GUERILLA *cannot bear. He lifts a glass and smashes it against the clock. The* AMBASSADOR *doesn't move. The* GUERILLA *sits in the armchair covering his face with his hands; without realising it he soon falls asleep.*

Time passes. The GUERILLA *dreams about something, cries in his sleep, wakes up and jumps out of the armchair. He looks around the room which he has disarrayed. He sees the* AMBASSADOR *standing quietly by the window, his arms against the sill. The* GUERILLA *feels his chest, his pistol is still in its place. Astounded, he looks at the old man. He doesn't understand. Why didn't the* AMBASSADOR *take advantage of his opportunity?*

GUERILLA *(to himself)*.
    I slept off eternity. He could have tied
    or killed me, why is he standing still,
    as if he was my guard . . . Good grief,
    what am I, what is he this minute?
    (to himself, but unexpectedly loud)
    What can you do when you cannot do?
    What did we talk about last night?
AMBASSADOR. I hear you.
GUERILLA.   I didn't say anything.
AMBASSADOR. I heard some words.
GUERILLA.   It was semantic hum.
AMBASSADOR. You made this hum into a medium, though,
    for quite a hot message, since you hurry to hush it up.
GUERILLA. Nothing hot any longer nor worth reheating.
AMBASSADOR. You fear to part with your part in the party,
    or with your party in the part you played with nerve?
GUERILLA. I see you keep being smart under the circumstances.
AMBASSADOR. You are too bright to play the null.
    If you are a figure, how come you're troubled with me?
GUERILLA. Not troubled really, thought to thought I pull.
    (after a while)
    This was my Self giving myself a cry,
     you shouldn't have heard it. I am stripped bare.
AMBASSADOR. A mote that fell in the apple of your mind's eye
    becomes a beam which your fellow-men
    are quick to pluck out and fit into your scaffold.
    How long will you, nutcase, in your nutshell dwell?
    (standing) You hold a skeleton-key in your brain.
GUERILLA. Rather—that loam to stop a beerbarrel.
    (pauses) They went away lest they lure the deuce,
    or else they don't exist.
AMBASSADOR.   Do not take in vain
    a name you trust not. Let's get out of here.
GUERILLA. You are the wolf's deathtrap.

AMBASSADOR. I'm sorry.
    You smashed the clock that too slow did spell
    our get-away from this rat-decoy.
    Alcohol failed your fearful tremor to quell—
    try where you wish to step—there'll be a chasm.
    Are you Alexander, God's scourge—a loampeg in a hole?
    Nobody's in, and therefore we're not in.
    A childish syllogism police have drawn.
    Two fellow humans who each other own.
GUERILLA. A syllogism which turns into a dilemma
    is a dilemma still. That's logic, dear sir.
    Once you failed already when I fooled logic.
AMBASSADOR. In a game of chess.
GUERILLA. Ariston of Chios could not care
    less about logic, said it was dangerous.
    Once you've made a break with Kant and Mach
    in fuzziness you soar, You know your *modus
    ponens.* You are pure fuzziness. Leave logic alone.
    Look at the mote my eye has grown:
    how big it swells even as Hamlet's beam . . .
    Your silence is heavy, such silence is shame.
    When the radio is silent, the deaf are on the phone,
    when the flowerpot stinks with our urine,
    with such a view, my king, I dare thee to entwine:
    here is a mountain, its peak I try to near,
    dragging along the last of Sysyphian stone
    and there you are, breathing in my ear:
    push! push! O brother, push on your ordeal—
    at the top, in festive masses, you'll see the real!
    I push, and so grow weaker, meek,
    stop . . . My stone slips from this grasp of mine:
    crushes me, my vanity, and my world's design.

Police sirens scream again, single shots are heard.

AMBASSADOR. Sirens are back. Some wretches die again,
    for one's true vanity, or some truth in vain.
    You barefoot, barefoot with me, at one,
    discuss the top you wish to smash with the stone
    that laid upon your heart so firm,
    and how to be humble you refuse to know.

*The GUERILLA stands up and moves pieces of broken glass with his
bare foot.*

GUERILLA. Here's glass. Shall we to glass a parallel draw?
    Will you put on your shoes? The streets take bets
    on your Grace's life.
AMBASSADOR. High bidding I expect.

GUERILLA. Amok runs his shooting. Amok his hour frets!
Time's an empty projection, the mind's hollow weight.
I am your perceiver, you are but a trace
of some non-essence which equals the non-essence
you perceive in me: about me a little speck,
you knew nothing. All I saw in you
was a vehicle for our group tour.
As far I am as here and now I am: the past
eternally I miss, the future matters little . . .
Man is himself here and now, no more,
the past is but a load, the memory's junk,
while fear and hope are watchwords for the future.
You help uncover this game's many rules
at which play those who seek the taste of self.
Contempt for those players I obviously bear
marks the reverse of my deck so clear
that I can only lose. My aims?
Yes, I have some—to be myself throughout,
intense, concise, in sharpest fócus,
to be my self within self—no mirror reflection
inherited from some unwanted grannies.
I want to be myself so that my scent
can be discerned, by you, by them, time's travellers . . .
This is "being" to me. You?—are but a spray
of flowers, while they—nontransparent plates
which our portrayals to the world betray.
This is what it means to live in a community:
a separate self, I pay some tribute
to a multitiude for which I feel sorry.
Listen, the Conscious hardly sign alliance
with any such player who sees but pawns in us.
Prey of no illusion, for the multitude
needful of street Pole-stars—I shine.
Your keen awareness of those chain connections
lets you dive into the depth of my conscience,
and thus myself is lined out in your focus:
a case you note of the grey life's exclamation
flexing its weary cross to question mark:
its hope for an answer has no chance,
but should fear reprehension for breaking taboo.
So, sir, under the clock my case had broken too,
you sink, plunged in the quagmire of my utterance,
and say nothing.
AMBASSADOR. You need my diagnosis?
GUERILLA. I am not raving. My pulse as much as yours
measures the time which flows by.
A Knower. I feel guilty.

224

AMBASSADOR. Such feelings cease!
GUERILLA. Yet we are just at the initial stages.
My light-deprived nation these shells will illumine.
God save the salvos. Hail the fire sermon
tearing in pieces the belly of this night.
With David's catapult, Most High begins his fight.
The awakened by volleys install the law of talion.
True comes at last my life's longest dream,
and I owe this to you, my Grace, my King.
Long live our terror. Long live the shooting.
AMBASSADOR. This is said in dotage. You put me aghast.
Relax! Get dressed, beware of glass.
GUERILLA. Sinless sheep die, and wake 'mong their class.
Bye bye to slumber. Bye bye to abuse.
These volleys shan't be cooled by the dead.
Fire! The killed become a fuse!
AMBASSADOR. If only you were my son!
GUERILLA. I'm not alas.
AMBASSADOR. I'd bash your face in.
GUERILLA. Do hit me, my treasure,
see how from pain one sucks the greatest pleasure.
You're a manifesto of chaps who trigger press
against protesters: for you this bleeding hour.
Please crash to the end, tear off
the armour that round my soul has grown . . .
You have no courage?
AMBASSADOR. He's a lunatic.
GUERILLA. You wait?
Down there has begun a pitched showdown.
People can only enter the path of the great
when they die for rights of their own.
They're ennobled by dying.
AMBASSADOR. Only by this, o page?
GUERILLA. Seven twenty. How many minutes more?
Less than three quarters. The nation takes avenge.
What ecstasy of joy does pain have in store!
AMBASSADOR. In these forty minutes what will you spin?
Your thread ends?
GUERILLA. A thread of which you're worthy.
AMBASSADOR. Whisky all gone, not a drop of gin.
GUERILLA. The wine of hope ripens in this jar
—one whose handle is an ear of Saracen steel.
AMBASSADOR. All right, lots of bells we still could peal,
before comes what is written in your star.
The truth seems close, then it slips, as it were:
it's nervous energy, the guardian of your snare.
Corpses amuse you, because they detonate

your bombs—insane crazy boy—
detonators you see, not the human dead.

GUERILLA.   Nice that my vice instead of me you hate,
and that into your heart these arrows are fled
which from my quiver I so deploy.
Do quench my eye covered with flaming rage!
What am I?

AMBASSADOR.   A bar in my cage.
You ought to be closed up in a room with some girl
so I could hear your speeches in whispers still.
You're either a madman, or plain overactive . . .

GUERILLA.   A madman—'cause naked appears 'fore his captive.
Too active—'cause obedient to one power: will.
Yes, I never had a girl truly cognizant
of a complete sentence with a few words' text.
Hers would be body language, a lengthy pageant
of faces, poses, leading through drink to sex.
How strange, o sir, that I with mind so free
die in genitals' snare . . .

AMBASSADOR.   I agree.

GUERILLA.   Do you know sonnet one hundred and thirtysix?
"Will" stands for his name, penis and power.
Thinking one thing, Shakespeare more than one did cover.
Thus in myself divided flies a uniting dove:
God gave me a body, this body wants love,
which by very nature making lofty passes
must don a soul that makes sages asses!

AMBASSADOR.   I don't know who you are, you me no more.
You hold me in hand, I held you in check.

GUERILLA.   Seven fifty, the game is a draw.

RADIO ANNOUNCER.   Here is a special announcement:
despite many lobbies and official pressures from governments
to exchange the bandits sentenced to death for Baron van den
Bergh who was recently kidnapped, the President has decided as follows:
first, according to the legal and unreversible pronouncement
of the military court, the sentences: execution by firing squad—
for subversive action—and imprisonment under a severe regime
for the time established— in the case of the other prisoners, will
continue to be carried out. The execution will take place this
evening at eight pm precisely. Secondly, during a two-day
round-up of bandits, many who were involved in the kidnapping
of the ambassador were seized. Unless the ambassador is freed
immediately, they will also be treated as hostages and will be
severely penalised according to the law. This is the final
decision. Law and order will be resumed at any cost and no price
appears to be too high. This is the end of the special announcement.

Music.

AMBASSADOR.   Let's break down the door.
GUERILLA.   It's made of steel.

He patters to the rhythm of the music.

AMBASSADOR.   Please don't patter.
GUERILLA.   Care to suck on a bone?

The AMBASSADOR *sits up on the sofa.*

Don your tie and shoes.
AMBASSADOR   I do not beg your pardon,
    remember them, Hamlet!

The GUERILLA *throws away the bone he has been sucking and
cleans his fingers on his trousers. He helps the* AMBASSADOR
with his tie and tucks his shirt in for him.

AMBASSADOR.   I am under immunity. Stop pretending.
GUERILLA.   Yes, my visitor, but stop moaning.
AMBASSADOR.   You forgive yourself, they're degenerates.
GUERILLA.   Listen father, I have to do it.
AMBASSADOR.   You will kill them then.
GUERILLA.   No, those were just threats.
    I must do it, none of us would give in
    alive. They're holding innocent prisoners.
AMBASSADOR.   For two days they've been hunting.
GUERILLA.   I've got to do it.
    If they kill them they'll cast the die.
    We've got to do it, come on, sacrifice!
    You aren't young , come what may.
AMBASSADOR.   You won't do it.
GUERILLA. *(aiming at the* AMBASSADOR'*s chest)*
                          There is no getaway.
AMBASSADOR.   You won't do it.
GUERILLA.   Any last requests?
AMBASSADOR.   Young fellow, your nation will not lift a finger.
    My body is a poor, dud fuse.
GUERILLA.   If all principles are dead, good man,
    if law is only mockery of law,
    if whores alone have lofty principles,
    if God to their prayers puts a ready ear
    instead of sending thunder 'gainst their citadel—
    being a murderer I no longer fear—
    worse than any before—may all go to Hell.
    I must have faith. In what? In this lava
    on which they lavishly spit with contempt,
    before it breaks, to cover and bury with fire
    the cancer of this planet. I'd rather shave

off your laws and burn them. On the immunes I shit
and will tie a love-knot in our black banner
and my words in knuckle-dusters with which I'll hit . . .
for all your verbiage is the world's pimp.
AMBASSADOR. Natus oppressor's whip. Hamlet obiit?
The poor tragic bedlamite!
GUERILLA.   I consent
to stick to the "poor", dad, but not to the "tragic".
The tragic holds good only where free choice
abides, and as you know, this is not the case.
AMBASSADOR. They will not blink, you yield all your heart
to them: they stay in their fetid pond—
is this what you call your people's noble bond?
GUERILLA. Five to eight. Still silence on the air.
RADIO ANNOUNCER. It's five minutes to eight pm.
AMBASSADOR. Stealthy he does after you trail.
A war of nerves: whose heart will first quail?
GUERILLA. You are a stone, mark the avalanche!
AMBASSADOR. Rubbish! Go on! Uncock and shoot,
nothing special will follow, no finger will move
except those ruffians': the hungry—for want
of light, the enlightened—for excess of food.
Should you do this and one day on my grave be stood
you, clean, will say: defeated by him I am.
To arms, my son!
RADIO ANNOUNCER.   Four minutes to eight.
AMBASSADOR. Where is your footing? Remember Guevara's end?
He went waking up and how did it fare?
He found Judases and you're in his footsteps.
GUERILLA. You're trying to scare.
AMBASSADOR.   I to scare?
You fear the death of others, my friend?
The eternal fiesta in heaven does wait,
only who are the servants and who are the served?
RADIO ANNOUNCER. It is two minutes to eight.
AMBASSADOR. Who are you all? The planet forswears you.
Shoot me, and your mountain breaks.
GUERILLA. A man there once was, his head ashook, too bad.
RADIO ANNOUNCER. It is exactly one minute to eight.
AMBASSADOR. Fancy, the way they tell the time!
GUERILLA. This is the way they wind people up.
AMBASSADOR. Skip hence, my friend!
GUERILLA.   I called you father.
AMBASSADOR. You are too conscious not to be aware,
verily too aware not to be conscious:
to bargain this solid flesh I do not care.
The way I was to go I covered double,

228

yet I'd rather not preside over the host of spectres
to worry the life out of you. Yes, I share
your view of yourself.
GUERILLA.   Yet no more acquit?
AMBASSADOR. I did acquit you of your thoughts, not actions.
GUERILLA. My thoughts? I thought I loved you, man.
AMBASSADOR. Then I forgive this thought twofold
which will turn prosecutor at your conscience's court.
GUERILLA. "Give me your pardon, sir, I have done you wrong",
and yet this evil done can turn a salve
to those from whom th'Almighty withdrew his remembrance.
AMBASSADOR. You shall not shoot, because within your soul
the world's Redeemer struggles with a maniac.
GUERILLA. Thank you, Your Grace. I'm already dead,
after me—only hope remains.
AMBASSADOR.   So very much?
Wishful thinking, my boy.
GUERILLA. Your star shines quick.
Let's count the seconds, the gong ere long.

The GUERILLA *cocks his pistol. The* AMBASSADOR *and the camera focus on the barrel.*

AMBASSADOR. I trust the dictator will grant clemency.
GUERILLA. What shall I transmit to your wife and the police?
AMBASSADOR. Words, words that cease.
GUERILLA. You tremble father.
RADIO ANNOUNCER. The time is eight pm. As decreed by the
authorities, the execution of the bandits will be carried out in a few
seconds. The salvo will reverberate in your homes, hearts and
consciences as a warning to all those who raise their arms against legal
power, law and social order. Attention: five, four, three, two, one . . .
(The salvo is heard. The GUERILLA *pulls the trigger.)*

*This fragment is filmed focusing on the faces of the two characters, on the
details of their clothes, the room, the window, and on a fly lazily
walking across the window-pane below which children are playing and the
normal life of the city goes on. Stark silence as after a violent explosion.
The* GUERILLA *stands stiffly over the dead body,his arm holding the
pistol fallen limply to his side, he stares into the open eyes of the corpse.
Suddenly, a piercing successive whistle breaks the silence: a second,
a third. The* GUERILLA *shudders and dashes to the window—below a
boy is blowing a whistle, making the air-stabbing sounds. Two girls are
holding a skipping-rope for a third who jumps it to the rhythm of the whistle.
All else is still. Close-up on the* GUERILLA*'s face, full of pain, and
despair in his eyes. The noise continues in regular rhythm. Against this
background the final credits appear to the same rhythm while the* GUERILLA
speaks his final monologue in broken and unfinished sentences.

229

Hamlet 70 by Bohdan Drozdowski, directed by Jerzy
Krasowski, at the Panstwowy Theatre, Cracow, 1978.
Photo: Wojciech Plewinski

GUERILLA *(over the dead body).*
  Thus, the knee-fallen, your warmth unspoken,
  one of good trust, one of subtle sense . . .
  In the street's abyss around the jail's fence
  the mob goes berserk, fearing the next salvo.
  From the volcano of my extinct conscience
  I gather evil flowers, which breed in the inferno,
  to cast them on your body which lived so fully, truly—
  a world, a cosmos, of bitter beauty wrought . . .
  Who am I, Hamlet, son of childless thought?

Hamlet 70 by Bohdan Drozdowski, directed by Jerzy
Krasowski, at the Panstwowy Theatre, Cracow, 1978.
Photo: Wojciech Plewinski

A bully?
To pyramids' brows this path I pave.
and thus I revile the kings of misrule,
and so with murder the world I save.
How many faces can my malice pull?

This planet gripping with a new wave.
Silence below. My deed—an empty gimmick?
Take my defeat, father, to the grave.
You are the dead . . . Who am I, the quick?

231

Finis. Blackout. For a few moments in the dark the boy's whistling can be heard making the rhythm for the girls' innocent skipping.

BIBLIOGRAPHY OF POLISH PLAYS IN ENGLISH TRANSLATION

Classic

Józef Bliziński (1827–1893)
Pan Damazy. Orig. pub. in *Tygodnik Ilustrowany,* 1877. Re-pub. as a book
in 1878. Trans. by Elizabeth Clark Reiss. MS. Available from the translator:
305 East 88th St., New York 28, N.Y., U.S.A.

Jan Checiński (1826–1874)
Verbum nobile. Libretto to the opera by Moniuszko. Translator unknown.
MS. or pub. Available from: Reference Dept., Slavonic Division, The New
York Public Library, 42nd St. & 5th Avenue, New York 18, N.Y., U.S.A.

Aleksander Fredro (1793–1876)
Ladies and Hussars (Damy i huzary). Orig. pub. 1825. Trans. by F. Noyes
and G.R. Noyes. Pub. French, New York, 1925. Another translation of
the same work, by Harold B. Segel.
Maidens Vows (Śluby panieńskie). Orig. pub. 1833. Trans. by A.P. Coleman
and Marion M. Coleman. Pub. Electric City Press Inc., Schenectady, N.Y.,
1940. Obtainable from the translators: 202 Highland Avenue, Cheshire,
Conn., U.S.A. Another translation of the same work by Harold B. Segel.
Vengeance (Zemsta). Orig. pub. 1833. Trans. by May Bamforth. Pub. in
Alliance Journal, VII, 1957. Obtainable from: Alliance College, Cambridge
Springs, Penna, U.S.A. Another translation of the same work, by Harold
B. Segel. Verse.
Husband and Wife (Maz i żona). Orig pub. 1826. Trans. by Harold B. Segel.
The Life Annuity (Dozywocie). Orig. pub. 1835. Trans. by Harold B. Segel.
Another translation of the same work, by Mieczyslaw Lisiewicz. MS. Available
from the translator: 20 Alexander Place, London S.W.7. England.
The Major Comedies of Alexander Fredro, tr. by Harold B. Segel.
(Princeton, Princeton Univ. Pr., 1969).

Jan Kochanowski (1530–1584)
The Dismissal of the Grecian Envoys (Odprawa posłów greckich). Orig. pub.
1578. Trans. by R.E. Morrill. Pub. University of California Press, Berkeley,
Calif., U.S.A., 1928 (in the volume of Kȯchanowski's *Poems*). Another
translation of the same work in prose, by Robert Temple. M.S. Available
from the translator: 2038 Locust St., Philadelphia, Pa. 19103, U.S.A.
Libretto after Jan Kochanowski's drama, by Bogdan Ostromecki, to a one
act opera by Witold Rudziński. Trans. by Eugenia Tarska. Available from:
Author's Agency, Warsaw, Hipoteczna 2, Poland. The work was prod. in
Polish by Polish Radio and Television in 1964.

Zygmunt Krasiński (1812–1859)
The Undivine Comedy (Nieboska komedia). Orig. pub. 1835. Trans by
C.F. Henningsen. Pub. (excerpts only) in *Eastern Europe,* London, 1846,
vol. 2, pp. 79-113. *The Profane Comedy.* Another translation (incomplete)

233

of the same work, by Mary Lowell Putnam. Pub. in *North American Review*, 1848, vol. 67, pp. 26-84. *The Undivine Comedy*. Another translation of the same work, by Martha Walker Cook, in prose. Pub. in *The Continental Monthly*, vol. VI, nos. 3-5, Sept.-Nov., 1864. Another translation of the same work, by Martha Walker Cook, in verse. Pub. in *The Undivine Comedy and other Poems*, Philadelphia, 1875. Repub. in *The Universal Anthology. A Collection of the Best Literature Ancient, Medieval, and Modern*, with bibliographical and explanatory notes, ed. by Richard Garnett, Leon Valleé, Alois Brandl. London-New York-Paris-Berlin, 1899, vol. 29, pp. 37-130. *Orval, the Fool of Time*. A free paraphrase translation of the same work, by Owen Meredith (Robert Bulwer, The First Earl of Lytton), London, 1869. *The Undivine Comedy*. Another, now the standard, translation of the same work, by H. Kennedy and Z. Umińska. Preface by G.K. Chesterton. Pub. Harrap, London, 1924. *The Un-Divine Comedy*. Tr.by Harriette Kennedy and Zofia Umińska (Westport, CT; Greenwood, 1976).

The Un-Divine Comedy. Trans. by Gordon Wickstrom. MS. Available from the translator, 1937 Temple Ave., Lancaster, Pa., U.S.A.

Iridion (Irydion). Orig. pub. 1836. Trans. by Florence Noyes. Pub. Oxford University Press, London, 1927. Another translation of the same work, by Martha Walker Cook. Pub. in *The Undivine Comedy and Other Poems*, Philadelphia, 1875. Another translation of the same work, by Edmund Obecny. MS. Available from: Professor Edmund Ordon, Department of Slavic and Eastern Languages, Wayne State University, Detroit 2, Mich., U.S.A. *Iridion*, ed. by George R. Noyes, tr. by Florence Noyes (Westport, CT; Greenwood, 1975).

Adam Mickiewicz (1798–1855)
Forefathers' Eve (Dziady). Part II. Orig. pub. 1823. Trans. by Dorothea P. Radin. Pub. University of California Press, Berkeley, Calif., 1925 (in *Konrad Wallenrod and other writings*). Part III. Orig. pub. 1832. Trans. by Dorothea P. Radin. Pub. for the School of Slavonic and East European Studies by Eyre & Spottiswood, London, 1928. The complete poem. Pub. by the Polish Institute of Arts and Sciences in America, New York, 1944 (In: *Poems*, translated by various hands and ed. by George R. Noyes). Another translation of Parts I and II of the poem, by Count Potocki of Montalk. Pub. in *The Right Review*, 1944. The whole drama pub. by Polish Foundation, London, 1968. Apply for rights: W. Potocki, Draguignan, Villa Vigoni, Chemin de Fouisses, Haute-Provence, France. The Great Improvisation. Another translation, by Louise Varese, of the Great Improvisation–the most important poetic fragment of Part III of the poem. Pub. Voyages, 35 West 75th St., New York 23, N.Y., U.S.A., 1955.

Konrad Wallenrod. A dramatic poem. Orig. pub. as a narrative poem in 1828. Trans. (in cooperation with George R. Noyes) by Jewell Parish. Available from the adaptor: A. Janta, 88-28 43rd Avenue, Elmhurst 73, L.I., N.Y., U.S.A. *Konrad Wallenrod & Other Writings*, George R. Noyes, ed. (Westport, CT, Greenwood, 1975).

Pan Tadeusz, tr. by Watson Kirconnell (New York, Polish Inst. of Arts & Sciences in America, 1962). *Pan Tadeusz*, tr. by Kenneth MacKenzie. (New York, Dutton, 1966).

Krystyn Ostrowski (1810–1882)
John Sobieski. Part II. The Siege of Vienna (Jan Sobieski. Cześć II. Odsiecz Wiedeńska). Verse. Trans. by Lucia Duncan Cook Pychowska. Pub. Paris, 1879.

Włodzimierz Perzyński (1878–1930)
Giving Notice (Dziękuję za służbę). Orig. pub. 1929. Trans. by Floryan Sobieniowski. MS. Availability unknown at present.

Tadeusz Przeworski (1890–1916)
Vaclav the Bandit. Trans. by Winifred Katzin and Milda Robin. Pub. in *Short Plays from 12 countries,* ed. W. Katzin Harrap & Co., London, 1937.

Stanisław Przybyszewski (1868–1927)
For Happiness (Dla szczęścia). Orig. pub. 1900. Trans. by Lucille Baron. Pub. in *Poet Lore. A Monthly Magazine, devoted to Shakespeare, Browning and the comparative study of literature,* vol. xxiii, pp. 81-110, Boston, 1912. Available from: *Poet Lore,* 30 Winchester St., Boston, Mass.,U.S.A.
Homo Sapiens, tr. by Thomas Seltzer. New York, AMS Press, 1970.
Snow (Śnieg). Orig. pub. 1903. Trans. by O.F. Theis. Pub. by Nicholas L. Brown, New York, 1920.

Stanislawa Przybyszewska (1901–1935)
The Danton Case (Sprawa Dantona). Orig. pub. 1975. Trans. by Boleslaw Taborski. MS. Available from the translator, 66 Esmond Road, London W.4., England.

Tadeusz Rittner (1873–1921)
The Human Touch (Wilki w nocy). Orig. pub. 1914. Trans. by Floryan Sobieniowski and Hesketh Pearson. MS. Availability unknown at present.
Don Juan. Orig. pub. 1914. Trans. by S. Wuyastyk. MS. Available from the translator: c/o Glyn Mills & Co., Holt's Branch, Kirkland House, Whitehall, London S.W.1.
Stranger and the Dark (Nieznajomy o zmroku). Trans. by S. Wuyastyk. MS. Available from the translator, as above.

Lucjan Rydel (1870–1918)
Polish Bethlehem (Betlejem polskie). Orig. pub. 1905. Trans. by Viola Wojnarska Piszczek. Pub. 1957 by Wilkes College, Wilkes Barre, Pa., U.S.A.

Harold B. Segel
Polish Romantic Drama. (Ithaca, NY; Cornell Univ. Pr., 1977) contains translations of *Forefathers' Eve, Part III,* by Adam Mickiewicz; *The Un-Divine Comedy,* by Zygmunt Krasiński; and *Fantazy,* by Juliusz Slowacki.

Henryk Sienkiewicz (1846–1916)
On a Single Card (Na jedną kartę). Orig. pub. 1881. Trans. by Jeremiah Curtin. Pub. in the volume *Sielanka: A Forest Picture, and Other Stories,* Dent, London, 1898, pp. 173-252.
Whose Fault? (Czyja wina?) Orig. pub. 1880. Trans. by Jeremiah Curtin. Pub. in the volume *Sielanka: A Forest Picture, and Other Stories,* Dent, London 1898, pp. 137-156.
I Must Take a Rest (Muszę wypocząć). Orig. pub. 1897. Translator anonymous. Pub. in *Current Literature,* vol. XLI, July 1906, pp. 114-116.

Quo vadis. A play adapted from the novel of Henryk Sienkiewicz by Marie Doran. Pub. French, London-New York, 1900. An opera adapted by Henri Cain from the novel of Henryk Sienkiewicz. English libretto by A. St. John Brenon. Pub. Enoch & Sons, London,1911. Trans. by C.J. Hogarth, adapted for radio in ten parts by Felix Felton and Susan Ashman. Broadcast on the BBC Home Service in ten one-hour episodes from July 4, 1965, and from July 17, 1966. Dir. R.D. Smith. Trans. by Jeremiah Curtin (New York, Airmont, 1969).

Juliusz Słowacki (1809–1849)

Mary Stuart (Maria Stuart). Orig. pub. 1832. Trans. by A.P. Coleman and Marion M. Coleman. Pub. by the translators: Alliance College, Cambridge Springs, Penna. U.S.A., 1937. *Mary Stuart,* tr. by A.P. Coleman and M.M. Coleman (New York, Greenwood).

Mazeppa (Mazepa). Orig. pub. 1840. Trans. by C.D. Wells and C.F. Wells. Pub. Alumni Press, University of Michigan, Ann Arbor, Mich., U.S.A., 1929.

Balladyna. Orig. pub. 1839. Trans. by M.M. Coleman. Pub. Alliance College, 1959. Available from the translator: 202 Highland Avenue, Cheshire, Connecticut 06410, U.S.A. Another translation of the same work, by Edmund Obecny. Edited by Edmund Ordon. MS. Available from: Professor Edmund Ordon, Department of Slavic and Eastern Languages, Wayne State University, Detroit 2, Mich., U.S.A.

Lilla Weneda. Orig. pub. 1840. Trans. by Edmund Ordon. MS. Available from the translator, as above.

The Constant Prince (Ksiaze Niezlomny). In the L. Flassen– J. Grotowski acting version. Trans. by Ludwick Krzyranowski. MS. Available from the translator, c/o The Polish Review, 59 East 66th St., New York, N.Y. 10021, U.S.A.

Wlodzimierz Wolski (1824–1882)

Halka. Libretto to opera by Moniuszko, considered his best. Trans. unknown. Pub. by Książnica Atlas, Glasgow, 1941.

Stanisław Wyspiański (1869–1907)

Meleager. Orig. pub. 1898. Trans. by G.R. Noyes and F. Noyes. Pub. University of California Press, Berkeley, Calif., 1933.

Protesilaus and Laodamia (Protesilas i Laodamia). Orig. pub. 1899. Trans. by E.M. Clark and G.R. Noyes. Repr. from *Slavonic Review* (London University) of January and April, 1933, by Eyre and Spottiswoode, 1933.

The Wedding (Wesele). Orig. pub. 1901. Trans by Floryan Sobieniowski and Hesketh Pearson. MS. Available from: B. Taborski, 66 Esmond Rd., London W.4, England, and from: The Drama School library of Yale University, by permission of Mr. Frederic Burleigh, Pittsburgh Playhouse, 222 Crafts Ave., Pittsburgh, Pa., U.S.A. Another translation of the same work, anonymous, was relayed over a simultaneous translation system while the play was performed in Polish by the company of Teatr Powszechny (Popular Theatre) of Warsaw, at the Aldwych Theatre, London, as part of the World Theatre Season, April, 1966.

The Return of Odysseus (Powrót Odysa). Orig. pub. 1907. Trans., with an Introduction by Howard Clarke. Pub. Bloomington, Indiana University, 1966. Pp. XXVIII, 74. Indiana University Publications: Russian & East European Series, vol. XXXV.

Acropolis (Akropolis). In the L. Flassen–J. Grotowski acting version.
Trans. by Ludwick Krzyranowski. MS. Available from the translator,
c/o˙The Polish Review, 59 East 66th St., New York, N.Y. 10021, U.S.A.

Gabriela Zapolska (1860–1921)
*The Morals of Mrs. Dulska (Moralność pani Dulskiej).*Orig. pub. 1907.
Trans. by Edwin B. Self. MS. Information as to availability can be
obtained from: Mr. A. Maciuszko and Mr. H. Mansfield, The Public Library,
Cleveland, O., U.S.A.
Miss What's Her Name (Panna Maliczewska). Orig. pub. 1912. Trans. by
Cecylia Wojewoda. MS. Available from the translator: Warsaw, Piwna
6 m. 1, Poland.
Sonya. Said to be based on a play by Zapolska, whose identity or
whereabouts cannot now be established. Trans. by Eugene Thomas
Wyckoff. MS. Availability unknown at present.
The Secret of Skiz (Skiz). Orig. pub. 1909. Trans. and adapted by Donald
Howarth. MS. Available from the translator: 19c Nevern Place, London
S.W.5, England; or his agents: Margaret Ramsay Ltd., 14 Goodwin Court,
London W.C.2.

Stefan Zeromski (1864–1925)
Breaking the Spell (Uciekla mi przepióreczka). Orig. pub. 1924. Trans. by
Floryan Sobieniowski and Hesketh Pearson. MS. Availability unknown at
present.

Modern–Poland

Jaroslaw Abramow (b. 1933)
Auction (Licytacja). A play. Orig. pub. in *Dialog,* no. 12, 1961. Trans. by
Eugenia Tarska. MS. Available from: Authors' Agency. Rights: the author,
Warsaw, Krasińskiego 16 m. 24, Poland.
High Above the Earth (Wysoko nad ziemią). A play for radio. Prod. 1965.
Trans. by Eugenia Tarska. MS. Available from: Polish Radio. Rights: as above.

Henryk Bardijewski (b. 1932)
The Lighthouse of the Ginger Cat (Latarnia pod rudym kotem). A play for
radio. 1960. Trans. by Edward Rothert. Available from: Polish Radio.
Rights: the author, Warsaw, Dobra 18/20 m. 48, Poland.
The Stairs (Schody). A play for radio. Trans. anonymous. MS. Availability
and rights: as above.

Roman Brandstaetter (b. 1906)
Return of the Prodigal (Powrót syna marnotrawnego). Orig. pub. 1948.
Trans. by S. Wuyastyk. MS. Available from the translator: c/o Glyn Mills
& Co., Holt's Branch, Kirkland House, Whitehall, London S.W.1, England.
Silence (Milczenie). Orig. pub. in *Dialog* no. 6, 1956; re-pub. as a book in
1957. Translator anonymous. MS. Script available from: BBC, Drama (S),
Broadcasting House, London W.1., England.
The Day of Wrath (Dzień gniewu). Orig. pub. 1962. Trans. by Ben Conrad.
MS. Available from the translator: 13 Queen's Gate Place,
London S.W.7, England. Another translation of the same work, by
H.C. (Harry) Stevens. MS. Availability unknown.

237

Twilight of the Demons (Zmierzch demonów). "An inhuman comedy in four acts." Orig. pub. in *Dialog*, no. 3, 1964. Trans. by H.C. (Harry) Stevens. MS. Availability unknown.

Roman Bratny (b. 1921)
The Columbus Boys: Warsaw 44-46 (Kolumbowie–rocznik 20). The orig. novel pub. 1957. Adapted from the novel, by Adam Hanuszkiewicz. Trans. by Krzysztof Jakubowicz. MS. Available from: Authors' Agency.

Jerzy Broszkiewicz (b. 1922)
Two Adventures of Lemuel Gulliver (Dwie przygody Lemuela Gullivera). Orig. pub. in *Dialog*, no. 8, 1961. Re-pub in *6 sztuk scenicznych*, Cracow, 1962. Trans. by Nicholas Bethell. *We are Very Sorry to Admit, or The Two Adventures of Lemuel Gulliver.* Another translation of the same work, by Stan Fedyszyn. MS. Prod. by Kanawha Players, Official State Theater of West Virginia, Charleston, W.V., U.S.A., 1964. Dir. Stan Fedyszyn. *All Saints' Cafe (Bar wszystkich świetych).* Trans. by Stan Fedyszyn. MS. *The Names of Power (Imiona wladzy).* A play in three one-act plays. Orig. pub. in *Dialog*, no. 7, 1957. Trans. by Magdalena Czajkowska and Boleslaw Taborski. MS. Another translation of the same work, by Leonidas Dudarew-Ossetyński. MS. *Philip.* Another translation of the middle act of the same work by Edward J. Czerwiński. MS. *Jonah and the Jester (Jonass i blazen).* Trans. by H.C. (Harry) Stevens.

Krzysztof Choinski (b. 1940)
Expedition (Krucjata). Orig. pub. in *Dialog*, no. 9, 1961. 1st prize at a First Play Competition, Ateneum Theatre, Warsaw, 1961. Trans. by M. Slabosz and A. Slabosz. MS. Availability and rights: Authors' Agency. *A Night's Tale (Nocna opowieść).* Orig. pub. in *Dialog*, no. 6, 1963. Trans by M. and A. Slabosz. MS. Availability and rights: Authors' Agency.

Michal Choromański (1904–1972)
Jealousy and Medicine (Zazdrość i medycyna). The original novel pub. 1932. Adapted from the novel by Walentyna Aleksandrowicz and Leopold Kielanowski. Trans. by E. and S. Wuyastyk. MS. Available from: L. Kielanowski, 6 Frognal Lane, London N.W.3, England. *The Crossword (Krzyżówka).* A play for radio. Trans. by Eugenia Tarska. MS. Available from: Polish Radio. Rights. Authors' Agency.

Marek Domański (b. 1921)
Woman in a Tight Spot (Kobieta w trudnej sytuacji). A comedy. Orig. prod. in 1960. Trans. by Barry Clayton. MS. Available from: Authors' Agency.

Bohdan Drozdowski (b. 1931)
The Funeral Convoy (Kondukt). Orig. pub. in *Dialog*, no. 11, 1960. Trans. by John Richards. MS. Available from International Theatre Club, 81 Elgin Crescent, London W.11, England. Rights: Warsaw, Plac Konstytucji 6 m. 89, Poland & Authors' Agency. *The Cage (Klatka).* Trans. by John Richards. Availability as above.

Edward Fiszer (b. 1916)
Golden Rain (Profesor i gangsterzy). A play for radio. Entered for the Italia Prize competition, 1962. Trans. by Barry Clayton. MS. Available from: Polish Radio. Rights: Authors' Agency.

The Violin and the Paragraph (Skrzypce i paragraf). "A poetic radio story based on fairy-tale motifs." Entered for the Italia Prize competition. 1958. Trans. anonymous. MS. Availability and rights, as above.

Daniel Gerould

ed.: *Twentieth-Century Polish Avant-Garde Drama* (Ithaca, NY; Cornell Univ. Pr., 1977) contains translations by Daniel and Eleanor Gerould of plays by Stanislaw Ignacy Witkiewicz, Andrzej Trzebiński, Konstanty Ildefons Galczyński, Jerzy Afanasjew, Slawomir Mrożek and Tadeusz Różewicz.

Stanislaw Grochowiak (1934–1976)

King IV (Król IV). Orig. pub. in *Dialog*, no. 1, 1963. Trans. by John Richards. MS. Available from: International Theatre Club, 81 Elgin Crescent, London W.11, England. Rights: Authors' Agency.
The Boys (Chlopcy). Orig. pub. in *Dialog*, no. 8, 1964. Trans. by John Richards. MS. Availability and rights, as above.

Zbigniew Herbert (b. 1924)

The Philosophers' Den (Jaskinia filozofów). Orig. pub. in *Twórczość* no. 9, 1956. Trans. by Paul Mayewski. Pub. in *The Broken Mirror, a Collection of Writings from Contemporary Poland*, Random House, New York, 1958.
The Other Room (Drugi pokój). Orig. pub. in *Dialog*, no. 4, 1958. Prize in Polish Radio Competition, 1958. Trans. by Halina Carroll. MS. Available from: M. Czajkowska, 46 Chiswick Way, London W.4, England.
Reconstruction of a Poet (Rekonstrukcja poety). Orig. pub. in *Więź*, no. 11-12, 1960. Trans. by Magdelena Czajkowska. MS. Available from the translator, as above.
Lalek. "A play for voices." Orig. pub. in *Dialog*, no. 12, 1961. Trans. by Magdelena Czajkowska. MS. Available from the translator, as above.

Irenevsz Iredynski (b. 1939)

Farewell, Judas (Zegnaj Judaszu). Orig. pub. in *Dialog*, no. 9, 1965. Trans. by Catherine Mulvaney in Mariusz Tchorek. MS. Available from the translators, 1 Tunstall Close, Bowthorpe, near Norwich, Norfolk, England.

Jaroslaw Iwaszkiewicz (b. 1894)

Summer at Nohant (Lato w Nohant). Orig. pub. 1936. Trans. by Celina Wieniewska. Pub. Minerva Pub. Co. Ltd., London, 1942. Available from the translator: 7 North End House, London W.14., England.
The Wedding of Balzac (Wesele pana Balzaca). Orig. pub. in *Dialog*, no. 1, 1959. Trans. anonymous. Act. II only pub. in *Poland*, July 1959.

Jerzy Janicki (b. 1928) and Stanislaw Stampfl (b. 1919)

The Operator Will Give Your Number (Centrala poda numer). A play for radio. Trans. anonymous. MS. Available from: Polish Radio. Rights: Authors' Agency.

Tymoteusz Karpowicz (b. 1921)

His Little Girl (Jego mala dziewczynka). Orig. publ. 1967. 1st prize in Polish Television Competition, 1963. Trans. by Andrzej Busza. MS.

Available from the translator: Dept. of English, University of British Columbia, Vancouver 8, B.C., Canada.

Stranger at the Door (Kiedy ktoś zapuka). Orig. publ. 1967. Awarded the prize for the best Polish Radio play of 1962. Trans. by Halina Carroll. Available from B. Taborski, 66 Esmond Rd, London W.4., England.

The Strange Passenger (Dziwny pasażer). Orig. pub. in *Dialog,* no. 6, 1964. A play. Trans. by Edward J. Czerwiński. MS. Available from the translator: Department of Slavic Languages, University of Kansas, Lawrence, Kansas 66044, U.S.A.

Tadeusz Konwicki (b. 1926)

Final Exam (Matura). A screenplay. 1966. Trans. by Christina Cenkalska. Pub. in *Poland,* no. 4, 1966, pp. 46-48.

Kazimierz Korcelli (b. 1907)

The Neophytes, or The Future of Literature (Neofici, czyli przyszłość literatury). A comedy for radio. Trans by Edward Rothert. MS. Available from: Polish Radio. Rights: Authors' Agency.

Janusz Krasiński (b. 1928)

Death in Instalments (Czapa). A radio play, subtitled "A Stereophonic Comedy". Orig. pub. in *Dialog,* no. 6, 1965. Trans. by Edward Rothert. Available from: Polish Radio. Rights: Author's Agency.

Leon Kruczkowski (1900–1962)

The First Day of Freedom (Pierwszy dzień wolności). Orig. pub. in *Dialog,* no. 11, 1959. Re-pub in collected edition of *Dramaty,* 1962. Trans. by Floryan Sobieniowski and John Coates. MS. Information on availability: B. Taborski, 66 Esmond Rd, London W.4., England.

The Germans (Niemcy). Orig. pub. 1949. Repub. in *Dramaty,* 1962. Trans. by M. Michalowska and J. Radker. Availability unknown.

Jerzy Krzyszton (b. 1931)

The Boys from Verdun (Chlopcy spod Verdun). A play for radio . Orig. pub. in *Współczesność,* no. 25-26, 1965. Trans. by Krzysztof Klinger. MS. Availability and rights: the author: Warsaw, Madalińskiego 21 m. 10, Poland, or Authors' Agency.

Necklace (Koralik). Orig. pub. in *Teatr Polskiego Radia,* no. 4, 1963. A play for radio. First prize in a Polish Radio competition, 1963. Trans. by Edward Rothert, MS. Available from: Polish Radio. Rights: the author as above.

Golden Wedding (Zlote gody) Prod. 1963. A play for radio. Trans. by Danuta Kuzian. MS. Available from: Polish Radio. Rights: the author, as above.

Comrade N. (Towarzysz N.). A play for radio. Orig. pub. in *Dialog,* no. 3, 1965. Trans. by H.C. (Harry) Stevens. MS. Available from: Author's Agency.

Jerzy Kuncewicz (S. Leonard)

Better to Dream (Lepiej sie nie Budzic). Trans. by H.C. (Harry) Stevens. Rights and text available from Mary Lide, Washington, D.C., U.S.A.

Jerzy Lutowski (b. 1923)

The Middle of the Operation (Ostry dyżur). Orig. pub. 1956. Trans. by

Carol Wilson and Walter Jeleń. MS. Available from: Play Library,
BBC, Broadcasting House, London W.1

Mariusz Maszyński (1888–1944)
Just Like That (Tak a nie inaczej). Written c/a 1930. Trans. by Elizabeth
M. Clark. Apply for rights to : Miss M.C. Slomczanka, The Vale, Vale Rd.
Mayfield, Sussex,England. Script available from: the translator,
Mrs. Elizabeth Clark Reiss, 305 East 88th St., New York 28, N.Y., U.S.A.
and B. Taborski, 66 Esmond Rd, London W.4., England.

Ludwik Hieronim Morstin (1886–1966)
Xanthippe (Obrona Ksantypy). Orig. pub. 1938. Trans. by A. Truscoe and
Z. Karpiński. MS. Available (rights for America only) from
Z. Karpiński, Apt. 3, 202 East 61 st., New York 21, N.Y., U.S.A.
Another translation of the same work, by Roman Rostowski. MS. Available
(universal rights, except America) from the translator: 131 Goldhurst,
London N.W.6., England.
Penelope (Penelopa). Orig. pub. 1945. Trans by A.F. Gray. MS. Availability
unknown at present. Another translation of the same work, by R. Hopen.
MS. Available from the translator: 103 Alexandra Rd, London N.W.8., England.
Cleopatra (Kleopatra). Orig. pub. 1956. Trans. by Robert Hopen. MS.
Available from the translator, as above.

Slawomir Mrożek (b. 1930)
The Police (Policja). Orig. pub. in *Dialog,* no. 6, 1958. Trans. by Edmund
Ordon. Pub. in *East Europe,* vol. viii, May, 1959. Another translation of
the same work, by Krystyna Griffith-Jones. MS. Another translation of the
same work, by Nicholas Bethell. Broadcast as a 60 minute play on the
BBC Third Programme February 27, 1964. Dir. J. Gibson. Prod. at
Central School of Speech and Drama, London. March, 1964. Prod. on
the BBC Television, May 27, 1964. Dir. W. Hussein. Prod. at the
Royal Lyceum Theatre, Edinburgh, October, 1965. Dir. Jan Kott. Prod.
at the University of Bristol Dramatic Society, April, 1966.
The Policemen. Another translation of the same work, by Leonidas
Dudarew Ossetyński. MS. The play was prod. in this translation at the
Phoenix Theatre, New York, November 21, 1961. Dir. L.D. Ossetyński.
At Sea (Na pelnym morzu). Orig. pub. in *Dialog,* no. 2, 1961. Trans. by
Ewa Markowska. Pub. in *East Europe,* vol. x, October 1961.
Out at Sea. Another translation of the same work, by Maia Rodman.
MS. The play in this translation was broadcast on the BBC Third
Programme, June 13, 1963. Dir. R.D. Smith. Prod. at the Mermaid Theatre,
New York, April, 1962. Dir. L.D. Ossetyński. Another translation of the
same work by Nicholas Bethell. Prod. in this translation at the Royal
Lyceum Theatre, Edinburgh, October 1965. Dir. Jan Kott. Prod. at the
Oxford University Experimental Theatre Company, Oxford, November
1966, February 1967. Dir. James Ware. *On the Open Sea.* Another
translation of the same work, by Eugenia Tarska. MS.
The Martyrdom of Peter Ohey (Męczeństwo Piotra Oheya). Orig. pub.
in *Dialog,* no. 6, 1959. 2nd prize in the Polish Radio TV play competition,
1959. Trans. by Krystyna Griffith-Jones. MS. Broadcast on the BBC Third
Programme, January 31, 1964. Dir. R.D. Smith. Another translation of
the same work, by Nicholas Bethell.

The Enchanted Night (Czarowna noc). Orig. pub. in *Dialog,* no. 2, 1963.
Trans. by Nicholas Bethell. Broadcast on the BBC Third Programme,
December 4, 1964. Dir. John Tydeman. Prod. at the Traverse Theatre
Club, Edinburgh, August 28, 1964. Dir. Callum Mill.
Striptease (Strip-tease). Orig. pub. in *Dialog,* no. 6, 1961. Trans. by
I.A. Langnas and Robert O'Brien. Pub. in the *Odyssey Review,* vol. 3,
No. 2, June 1963. Another translation of the same work by Irene M. Sokol.
MS. Available from the translator, 54-27 69 St., Maspeth, N.Y., U.S.A.
Performed at the University of Kansas Experimental Theatre, October
26-31, 1964. Dir. Janusz Warmiński, Artistic Dir., Ateneum, Warsaw, Poland.
Another translation of the same work, by Edward Rothert. Pub. in
Polish Perspectives, no. 10, 1965, pp. 53-72, and *Tulane Drama Review,*
Vol. II, no. 3, Spring, 1967, pp. 52-59. *Striptease, Repeat Performance,
and Three Prophets: Three Plays.* (New York, Grove Pr., 1973).
Siesta. Orig. pub. in the book *Słoń (The Elephant),* Cracow, 1957, as
a short story. Trans. by Konrad Syrop. Adapted into a 20 mins.
"conversation piece" by Martin Esslin. Broadcast on the BBC Third
Programme on July 13, 1963. Dir. M. Esslin.
Charlie (Karol). Orig. pub. in *Dialog,* no. 3, 1961. Trans. by Nicholas
Bethell. Prod. at the Traverse Theatre Club, Edinburgh, 1964.
Party (Zabawa). Orig. pub. in *Dialog,* no. 10, 1962. Trans. by Nicholas
Bethell. The six translations from Mrożek by N. Bethell listed above have
been published in England by Jonathan Cape, London, and in USA by
Grove Press, New York, 1967. Prod. at the Traverse Theatre Club,
Edinburgh, August 28, 1964. Dir. Callum Mill.
Tango. A play. Orig. pub. in *Dialog,* no. 11, 1964. Trans. by Nicholas
Bethell, adapted by Tom Stoppard. Published by Johnathan Cape of
London and Grove Press of New York, 1968. Prod. by the Royal
Shakespeare Company at the Aldwych Theatre, London, May 25, 1966.
Dir. Trevor Nunn. Another tr. by Ralph Manheim and Teresa Dzieduszycka.
(New York, Grove Pr., 1968).
Kynologist in a Dilemma (Kynolog w rozterce). A comic opera in one act
by Henryk Czyż, based on a play by Slawomir Mrożek, orig. pub. in *Dialog,*
no. 11, 1962. Adapted for radio by W. Opalek. (Text of the play abbreviated.)
Trans. by Krzystof Klinger. MS. Available from: Polish Radio. Rights:
Authors' Agency.
Home on the Border (Dom na granicy). A short play in 12 scenes, subtitled
"burlesque". Orig. pub. in *Dialog,* no. 5, 1967. Trans. by Edward Rothert.
Pub. in *Polish Perspectives,* no. 8-9, 1967.
Vatzlav, tr. by Ralph Manheim. (New York, Grove Pr., 1970).
Six Plays, tr. by Nicholas Bethell. (New York, Grove Pr., 1967) Includes
"The Police", "The Martyrdom of Peter Ohey," "Out at Sea," "Charlie",
"The Party," and "Enchanted Night."

Zofia Nalkowska (1885–1954)
The Day of His Return (Dzień jego powrotu). Orig. pub. 1931. Trans. by
Maria Celina Slomczanka. MS. Available from the translator: The Vale,
Vale Rd, Mayfield, Sussex, England.
The House of Women (Dom kobiet). Orig. pub. 1930. Trans. by Benn Wynd
and Forbes Walsh. MS. Available from: Ben Conrad, 13 Queen's Gate Place,
London, S.W.7., England.

Adam Niemczyc (b. 1919)
Love in abundance (Zaduzo milosci). Trans. by S.J. Radecki. MS.
Available from J. & M. McClafferty, 44 Jasper Road, London
S.E.19, England.
Nothing Important (Blahostlea). Trans. by John and Maria
McClafferty. Available from the translators as above.

Bogdan Ostromęcki (b. 1911)
Poem in the Making (Poemat otwarty). A poetic play for radio based on a
cycle of poems by Tadeusz Różewicz, orig. pub. in 1965. Trans. anonymous.
MS. Available from: Polish Radio. Rights: B. Ostromęcki, Warszawa, Al.
Armii Ludowej 6 m. 137, Poland, or Authors' Agency.
"Et in Arcadia ego . . . " A poetic play for radio, based on a poem by
Tadeusz Różewicz, orig. pub. in 1961. Entered (with music set by Zbigniew
Wiszniewski) for the Italia Prize, 1962. Trans. by Edward Rothert and
Jerzy S. Sito. MS. Availability and rights: as above.

Jerzy Przeździecki (b. 1927)
Handful of Sand (Garść piasku). Orig. pub. in *Dialog,* no. 11, 1963. Trans
by Jan Conrad. MS. Available from the translator: 49 Nassington Road,
Hampstead, London N.W.3., England.

Jeremi Przybora (b. 1915)
The Man with a Halo (Aureola). A play for radio. Trans. by Danuta Kuzian.
Available from: Polish Radio. Rights: the author, Warsaw, Dąbrowszcaków
12 m. 110, Poland, or Authors' Agency.

Tadeusz Różewicz (b. 1921)
The Card Index (Kartoteka). Orig. pub. in *Dialog,* No. 2, 1960. Re-pub. as
a book in 1961. Trans. by Bronislaw Zieliński. MS. Available from: Authors'
Agency. Another, authorized, translation of the same work, by Adam
Czerniawski. Prod. in this translation at the Oxford University Experimental
Theatre Company, Oxford, February 27, 1967. Dir. J. Ware. *The Card
Index and other plays,* tr. by Adam Czerniawski. (New York, Grove Pr., 1970)
includes also "The Interrupted Act" and "Gone Out". London, Calder &
Boyars. *The Dossier.* Another translation of the same work, by Barbara
Vedder. Pub. in *East Europe,* vol. IX, Sept. 1960. Produced in this translation
at the Unicorn Theatre, New York, 1961.
The Group of Laocoon (Grupa Laokoona). Orig. pub. in *Dialog,* no. 8, 1961.
Trans. by Sheila Patterson. MS. Available from: Authors' Agency. Another,
authorized, translation of the same work, by Adam Czerniawski.
*The Witnesses, or Things are Almost Back to Normal (Świadkowie, albo
nasza mala stabilizacja).* Orig. pub. in *Dialog,* no. 5, 1962. Trans. by Ann
and Adam Czerniawski. Broadcast on the BBC Third Programme (as a 60
mins. play), March 22, 1964. Dir. M. Esslin. *The Witnesses or Our Period
of Minor Stability.* Another (anonymous) translation of the second scene
of the same play. Pub. in *Poland,* no. 3, 1963, pp. 31-33. *The Witnesses and
other plays,* tr. by Adam Czerniawski. (London, Calder & Boyars, 1970)
includes also "The Funny Old Man" and "The Old Woman Broods".
The Funny Old Man (Śmieszny staruszek). Orig. pub. in *Dialog,* no. 2, 1964,
A comedy in two scenes. Trans. by Edward J. Czerwiński. MS. Available
from the translator: Department of Slavic Languages, University of Kansas,
Lawrence, Kansas 66044, U.S.A.

Gone Out (Wyszedl z domu). "A so called comedy." Orig. pub. in *Dialog,* no. 10, 1964. Trans. by Adam Czerniawski. Pub. in *Tulane Drama Review,* vol. 11, no. 3, Spring, 1967. London, Calder & Boyars.
The Interrupted Act (Akt przerywany). "A non-theatrical comedy in one act." Orig. pub. in *Dialog,* no. 1, 1964. Trans. by Adam Czerniawski. London, Calder & Boyars.

Kazimierz Strzalka (b. 1922)
Footsteps on the Sand (Ślady na piasku). A play for radio. Received a television award, 1959. Trans. unknown. Availability and rights: Authors' Agency.

Artur Marya Swinarski (1900–1965)
Alcestis Comes Back (Powrót Alcesty). Orig. pub. 1958. Trans. by Anthony Patrick Smith. MS. Available from the translator, 150 W. 21 St., New York 11, N.Y., U.S.A.
Ararat. Orig. pub. in *Dialog* no. 2, 1956. Re-pub. as a book, Warsaw, 1957. Trans. by Ben Conrad. MS. Available from the translator: 13 Queen's Gate Place, London S.W.7., England.
Achilles and the Maidens (Achilles i panny). Orig. pub. 1956. The play forms part I of a *Trojan Trilogy* but is a complete play in itself. Trans. by Ben Conrad. MS. Available from the translator, as above. Another translation of act II only, by Ilona Ralf Sues. Pub. in *Poland,* no. 24, August 1956.
The Golden Tower (Zlota wieża). Orig. pub. 1958. Part II of the *Trojan Trilogy.* Trans. by Ben Conrad. MS. Available from the translator: 13 Queen's Gate Place, London, S.W.7., England.
Epilogue in Egypt (Epilog w Egipcie). Orig. pub. 1958. Part III of the *Trojan Trilogy,* and direct sequel to the former, often produced with it in a single performance. Trans. by Ben Conrad. MS. Available from the translator, as above.

Jerzy Szaniawski (1887–1970)
The Bridge (Most). Orig. pub. 1933. Trans. by Maria Celina Slomczanka. MS. Available from the translator: The Vale, Vale Rd., Mayfield, Sussex, England.
The Lawyer and the Roses (Adwokat i róże). Orig. pub. 1929. Trans. by Ruth Collins Allen. MS. Availability unknown at present. Prod. at the Arts Theatre Club, London, May, 1934.
The Two Theatres (Dwa teatry). Orig. pub. 1946. Trans. by Anthony F. Gray. MS. Availability unknown at present.
Mother (Matka). Another (anonymous) translation of one of the two one-act plays contained in *The Two Theatres.* Pub. in *Poland,* October 1955..
The Flood (Powódż). Another translation, by Eugenia Tarska, of the other one-act play contained in *The Two Theatres.* MS. Available from: Polish Radio. Rights: Authors' Agency.

Maria Morozowicz-Szczepkowska (1889–1968)
Doctor Monica (Sprawa Moniki). Orig. pub. 1933. Trans. by Laura Walker. MS. Information on availability to be given at: The New York Public Library, 42 St. & Fifth Avenue, New York 18, N.Y., U.S.A.

Wladyslaw Lech Terlecki (b. 1933)
Archeology (Archeologia). A play for radio. Trans. unknown. Availability and rights: Authors' Agency.

Michal Tonecki (Noe Wertzchajzer) (b. 1915)
The Fifth for the Bridge (Piąty do bridge'a). A play for radio. Trans. by
Krzysztof Klinger. Available from: Polish Radio. Rights: Noe Wertzchajzer,
Warsaw, Sielecka 3, Poland, or Authors' Agency.
I'll Go to Him (Pójdę do niego). 1959. A monologue for radio. Trans. by
Krzysztof Klinger.. Availability and rights: as above.
Gabriel's Dolls (Lalki mistrza Gabriela). A play for radio. Trans. by Hilda
Andrews. MS. Availability and rights: as above.

Andrzej Wajda
Ashes & Diamonds, Kanal, The Generation, tr. by Boleslaw Sulik. (New York,
Simon & Schuster, 1972) Scripts to movies directed by Wajda.

Bronislaw Wiernik (b. 1909)
A Star on a String (Gwiazdy na nitce). A play for radio. Trans. unknown.
Availability and rights: Authors' Agency.

Bruno Winawer (1883–1944)
The Book of Job (Księga Hioba). Orig. pub. 1921. Trans. by Joseph Conrad.
Pub. Dent, London, 1931.

Stanislaw Ignacy Witkiewicz (1885–1939)
The New Deliverance (Nowe Wyzwolenie). Written 1920. Orig. pub. in
Zwrotnica, no. 3, 1922 and no. 4, 1923. Trans. by Adam Turyn. Pub. in
Polish Perspectives, no. 6, 1963, pp. 45-48.
*Madman and the Nun (Wariat i zakonnica, czyli Nie ma zlego, co by na
jeszcze gorsze nie wyszlo)*. Written 1923. Orig. pub. in *Skamander*, no. 39,
1925. Trans. by C.S. Durer and Daniel C. Gerould. Pub. in *First Stage*,
Spring 1966. *Lunatic and the Nun*. Another translation of the same work, by
Edward J. Czerwinski. MS. Available from the translator: Department of Slavic
Languages, University of Kansas, Lawrence, Kansas 66044, U.S.A. *The Madman
and the Nun & Other Plays*. Tr. and ed. by Daniel Gerould & C.S. Durer.
(Seattle, Washington Univ. Pr., 1968) Includes also "The Water Hen,"
"The Crazy Locomotive", "The Mother," "They," and "The Shoemakers."
Tropical Madness. Tr. by Daniel & Eleanor Gerould. (New York, Winter
House, 1973) Includes also "The Pragmatist," "Gyubal Wahazar," and
"Metaphysics of a Two-Headed Calf".
The Cobblers (Szewcy). Written 1934. Orig. pub. Cracow, 1948. Trans. by
Edward J. Czerwiński. MS. Available from the translator, as above.
The Shoemakers. Another translation of the same work, by C.S. Durer
and Daniel C. Gerould.
The Water Hen (Kurka wodna). Written 1921. Orig. pub. in *Dramaty*, 1962.
Trans. by C.S. Durer and Daniel C. Gerould. Published in *First Stage*,
Summer 1967.
The Crazy Locomotive (Szalona lokomotywa). Written 1923.
The original MS had been lost, but the play was re-translated
into Polish by Konstanty Puzyna from two preserved French translations
and pub. in *Dramaty*, 1962. Trans. by C.S. Durer and Daniel C. Gerould.
The Cuttlefish (Mątwa czyli Hyrkaniczny światopogląd). Written 1922.
Orig. pub. in *Zwrotnica*, no. 5, 1923. Re-pub. in *Dramaty*, 1962. Trans.
by C.S. Durer and Daniel C. Gerould.
They (Oni). Written 1920. Orig. pub. in *Dramaty*, 1962. Trans. by C.S. Durer
and Daniel C. Gerould.

The Mother (Matka). Written in 1924. Orig. pub. in *Dramaty,* 1962. Trans. by C.S. Durer and Daniel C. Gerould.

Karol Wojtyla (b. 1920)

In Front of the Jeweller's Shop (Przed Sklepem jibilera). Orig. pub. in *Znak,* no. 12, 1960. Trans. by Boleslaw Taborski. MS. Available from the translator, 66 Esmond Rd., London,W.4., England, in conjunction with Hutchinson Publishing Group, London, and Libreria Editrice Vaticana, The Vatican (pending publication).

Jerzy Zawieyski (1902—1969)

The Deliverance of Jacob (Ocalenie Jakuba). Orig. pub. 1947. Re-pub. in *Dramaty wspólczesne,* 1962. Trans by Boleslaw Taborski and Lance Wright. MS. Available (in both stage and radio versions) from: B. Taborski, 66 Esmond Rd., London W.4., England. Produced at University of Bristol Drama Department Studio, Bristol, England, February 7, 1952. Dir. by B. Taborski.

The Cross Roads of Love (Rozdroże milości). Orig. pub. 1947. Re-pub. in *Dramaty,* Poznań, 1957. Trans. by Boleslaw Taborski. MS. Available from the translator, as above.

Socrates (Sokrates). Orig. pub. in *Tygodnik Powszechny,* 1950. Re-pub. in *Dramaty,* Warsaw, 1957. Trans. by Janusz. A. Ihnatowicz. MS. Available from: B. Taborski, as above.

Protest. Written in 1963. Translated by Marcus Wheeler. MS. Available from B. Taborski, as above.

Modern—Abroad

Andrzej Bobkowski (1913—1961)

Black Sand (Czarny piasek). Orig. pub. in *Kultura,* no. 145, November, 1959. Trans. by Ben Conrad. MS. Available from the translator: 13 Queen's Gate Place, London S.W.7., England.

Antoni Cwojdziński (1896—1972)

The Einstein Theory (Teoria Einsteina). Orig. pub. 1934. Trans. by George R. Noyes. MS.

Freud's Theory of Dreams (Freuda teoria snów). Translator anonymous. MS. Available from: Rider Alex (Adrianne Foulke) Agency, 301 East 73 St., New York 21, N.Y., U.S.A.

Life and Dreams (Życie i sny). Translator anonymous. MS.

The German (Niemiec). Translator anonymous. MS.

Ferdynand Goetel (1890—1961)

Mr. Gill Rejuvenated (Odmlodzony Mr. Gill). Orig. pub. 1956. Translator anonymous. MS. Available from: Dr. Maria Kopff, Cracow, Świerczewskiego 23, Poland.

Witold Gombrowicz (1905—1969)

Ivona, Princess of Burgundy (Iwona księżniczka Burgunda). Orig. pub. in *Skamander,* 1938; re-pub. as a book, Warsaw, 1958. Trans. by Krystyna Griffith-Jones. MS. Available from the translator: The Manor House, Chatsburn, near Clitheroe, Lancs., England. Another translation by Krystyna Griffith-Jones and Catherine Robins. New York, Grove.Pr., 1970.

The Marriage, trans. by Louis Irbarne. New York, Grove Pr., 1969.
Operetta, trans. by Louis Irbarne. London, Calder & Boyars, 1971.

Waclaw Grubiński (1883–1973)
Diogenes. Orig. pub. 1914. Trans. by Floryan Sobieniowski and Hesketh Pearson. MS. Availability unknown at present. Another translation of the same work, by Maria Lilien. MS
The Lovers (Kochankowie). Orig. pub. 1915. Translator anonymous. MS.
The Beautiful Helen (Piękna Helena, albo o zmienności powodów toczącej się wojny). Orig. pub. 1917. Trans. by Floryan Sobieniowski and Hesketh Pearson. MS. Availability unknown at present.
Ulysses' Fancies and Agamemnon's Reality. A film script based on the author's play *The Beautiful Helen.* Translator anonymous.
Lenin. Orig. pub. 1921. Trans. by Floryan Sobieniowski and Hesketh Pearson. MS. Availability unknown at present. Another translation of the same work. Translator anonymous.
Lola Montez. Orig. pub. 1925. Trans. by Kate Zuk-Skarszewska. MS. Availability unknown at present. Another translation of the same work. Translator anonymous.

Marian Hemar (1901–1972)
Poor Man's Miracle (Cud biednych ludzi) Orig. pub. 1939. Trans. by F.B. Czarnomski. Pub. Minerva, London, 1943. Available from the author: Fig Tree Cottage, Leith Field, Dorking, Surrey, England. Broadcast on the BBC Home Service in 1943, 1944, 1947, 1952. Prod. at the Questors Theatre, London; Abbey Theatre, Dublin; Repertory Theatre, Birmingham, November, 1959; broadcast on the CBS Television.

Zygmunt Jablonski (b. 1920)
Before You Die (Zanim umrzesz o 3-ej). MS. Trans. by Andrzej Wojciechowski. MS. Available from the author: c/o Midland Bank, London; or: Siegfriedstr. 3, München 23, West Germany.
Avalanche in Speculum (Uczciwy zlodziej). MS. Trans. by the author. MS. available from the author, as above.
To Murder and Cherish. MS. Trans. by the author. MS. Available from the author, as above.

Aleksander Janta (1908–1974) and Leon Kostecki (b. 1916)
Blue Blood and Gasoline (Blekitna krew i gazolina). MS. Based on A. Janta's long short story *Wielka gafa księżny Balaganow,* Buenos Aires, 1961. Trans. (with the cooperation of W. Stanley Moss) by L. Kostecki. MS. Available from: L. Kostecki, 17 rue Saint-Romain, Paris VI, France.

Ryszard Kiersnowski (1912–1977)
A Night in Alicante (Noc w Alicante). MS. 1st prod. in 1961. Trans. by R.M. Montgomery. MS. Available from the author's widow: 3 Tangier Rd, Richmond, Surrey, England.

Leszek Kolakowski (b. 1927)
The Expulsion from Eden (Wygnanie z raju). Orig. pub. in *Dialog,* no. 6, 1961. Trans. by Halina Carroll. MS. Information on availability: B. Taborski, 66, Esmond Road, London W.4., England.
The System of Jensen the Priest, or Entry and Exit (System ksiedza Jensena

albo Wejscie i Wyjscie). "A farce in 2 acts imitated from various authors, unoriginal. Optimistic polemics with Beckett." Orig. pub. in *Dialog,* no. 6, 1965. Trans. by Nicholas Bethell. MS. Available from the translator: 73 Sussex Sq., London W.2., England.

Mieczyslaw Lisiewicz (b. 1897)
Unfathomed Caves (Niezgłębione jaskinie). MS. Trans. by D.M. Patrick. MS. Available from the author: 20 Alexander Place, London S.W.7., England.
Dreams for Sale (Sny na sprzedaż). MS. Trans. by Adam Truscoe. MS. Available from the author, as above.

Teodozya Lisiewicz (b. 1903)
Sunflowers (Sloneczniki). MS. Trans. by Adam Truscoe. MS. Available from the author: 312 Finchley Rd, N.W.3., England.
The Maple-Tree Boots (Jaworowe buty). MS. Trans. by A. Truscoe. MS. Available from the author, as above.
Madame X-ov. MS. Trans. by F.B. Czarnomski. MS. Available from the author, as above. Another translation of the same work, by A. Truscoe. MS. Available from the author, as above.
The Orange Peel (Skórka pomarańczy). MS. Trans. by A. Truscoe. MS. Available from the author, as above.
A Glass of Milk (Szklanka mleka). Pub. Trans. by C.S. Potocki. MS. Available from the author, as above.
Conspiracy of Things (Spisek rzeczy). Pub. Trans. by the author. MS. Available from the author, as above.
A High Bet (Wysoka stawka). MS. Trans. by the author. MS. Available from the author, as above.

Wlodzimierz Odojewski (b. 1930)
A Misunderstanding (Pomyłki). Written 1965. A play for radio. Trans. by Eugenia Tarska. MS. Available from: Polish Radio. Rights: Author's Agency.
A Really Lovely Summer (Bardzo udane lato). A play for radio. Orig. pub. in *Teatr Polskiego Radia,* no.8, 1962. Trans. unknown. MS. Availability and rights: as above.

Poplawski—Tenard
Little Kitty and Big Politics (Mala Kitty i wielka polityka). MS. Trans. by Ryszard Ordyński. MS. Available from: Reference Dept., Slavonic Division, The New York Public Library, 42nd St. & Fifth Ave., New York 18, N.Y., U.S.A.

R.R. Vincent (Roman Rostowski) (b. 1914)
The Colonel's Millions (Miliony pulkownika). MS. Trans.by the author. Available from the author: Dr. R. Rostowski, 131 Goldhurst, London N.W.6., England.

Kazimierz Wierzyński (1894—1969)
Comrade October (Towarzysz Październik). MS. Trans. by Norbert Guterman. MS. Available from the author: 83-40 Britton Ave., Apt 7 K, Elmhurst 73, L.I., N.Y., U.S.A.

Stanislaw Wuyastyk (b. 1914)
  The Strangler (Dusiciel). MS. Trans. by the author. MS. Available from
  the author: c/o Glyn Mills & Co., Holts Branch, Kirkland House, Whitehall,
  London S.W.1., England.
  The Banquet of Freedom (Bankiet wolności). MS. Trans. by the author.
  MS. Available from the author, as above.

For further information about these plays see *Polish Plays in English Translations*
by Boleslaw Taborski, The Polish Institute of Arts and Sciences in America, Inc.,
New York, 1968, from which this bibliography was extracted.